THE
FRICTION
PROJECT

To Marina and Sadhna, with our love.
For the joy they bring into our lives and
for putting up with us even when we
drive them crazy.

THE
FRICTION
PROJECT

**How Smart Leaders
Make the Right Things
Easier and the Wrong
Things Harder**

Robert I. Sutton &
Huggy Rao

ST. MARTIN'S PRESS
NEW YORK

First published in the United States by St. Martin's Press, an imprint of St. Martin's Publishing Group

www.stmartins.com

Design by Meryl Sussman Levavi
Pyramid illustration by Mapping Specialists, Ltd.

Library of Congress Cataloging-in-Publication Data

Names: Sutton, Robert I., author. | Rao, Hayagreeva, 1959– author.
Title: The friction project : how smart leaders make the right things
   easier and the wrong things harder / Robert I. Sutton, Huggy Rao.
Description: First Edition. | New York : St. Martin's Press, 2024. |
   Includes bibliographical references and index.
Identifiers: LCCN 2023036035 | ISBN 9781250284419 (hardcover) |
   ISBN 9781250284426 (ebook) | ISBN 9781250359209
   (international, sold outside the U.S., subject to rights availability)
Subjects: LCSH: Industrial management—Decision making. | Problem
   solving. | Leadership. | Organizational change.
Classification: LCC HD30.23 .S98 2024 | DDC 658.4/03—
   dc23/eng/20230911
LC record available at https://lccn.loc.gov/2023036035

Our books may be purchased in bulk for promotional, educational, or business use. Please contact your local bookseller or the Macmillan Corporate and Premium Sales Department at 1-800-221-7945, extension 5442, or by email at MacmillanSpecialMarkets@macmillan.com.

First U.S. Edition: 2024

First International Edition: 2024

10 9 8 7 6 5 4 3 2 1

Contents

Part IV. The Wrap-Up

Part I

SETTING
THE STAGE

Introduction

Why Friction Is Terrible and Wonderful. And How You Can Fix It

The email, all 1,266 words of it (not including a separate 7,266-word attachment), popped up in our inboxes on a Monday morning at 9:14, before the coffee had begun to kick in. Sent by a Stanford vice-provost to more than two thousand faculty, it invited us to spend the following Saturday brainstorming about the mission of our university's new School of Sustainability. We love the new school and were, at first, willing to give up a Saturday to help craft the mission—it's important to our students, faculty, and the planet. But the email left us annoyed and skeptical of any meeting convened by the big cheese who wrote it. That email was wordy, repetitive, confusing, and packed with defensive responses to picky past criticisms. Though it acknowledged how busy we all were, our struggles to decipher it sucked up more time than we would have thought possible.

With a little editing, the email could have been cut to five hundred or six hundred crisp words, and the attachment to two thousand words or so. Time would have been saved. Frustration spared. That leader's reputation wouldn't have taken a hit. And more Stanford faculty would have shown up that Saturday—including us.

Anyone who has tangled with organizations as an employee

or customer has had moments, days, and, sometimes, months and years when it felt as if the overlords who imagined and run the place have no respect for their time. Such as encounters with systems that seem designed to create maddening ordeals rather than give the simple answers, services, or refunds we need. Or unbearable meetings with ill-defined agendas and clueless blabbermouths that stretch on for hours. Or wrestling matches with rules, procedures, traditions, and technologies that once made sense but are now so antiquated, pointless, and inefficient that they make you want to pull your hair out. All are forms of friction that chip away at our initiative, commitment, and zest for work. That hurt our coworkers and the customers and clients we serve. And that undermine the productivity, innovation, and reputations of our organizations.

That's the bad news. The good news is that so much can be done to dampen the damage inflicted by friction problems, to reduce or eliminate such troubles, and to stop such ugliness from rearing its head in the first place. Every leader, whether you have influence over one or two people, or over hundreds or thousands, can be part of the solution.

The Friction Project is about forces that make it harder, slower, more complicated, or downright impossible to get things done in organizations. It's about why and when such friction is destructive, useful, or a mixed bag. Above all, it's about how to think and live like a friction fixer who makes the right things easier and the wrong things harder. So that work doesn't grind people down and drive them crazy.

We call it a friction project because we have, for the last seven years, made it our project to learn everything we can about the causes and cures for friction problems. Our goal is to help leaders craft homegrown projects that are tailored to fix the friction troubles in their organizations.

Too Much Bad Friction

We started this journey because we were deluged with stories and studies about the dark side of friction. We kept meeting people who were frustrated, pissed off, and exhausted by the organizations in their lives. No matter what we planned to cover during our research interviews, casual conversations, classes, workshops, and speeches—be it scaling, innovation, leadership, workplace jerks, or reinventing Human Resources—people kept talking about these soul-crushing obstacles and indignities. Here are a few examples:

- The healthcare CEO who bombarded thousands of employees with so many long, dull, and complicated email missives that they nicknamed him Dr. TLDR (too long; didn't read).
- The convoluted forty-two-page document inflicted on 2.5 million Michigan residents each year who applied for childcare, food, and healthcare support from the state. At eighteen thousand words and more than one thousand questions, it was the longest benefits form in the United States. Much of what it asked for was unnecessary, intrusive, and, sometimes, downright obnoxious. Why would the state need to know the date of conception of a person's child?
- Three hundred thousand hours a year. That's how much time executive-committee members and their underlings spent preparing for the weekly ExCom meeting at a big company. Bain, the management consulting firm, found that more than 150 intertwined weekly prep meetings rippled through the company, which culminated in pre-meetings to brief each ExCom member just before the

committee met. Then they all repeated the cycle again the next week.

- The exasperated service rep who showed us that, to serve just one customer, she struggled to switch among at least fifteen applications and twenty windows on the thirteen-inch screen of her company laptop. She was the victim of the unbridled IT managers at her biotech firm, who added more and more software applications to "help" reps do their jobs. Her company adopted so many efficiency tools that it rendered employees inefficient.

- "The people who can get away with wasting your time." That's what a group of sixty energy executives agreed—after much moaning and laughter—was the right answer to our question "Who are the most powerful people in your company?"

These friction horror stories rang true because our workplace, Stanford University, sometimes drives us crazy. Long and convoluted emails are just one problem. We are ground down by soul-crushing meetings. By oppressive rules and rule freaks that create ridiculous obstacles to raising and spending Stanford money. By the thicket of red tape for hiring and promoting faculty. In 2021, for example, to evaluate a fellow professor for promotion, our committee was required to create a 113-page document. It included twenty-seven recommendation letters that we solicited from scholars and past students. As well as thousands more words and numbers that we and Stanford administrators had to produce and edit over and over, to comply with a bewildering array of rules, traditions, and idiosyncratic preferences imposed by people who reviewed and approved the document. We attended perhaps a dozen meetings and sent at least two hundred emails. And that was, as one colleague put it, "one of easiest Stanford promotion cases in years."

A beleaguered corporate manager from HP summed up how we all feel during such episodes: "I am swimming in a sea of shit. I am just trying to stay afloat. They want me to show initiative. But it is impossible." We aren't alone. Every workplace is clogged with destructive friction—which grinds people down and undermines performance.

We set out to study this challenge and see whether we might be able to offer some solutions to the friction problem. We did case studies of companies like AstraZeneca, Uber, and JetBlue airline that struggled with friction troubles. We conducted and collected academic studies, taught dozens of classes and workshops, and developed solutions to friction problems—including a "meeting reset" tool with Asana's Work Innovation Lab to help people eliminate and revamp bad meetings.

Not Enough Good Friction

We soon learned that the goal of becoming a "frictionless organization" is misguided. Yes, the people who run most organizations create too much debilitating friction. But many also ignore the opposite side of the coin, making the wrong things too easy for employees and customers. We certainly love how simple it is to order a ride from Lyft or Uber, rent a place from Airbnb, or order goodies from Amazon. But at times organizations ought to make things harder or impossible to do.

That's how the parents of six-year-old Brooke Neitzel felt about their Amazon Echo Dot after Brooke asked this voice-activated gizmo, "Alexa, can you play dollhouse with me and get me a dollhouse?" Alexa, the ultimate frictionless entity, promptly confirmed Brooke's $162 order for a KidKraft Sparkle Mansion dollhouse, which arrived the next day. Brooke, understandably thrilled by this turn of events, declared her love for her virtual friend. Her parents were less enthusiastic.

Unfettered and overconfident leaders can squander a lot more cash than Brooke did when they fall in love with flawed ideas and there are insufficient organizational speed bumps to prevent them from rushing their half-baked creations to market. That's what happened to Google cofounder Sergey Brin in 2011 when he became smitten with the cool Google Glass prototype—wearable smart eyeglasses with a built-in camera, microphone, and screen. The result was a textbook case of spending money as a substitute for thinking. Despite protests from the Glass development team that it was an unfinished prototype, Sergey rushed it to market with massive fanfare. *The New York Times* reported that at a Google development conference in 2012, "Glass-wearing sky divers landed on top of the auditorium, raced across the roof on bikes and into the conference hall to thunderous applause."

Once people tried to use the eyeglasses, however, the truth reared its ugly head. Glass was plagued with hardware and software bugs, terrible battery life, and unresolved privacy issues. Tech reviewers deemed it "the worst product of all time." What might, with more thought and development, have become the next must-have device quickly became an avatar of uncool. Even Sergey soon stopped wearing it. Google pulled it off the market, and several disgusted and embarrassed members of the development team quit the company. The Glass prototype wasn't the problem; the problem was it was too easy for the impatient and powerful Sergey Brin to do the wrong thing at the wrong time.

There are other dangers to removing too much friction from the innovation process. We once heard a Disney executive complain about how much money and time the company wasted on developing new rides for their parks and new films—that the processes were horribly inefficient and needed to be streamlined. Yet, as piles of studies show, to do creative work right, teams need to slow down, struggle, and develop a lot of bad ideas to find a rare good one. During the thirty-two years that co-founder Ed Catmull was president of Pixar, the company produced a parade of hit films, including the *Toy Story* and *The Incredibles* series. Ed believes that, if Pixar followed that executive's advice, it would kill the goose that lays the golden eggs. He wrote us, "The goal isn't efficiency, it is to make something good, or even great. We iterate 7–9 times, with friction in the process."

Fad surfing also ought to be harder for leaders. An exasperated manager at a big insurance company told us that his CEO "falls in love with every flavor of the month, and every consultant who sells them." That manager had been taught design thinking, lean start-up, agile management, and digital transformation and was expected to somehow apply them all at once. He spent too much time in training sessions, task-force meetings, and working with colleagues to hone "the BS our executives want to hear." And too little time doing his job. Similar to Sergey Brin, it was too easy for those top bosses to make it too hard for their employees to do their jobs.

Technologies including Slack and Zoom that are meant to remove friction can also make it too easy for clueless leaders to inflict long and convoluted communications on colleagues and customers. We heard dozens of tales about senior execs like Dr. TLDR and our vice-provost who didn't realize or didn't care about the burdens that their technology-assisted blabbing imposed on their colleagues. In other workplaces, managers weaponize technologies to make their jobs easier, and everyone else's harder. Administrators who used to shield doctors, lawyers, and scientists from red tape such as approving budgets, expenses, and time sheets now use software that heaps such chores on the people they once served. Arizona State's Barry Bozeman shows that more and more of us are bogged down by such "robotic bureaucracy"—those relentless computer-generated administrative demands that cause "death by a thousand 10-minute tasks."

Warmth, caring, and human connections are also hampered when organizations remove too much friction. The leaders at Jumbo, a big Dutch supermarket chain, figured out that many older customers enjoyed their short interactions with cashiers, and because many were lonely, they felt such conversations were too brief. And with more Dutch stores using self-service counters where customers scan their purchases, grocery shopping now often entails no human interaction at all. So, Jumbo, as part of the Dutch government's One Against Loneliness Campaign for seniors, experimented at one store with a "slow checkout lane" for customers who were not in a rush and wanted to linger and chat with the cashier. This experiment was so successful that two hundred Jumbo stores now have slow lanes.

Developing deep commitment and affection for our organizations, teams, and one another requires far more time and effort than pausing for a few minutes to have a nice chat. Building strong and enduring attachments requires putting in long hours to grasp the nuances of what makes social systems and people tick. That's why, as the old Motown hit by the Supremes goes, "But mama said you can't hurry love. No, you just have to wait." Removing too much friction also can be a mistake because, as studies of everything from military boot camps to assembling IKEA products show, "labor leads to love." The harder we humans work at something, and the more we suffer, the more we come to value it (independent of its objective value) because of our need to justify all that work to ourselves and others.

Why We Wrote This Book

In short, friction problems squander the zeal, damage the health, and throttle the creativity and productivity of good people—and burn through company cash and other precious resources. All organizations, even the most renowned and successful, sometimes make the right things too hard and the wrong things too easy.

Unfortunately, as we've shown, such obstacles to excellence can fester because people with the power to fix them don't know or don't care about them. Other leaders know their organization is plagued with such maladies. And everyone else in the place knows such friction troubles are inflicting damage, too. Yet no one is assigned, rewarded, or feels accountable for repairing these orphan problems. Like the administrator and physician who complained to us about how long patient waiting times were in her hospital, how bad the information system was, and how little cooperation there was between departments. When we asked that leader who was responsible for fixing the mess, the answer was she wasn't sure but didn't think it was anyone's job, it wasn't her fault, and she didn't know who, if anyone, deserved the blame.

Sometimes, it seems as if Peter Drucker was right when he said, "Most of what we call management consists of making it difficult for people to get their work done."

We wrote this book because it doesn't need to be that way.

Our Friction Project

Our frustration and anger at the ridiculous obstacles that clog up our university, and at the idiocy we heard about, read about, and that people struggled to overcome in so many other organizations, prompted us to start this adventure. We devoted the last seven years to learning about the causes, consequences, and remedies for friction trouble in organizations. We cataloged the forms that it takes and the forces that cause leaders to create and cling to destructive impediments—and where and why they fail to add useful speed bumps and stop signs. As we dug into these studies and stories, our despair began to fade. There was more good news than we expected.

We were buoyed by the powerful language, beliefs, and tools used in organizations to avert and eliminate friction troubles. And by so many skilled people who create, find, and blend solutions to such challenges. We call them friction fixers. Sure, some are senior executives with formal responsibility for hundreds or thousands of people. But that doesn't let the rest of us off the hook. The deeds of a few top dogs aren't enough. Friction fixers also include middle managers, leaders of small teams, coaches, pilots, and directors of films and plays. Still others might be labeled "individual contributors" but are leaders, too, because they take it upon themselves to repair their workplaces and recruit others to join their cause.

All friction fixers are similar in that they start from where they are and use all the influence, talents, money, and tools they can muster to better their workplaces. They treat wrestling with bad and good friction as their job, not as an orphan problem that really ought to be somebody else's job (but isn't). They are the kind of folks who pick up that piece of trash that someone else has dropped rather than ignoring it or thinking that someone else ought to do it.

The Friction Project provides building blocks to help you be a friction fixer, too. The key to your success is learning to think and act like a friction fixer *and* motivating others to join you in building organizations where, day after day, people imagine, debate, and implement changes to make the right things easier and the wrong things harder.

Here's how we've learned and shared ideas about friction fixing during the last seven years. As academics, we're wired to produce and catalog academic research, case studies, and practical articles. For example, we tracked close to two thousand agile teams in a big software company to uncover forces that help and hamper efficiency. Huggy was also part of a research team that experimented with "prenups for start-ups." They created 348 remote teams and asked each to develop a business plan for a wellness product. These new teams could bolster performance when—rather than racing to start their work—members devoted their first meeting to writing a prenup or a "charter" to spell out agreements about the team's roles, norms, rules, and values. That way, rather than being mired in confusion and conflict about who ought to do what, and what was good and bad behavior, they were ready to charge ahead and develop their business plan.

We also wrote case studies about friction-fixing efforts, and the lessons that leaders can glean from them. We documented how AstraZeneca saved two million hours by scaling simplicity throughout this global pharmaceutical firm. How a new CEO at BHP (a big Australian mineral and energy company) turned the corporation around by taking things slow at first, telling his people, "We're not going to do anything today." And how Uber got in big trouble because executives didn't slow down and co-ordinate hundreds of fast-moving engineering teams—and the belated efforts they took to hit the brakes and pay down the re-sulting technical and organizational debt.

The reactions to our articles with practical advice revealed that people in every country and kind of organization felt belea-guered by friction troubles—and were hungry for solutions. We wrote four pieces for *The Wall Street Journal,* including "How Bosses Waste Their Employees' Time," which became the most downloaded article of the day when it appeared. We wrote a friction article for Gallup.com, "Too Many Teams, Too Many Bosses," and for *Times Higher Education,* "Our To-Do Lists Can't Grow Forever. It's Time to Try Subtraction." And the LinkedIn pieces "Why Your Job Is Becoming Impossible to Do" and "How Do You End a Meeting?"—each was viewed more than one hundred thousand times and generated more than four hun-dred comments. A piece for *Harvard Business Review,* "Meet-ing Overload Is a Fixable Problem," provided a "playbook" for "meeting resets" that we helped develop and test. The research and writing for such articles helped us to hone the approach that we present to you in this book.

Classic management writings address friction in its many guises—and offer timeless advice that guided our project. C. Northcote Parkinson's 1957 book, *Parkinson's Law,* proposed the "coefficient of inefficiency": Once a committee grows to more than eight members, it becomes less efficient with each new member added, becoming useless once it hits twenty. Yet, Parkinson observed, leaders still can't resist adding more and more members. A similar conclusion was reached by Frederick Brooks, Jr., in his 1975 classic, *The Mythical Man-Month*. Brooks led two of the largest computer hardware and software projects in IBM's history: the first developed their iconic 360 mainframe hardware systems and the second the massive OS/360 software system that runs on those computers. Brooks observed that, when projects are running late, leaders often add more people to speed things up—but the burdens of onboarding newcomers and coordinating more people make late projects run even later.

Numerous modern works wrestle with friction and were central to our project. Like Cass Sunstein's *Sludge*. A book, Cass reports, that was born out of his failure to reduce government paperwork when he led the White House Office of Information and Regulatory Affairs during the Obama administration. Cass confesses that he started working on the problem too little and too late—even though paperwork reduction was his office's responsibility. *Sludge* considers "what stops us from getting things done" and how "sludge audits" can track and motivate change, and proposes solutions including regulations to reduce paperwork in the courts, Congress, and federal agencies. *Administrative Burden* by Pamela Herd and Donald Moynihan digs deeper into the problems of bad government bureaucracy, paperwork, and convoluted regulations. This duo documents the damage that such sludge, ordeals, and red tape inflicts, especially on low-income, powerless, and vulnerable people. They propose an array of evidence-based solutions that policymakers can implement to reduce the learning, compliance, and psychological costs of such burdens—such as allowing people who seek services that require interviews with a civil servant to do so online or on the phone, as well as in person.

We are smitten with Leidy Klotz's *Subtract*, his book on "the science of less." It helped inspire chapter 5 here, "Addition Sickness." After we tracked Leidy down, we developed ideas together for our *Times Higher Education* piece on how colleges and universities can use subtraction. We proposed the "rule of halves": a thought experiment where you cut some burden by 50 percent (e.g., the number and length of standing meetings, the number of recommendation letters required for a job candidate, or the length of each letter), pause to fret awhile, then add back what you *really* need. We also learned what to make harder and slower from works including *The Necessity of Friction* by Nordal Åkerman, a collection of essays on the virtues of blocking, delaying, and stopping action that draws on fields including economics, organizational theory, physics, and artificial intelligence.

We taught more than a hundred classes and workshops on friction for varied audiences, including a Stanford online webinar for seven hundred executives from thirty-five countries, a Leading Innovation class for twenty-four Stanford students, a virtual presentation to eight hundred and fifty Google administrative assistants, a pair of "forums" for eight hundred Microsoft executives, a workshop for Bloom Energy's top team, a weeklong program for seventy Kraft Heinz executives, a retreat for the top eighty leaders of a big financial services company, and two friction workshops for a hundred executives who run credit unions. These gatherings gave us insights into the most debilitating pain points and made us optimistic that once friction is brought to the fore, people are enthusiastic to find solutions.

The president of a big restaurant chain described a weekly

senior-management meeting he'd attended for twenty-five years as a series of ritualized "Kabuki dances," where executives revisited decisions made at earlier meetings, replayed the same arguments, and arrived at the same decisions. Other groups joke about "leadershit," "being waterboarded by PowerPoint," "jargon monoxide," "fad surfing," "rule freaks," "death by meeting," "malicious compliance to stupid rules," and putting customers in "roach motels" (making it easy to sign up for a subscription or service, difficult or impossible to end). As we show in chapter 3, such dark humor helps people raise uncomfortable topics, release tension, and build social bonds.

Once participants wallow in and joke about their pain for a while, they are ready to move on to friction fixing. At the financial services company retreat, we talked about how "addition sickness" gums up the works and nudged the eighty executives in the room to brainstorm about impediments they ought to remove. The CEO surprised us by jumping up and offering each executive a $5,000 bonus for subtracting at least two routines, technologies, meetings, or roles from their business in the next month. We helped the CEO track those executives' progress: nearly all eighty earned that bonus, in part because, throughout that month, he celebrated execs who got rid of two or more obstacles ("Congrats to Sandra, who just earned her 5K!") and nagged laggards ("Hey, Tony, no word about subtraction from you yet, what's up?").

After our workshops for credit unions, staffers at Filene, the industry's research institute, spent several months writing the five-thousand-word "Friction: A Manifesto." And, as we wrote in the *Harvard Business Review,* when Saul Gurdus and Elizabeth Woodson were students in our Leading Innovation class, they spent about a month helping administrators at a California social services agency identify clients' friction-related pain points.

Especially the delay and despair experienced by people who applied for services. During the long and unpredictable gauntlet through the agency's silos, those clients reported "waiting," "still waiting," "call unanswered," and feeling "frustrated," "invisible," "helpless," and that "this is too hard." Then Saul and Elizabeth spent about six weeks working with administrators to improve communication across silos, which reduced clients' confusion and frustration and enabled them to get services faster.

We met Michael Brennan when he was a student in the same class a year later. He was taking a break from being CEO of the United Way for Southeastern Michigan to study at the Stanford d.school—where we teach human-centered design. Michael then left the United Way and joined two students he met at Stanford—Adam and Lena Selzer—to start Civilla, a Michigan-based nonprofit design firm. As Adam put it, they focus on getting "friction out of institutions and replacing it with greater humanity."

One of Civilla's first efforts entailed working with senior leaders from the State of Michigan, frontline employees, and residents to revamp that terrible forty-two-page benefits form we described earlier. They called it Project Re:form. The redesigned benefits form was 80 percent shorter, easing the burden on more than two million residents a year and thousands of state employees. Applications increased by 12 percent after the new form was introduced. Yet employees had far fewer errors to correct, and fewer citizens visited Health and Human Services offices for help—so lobby visits dropped by 50 percent.

We also learned and spread lessons from our *Friction* podcast, a series of twenty-two conversations with business leaders and academics produced by the Stanford Technology Ventures Program. Our guests included historian and Harvard Business School professor Nancy Koehn. Eric Reis of *The Lean Startup* fame. Filmmaker Sheri Singer, producer of more than forty TV movies—each filmed in two to three weeks (including *Halloweentown* and *Death of a Cheerleader*). And we interviewed restaurateurs Annie and Craig Stoll, who run the Delfina pizza chain in the San Francisco area.

Along the way, we've assembled a sprawling network of practitioners, researchers, and students who teach us about the twists, tricks, and pitfalls of friction fixing. They've used, helped develop, refined, and critiqued many of the ideas and tools in this book.

The Friction Project weaves together the best stories, studies, and—above all—solutions that we found during this adventure. We focus on lessons that can help you, dear reader, understand how friction fixers think about and practice their craft, and how you can be a friction fixer, too, and entice others to join your quest. This craft entails understanding *what* ought to be quick or effortless versus difficult, slow, or downright impossible to do. *Why* certain things ought to be easy and others hard. *How* each of us can remove bad friction and inject good friction. And *how* to build teams and organizations where friction fixing is baked into the norms, roles, rules, rituals, and incentives.

Practitioners of the Craft

Here's what friction fixing looks like. Dr. Melinda Ashton, the chief quality officer at Hawaii Pacific Health, was mighty unhappy because her nurses and doctors were devoting too much time to updating patients' electronic health records and too little time examining, treating, and comforting patients. Many other healthcare workers face the same predicament. A 2019 study in the *Journal of the American Medical Association* found that doctors devoted 43 percent of their time to updating patients' electronic medical records and only 13 percent to providing direct patient care.

Dr. Ashton realized that Hawaii Pacific's health records system kept getting more complicated and time-consuming. For example, nurses who cared for newborns weren't initially asked to document diaper changes. Over the years, as the system was "upgraded," multiple mouse clicks were required after changing each diaper. Dozens of other chores arrived courtesy of lawyers, IT administrators, human resources, and nurses and doctors, too. Some were necessary. But many additions (and original requirements) were too complicated or pointless. Many Hawaii Pacific employees complained about the time they were wasting. Yet it was a classic orphan problem, and no one stepped up to reduce these ballooning burdens.

In 2017, Dr. Ashton and her team decided that if nobody else would do it, they would. These friction fixers launched the Getting Rid of Stupid Stuff program (yes, the acronym is GROSS). It began with a call for nurse assistants, nurses, and doctors to nominate anything in the records system "that they thought was poorly designed, unnecessary, or just plain stupid." The team received 188 nominations and implemented 87 improvements by the time Dr. Ashton's "Getting Rid of Stupid Stuff" article appeared in *The New England Journal of Medicine* in 2018.

Fixing all that stupid stuff freed up a lot of time. One change reduced the required clicks for documenting a diaper change from three to one. Another tweak eliminated just one mouse click that every nurse and nurse assistant was required to make for every patient during hourly rounds. That saved twenty-four seconds per click—which, Dr. Ashton reports, "consumed approximately 1,700 nursing hours per month at our four hospitals." Throughout *The Friction Project*, we document how friction fixers drive changes that save others massive amounts of time, such as Project

Re:form by Michael Brennan's team at Civilla, who revamped that Michigan benefits form completed by millions of residents each year so it was 80 percent shorter and a lot easier to understand.

Then there are the friction fixers who feel accountable for hitting the brakes and knowing how and when to add necessary complexity, and for making the wrong things harder, or downright impossible, to do. And when to slow things down to protect people's mental health or to give them more time to connect with others and enjoy the sweet things in life.

In *Thinking, Fast and Slow*, Nobel Prize winner Daniel Kahneman argues that when people are in a "cognitive minefield," when they are confused, overwhelmed, or things are falling apart, it is wise to slow down and assess the situation rather than doing something rash, dumb, or dangerous. That's what Waze CEO Noam Bardin did in 2010 after his navigation software start-up got $25 million in funding. Bardin's investors pressured him to use that money to hire new employees, add features, and expand to new markets. But Waze was losing new U.S. customers at a rapid rate, and Bardin wasn't sure why. He ignored the investors' advice, froze hiring, and asked all employees to stop what they were doing and help figure out what was driving users away in the crucial U.S. market. After six weeks of talking to customers and analyzing data, Waze employees identified customer pain points and began to remove them. Then the company hit the accelerator and started hiring people and releasing a new version of Waze about once a month for six months. Customers loved the changes, and millions became loyal Waze users. Google bought the company for a billion dollars in 2013.

We've also found that veteran friction fixers use rules, regulations, and other roadblocks to prevent unethical and unwise actions. Consider the staffers at the U.S. Department of Defense

(DOD) who, in 2012, prevented former Theranos CEO Elizabeth Holmes from installing her company's unproven blood-testing device on army medical-evacuation helicopters. They were right to put up a fight, because that Edison machine was never able to run accurate blood tests on a single drop of blood despite Theranos's claims that it could. The company is now defunct, and Holmes was convicted on four felony counts of defrauding investors in 2022.

John Carreyrou's *Bad Blood* describes Holmes's indignation when Lt. Col. David Shoemaker (a DOD administrator with a Ph.D. in microbiology) asked her tough questions about the device's capabilities. Holmes was dismayed when—despite advice about circumventing the rules from her high-priced attorneys and support from four-star general Jim "Mad Dog" Mattis—she couldn't steamroll Shoemaker when he insisted that, before the device could be used on the choppers, it had to be approved by the U.S. Food and Drug Administration. Holmes wrote Mattis a "blistering email" about her company's allegedly unfair treatment from the lowly lieutenant colonel and his coworkers who dared to get in Theranos's way. Mattis demanded an in-person meeting with Shoemaker, but came away convinced Shoemaker had applied the rules properly to the Theranos gizmo. In 2013, when Lieutenant Colonel Shoemaker retired from the DOD, his colleagues presented him a "certificate of survival" for having the courage to stand up to General Mattis.

Friction fixers also slow things down so that people take time to care for one another, get to know one another, and enjoy the good things in life. Like Colette Cloosterman–van Eerd, chief customer officer at Jumbo, the big Dutch grocery store chain that installed two hundred "slow lanes" where cashiers take time for leisurely chats with seniors who crave social interaction. Cloosterman–van Eerd is the driving force behind these "chat checkouts." She explained, "Our stores are an important meeting place for many people, and we want to play a role in identifying and reducing loneliness." She sees this effort as a "small gesture, but very valuable, especially in a world that is digitizing and getting faster and faster."

How to Think Like a Friction Fixer

Our seven-year project taught us that a bedrock belief of friction fixers is that *if we focus on what to make easier and faster and what to make harder and slower, life will be better for workers and the people they serve.* And if we turn our attention to finding when and where friction troubles arise, understanding the causes, and developing remedies, then our organization will be more humane, productive, innovative, and profitable. That's what Dr. Melinda Ashton's team did when they invited their colleagues to stop and think about stupid stuff that was clogging up Hawaii Pacific's health records system. And what Michael Brennan's team at Civilla did during Project Re:form, when they involved numerous government leaders, civil servants, and citizens as they revamped Michigan's benefits application form.

The power of pausing to think about removing needless complexity is seen in research by Gabrielle Adams of the University of Virginia and her colleagues in the prestigious publication *Nature*. They document the human penchant to add rather than subtract—and show how to overcome that baked-in bias. In a series of twenty studies, these researchers found that—in tasks ranging from building LEGO models to improving a university—peoples' default problem-solving mode is to add rather than subtract complexity. Even when people were asked to build LEGO models where the best solution was to remove pieces at a key juncture (and were charged ten cents for each LEGO brick used), they still added more pieces. *But* when the researchers added a cognitive speed bump—and reminded people that they could either add or subtract pieces from the LEGO model—they were far more likely to remove pieces at the key juncture.

Sounds obvious, doesn't it? It is. Friction fixers pride themselves in being masters of the obvious. They are mighty skeptical of secret solutions, shocking surprises, and miracle cures.

This bedrock belief, this dogged dedication to making the right things easier and wrong things harder, is sharpened by three convictions that emerged from our project and run through this book. These beliefs help friction fixers to avoid wallowing in vague platitudes, take concrete action instead, and inspire others to join their mission. The first conviction is *I am accountable for friction fixing, and so are you.* Friction fixers feel obligated to prevent themselves and their colleagues from being oblivious of friction that they and their organizations generate. They battle decisions and designs that treat such obstacles and opportunities as orphan problems. They take responsibility for fixing things, encouraging others to join them, and discouraging free riders.

That's what Noam Bardin did when he pressed pause at Waze and made it everyone's job to figure out what was wrong with the company's app and how to repair it. As we wrote in *Scaling Up Excellence,* such accountability means everyone presses everyone else to talk and act as if "I own the place and the place owns me." Friction fixers see themselves as part of a movement that recruits, teaches, and rewards everyone around them—whether their zone of influence is modest or massive—to step up and figure out what is broken and how to mend it.

The second conviction is that *we are trustees of how people spend their time.* That's our focus in chapter 1, "A Trustee of Others'

Time." Fixers are preoccupied with how to design work and organizations, and how to treat others, to make the best use of employees', customers', and citizens' time. It paves the way for two other key elements of friction fixing. Chapter 2, "Friction Forensics," digs into figuring out what ought to be hard and what ought to be easy—which is essential for determining where people ought to spend more time and less time, and where to inject more and less friction. Chapters 1 and 2 set the stage for chapter 3, "How Friction Fixers Do Their Work," where we unpack our "help pyramid," which ranges from helping people to cope with friction troubles that they can't remove (at least for now) to implementing local and systemwide changes for the better. Our pyramid helps you decide when redesigning or repairing a broken system is a good use of time. Or when doing so is futile and it's better to help people keep their dignity intact, to avoid blaming themselves, and to stave off despair and helplessness. And to spend their time finding the least bad paths for traveling through lousy systems rather than squandering time tilting at windmills.

The third conviction is that *friction fixing is a craft that we learn, practice, develop, teach, and spread to others.* We unpack the details of this craft in chapters 4 through 8. Friction fixers know that their work entails finding, mastering, and applying specific skills and tools, having successes and setbacks that help them refine their craft, and learning from and teaching fellow travelers. That there are no one-size-fits all solutions for the minor hassles and massive messes that they tackle. Fixers develop custom projects that are suited to them, their team, and their organization.

To help you develop this craft, *The Friction Project* dissects five prevalent and destructive traps: Oblivious Leaders, Addition Sickness, Broken Connections, Jargon Monoxide, and Fast and Frenzied. We devote a chapter to each of these bundles of afflictions. We dig into why each plagues organizations and provide tactics, tools, rituals, and design principles to help you avoid, dampen, and remove each trap—without leaving people feeling frustrated, helpless, or defeated.

In short, too many of our teams and organizations are mired in muck because the wrong things are too easy and the right things are too hard. It doesn't need to be that way. *The Friction Project* fortifies you to band together with others to avoid, escape, and remove such obstacles to productivity, innovation, dignity, and sanity. To create a virtuous circle that is stoked by the feeling that, to earn others' respect and the right to be proud of myself, I've got to be part of the friction solution rather than part of the problem.

Part II

THE ELEMENTS OF FRICTION FIXING

A Trustee of Others' Time

In August 1940, as his country prepared for waves of attacks by German planes, Winston Churchill set out to address a different enemy. In his 234-word "Brevity" memo, he implored his colleagues to "see to it that their Reports are shorter." The British prime minister urged them to write "short, crisp paragraphs," to move complex arguments or statistics to appendices, and to stop using "officialese jargon" and "woolly phrases." A few months later, Churchill asked bureaucrats to hear his "cry of pain" and remember that "the number and length of messages sent by a diplomat are no measure of his efficiency."

More than seventy years later, we sat down with our teaching team to discuss how to run our "customer-focused innovation" class for sixty executives. As people weighed in with various ideas about the content, our colleague Jeremy Utley suddenly roared, "I hate wasting people's time. Let's make every minute good for them."

During the friction project, we returned to Churchill's memo and Jeremy's words again and again because both illustrate a hallmark of skilled friction fixers: being a trustee of other people's time. Trustees take pride in spotting and removing obstacles that squander people's time and money, frustrate them, and leave them feeling helpless and exhausted. And they take pride in knowing when to slow down, struggle, or stop—in creating constructive friction.

The Cone of Friction

Trustees are leaders who focus on and fret over who is—and could be—influenced by their powers to make things easier or harder, and whom they might be unwittingly hobbling by their words, deeds, and designs. This zone of potential impact is your "cone of friction." Churchill used his position as prime minister to press public servants in his cone to practice "short-windedness." Jeremy pressed our team to eliminate needless boredom, frustration, and downtime for the sixty executives in our "cone." Dr. Melinda Ashton and her team that launched the Getting Rid of Stupid Stuff program at Hawaii Pacific Health served as trustees of their nurses', doctors', and patients' time.

In 2013, Dropbox CEO Drew Houston and his top team used their powers over all employees of this file-sharing company to cancel hundreds of time-sucking meetings. Employees were wasting so much time in meetings that they kept missing crucial deadlines, especially shipping dates. Drew's team decided to help Dropbox employees avoid heaping unnecessary meetings on themselves. Dropbox IT folks removed nearly all standing meetings from employees' calendars and made it impossible for them to add new meetings to their calendars for two weeks. Employees were notified via an email titled "Armeetingeddon has landed." After explaining why their calendars were "a bit light," the email asked, "Ahhh, doesn't it feel fantastic?" Dropbox also developed guidelines that included such directives as "schedule meetings if (and only if) other forms of communication won't cut it" and "invite only key stakeholders, not spectators," and if people realized a meeting was useless, or they were adding nothing, they were encouraged to leave early.

Trustees also scout for signs that it's time to inject healthy friction, including when to hit the brakes and slow down or stop. That's a lesson from research on "stealth CEO factories," obscure companies that produce scores of successful CEOs for other companies. Consultants Elena Lytinkia Botelho and Sanja Kos found that one of the most productive of these factories is Rohm and Haas (a chemical manufacturer now part of Dow Chemical). Companies led by CEOs groomed at Rohm and Haas "performed 67 percent better than those companies did when other CEOs were in charge."

Rohm and Haas teaches its leaders that when they face a decision with broad and enduring consequences, taking speedy, narrow, and impulsive action is a recipe for disaster. Instead, Rohm and Haas preaches the Five Voices method. Before making a big decision, leaders slow down, do careful research, and talk to people until they understand five key stakeholders: the customer, the employee, the owner, the community, and the process. Time at this leadership finishing school helped alum Pierre Brondeau as CEO of the FMC Corporation. The Five Voices taught him, "It's not about pleasing your boss—it's about doing the right thing by your stakeholders."

Trustees also create red tape that makes the wrong things difficult or impossible to do. For example, the leaders of Blue Cross Blue Shield of Massachusetts (the state's largest private insurer) decided to take action because deaths from opioids in the state increased 45 percent between 2012 and 2013, and the death rate in Massachusetts from opioids was two and a half times the national average.

Many of these deaths resulted from opioids prescribed to

Blue Cross Blue Shield members. The company implemented policies to make it harder for physicians to prescribe opioids. Doctors were required to discuss treatment options other than opioids and to sign written agreements with patients about their treatment plans. Doctors also had to provide a written rationale for prescribing opioids, which was reviewed and approved (or rejected) by a clinician with expertise in opioid addiction. The company also implemented a ban on pharmacy mail orders for opioids.

By 2015, opioid prescriptions for Blue Cross Blue Shield members had dropped by 15 percent. That meant, as a team of researchers led by Dr. Macarena C. García reported, "twenty-one million fewer opioid doses were dispensed in the first three years after implementation."

The Massachusetts program was led by top company executives including Dr. Bruce Nash, their chief physician executive. We've also been inspired by many trustees who have more modest influence and are closer to the bottom than to the top of the pecking order. All of us have the power to help people in our cone of friction, whether it is big or little.

That's what happened when one of us, Bob Sutton, visited his local Department of Motor Vehicles (DMV) office in Redwood City, California, to change the registration on his late mother's Toyota Camry. He was dreading a long ordeal with grumpy civil servants. When Bob arrived at 7:30 A.M., a half hour before the branch opened, fifty people were already in line outside. At about 7:45, a friendly DMV employee set up a table near the entrance and began walking down the line asking everyone the purpose of his or her visit—something, we learned later, DMV employees did there every morning and was one of many systemic changes aimed at making California DMVs more effective and customer friendly. That employee told at least fifteen

people they could complete a form instead of waiting in line—
and even handed them the right form and a pen (!) so they could
complete it on the spot. The employee sent the rest, including
Bob, inside and told them which of the seven windows to wait at
and provided forms and tips to get ready—so our transactions
would be quicker for us and the clerk. Bob completed his rather
complicated transaction by 8:15 A.M.

Yes, to our amazement, one of the best customer service experiences either of us had during our project was at the DMV!
And it was largely due to that skilled (and warm) trustee of time
who helped people negotiate the bureaucratic maze.

The Five Commitments

Mottos for Trustees

Five mottos emerged from our friction project that help trustees protect the time—and bolster the dignity, zest for life, and
performance—of people in their cone of friction. These commitments guide how trustees practice their craft, teach it, and
recruit others to join them. Friction fixing works best when
people are encouraged, praised, and rewarded for banding together. The antics of lone heroes are rarely sufficient for averting
and repairing such vexing and messy problems.

1. It's like Mowing the Lawn

We love the dramatic flair and instant relief evident in Churchill's
"Brevity" memo and "Armeetingeddon" at Dropbox. The after-
math of both stories, however, reinforces a second, more som-
ber, lesson: friction requires constant vigilance. When Winston
Churchill returned for his second term as prime minister in 1951
(he was voted out in 1945), he re-sent his 1940 "Brevity" memo,
because official papers were still "too long and diffuse." Churchill

also attached a memo from his foreign secretary urging diplomats (yet again) to send fewer telegrams and make them shorter.

Similarly, at Dropbox, in the months after Armeetingeddon, people scheduled fewer meetings, meetings were smaller, and people routinely declined invites. But they soon slipped back into their old ways. Drew Houston told us that by 2015 "things were worse than ever," and added that the battle against too many big bad meetings was like mowing the lawn. Constant maintenance was required to stem the ugly and excessive growth.

This never-ending game of Whac-A-Mole entails injecting friction at the right times and places. Friction fixers think like the crew chiefs of NASCAR or Formula One racing teams, scheduling regular pit stops while searching for signs that it's time for emergency repairs. We interviewed a vice president at a big software company who used this "pit stop" perspective to manage his dozen direct reports, who were spread across nine countries and six time zones—and, together, led four hundred engineers. The VP cut regular meetings with this team from once a week to once a month, replacing meetings with a rhythm where team members wrote a shared (and collectively edited) document with schedules, responsibilities, goals, red flags, and updates. It was due every Friday. Relying more on writing and less on talking improved communication and coordination and forced people to think more deeply about their work—the team functioned better than ever.

But, after using this system for a few months, the VP learned that some flare-ups and fiascoes couldn't wait for the monthly meeting. Such as when a team member got in a nasty argument with a client and threatened to quit the company if the client wasn't fired—the VP called an emergency meeting to work through the anger and figure out how to save the relationship with the client.

2. Organizations Are Malleable Prototypes

Rather than feeling powerless to tinker with or toss out prevailing rules, procedures, and structures, friction fixers treat such organizational features as temporary and changeable—as just the best they can do right now. That's akin to how skilled designers treat the products and services they develop—as ever-changing and (they hope) ever-improving prototypes. Friction fixers live this mindset by asking such questions as: Do people know how to use the company? Is it simple? Complex? Is it obvious how it works? What is slow about it? Are there bugs? What can we fix quickly, and what's going to take a long time?

We learned the power of treating organizations as prototypes some twenty years ago from David Kelley, when we did an eighteen-month ethnographic study of IDEO—a renowned innovation firm that David cofounded and was CEO of at the time. David realized that unhealthy friction was rising at IDEO because the system that had worked for staffing projects when the company had 50 designers didn't work with 150. The committee that staffed projects was taking longer to make decisions and making mistakes because they didn't know enough about the work, the clients, or how long each project would take. Tempers flared as designers battled over who ought to work on which projects.

David introduced a prototype in hopes of fixing this mess at an all-hands meeting that we attended. He began by acknowledging that IDEO's structure was no longer working. Then he introduced three leaders, each charged with heading a new "studio." Each made a pitch about "why you should join my studio." Designers then selected which studio they wanted to join: each listed their first, second, and third choices (all got their first choice).

Before the pitches began, David reminded people that IDEO's philosophy was "enlightened trial and error outperforms the planning of flawless intellects." The new studio model, he noted, was a changeable prototype, just like the products, services, and experiences they designed for clients. To reinforce this message—in a move that shocked all—David shaved off his trademark Groucho Marx–style mustache just before the meeting. He said, "The changes we are trying are just like shaving off my mustache; they are temporary and reversible experiments."

David grew back that mustache a few months later, and IDEO has experimented with numerous other structures over the years. But David still reminds folks at IDEO and elsewhere to treat organizations as imperfect and unfinished prototypes.

When some policy or practice annoys or drives people crazy, friction fixers need the courage and sway to try something different. And if that doesn't work, to change it, or toss it out, and try something else.

3. Celebrate and Reward Doers, Not Posers

We call Becky Margiotta a friction fixer. She uses more graphic language. From the time Becky was a young U.S. Army officer, then as leader of a campaign that found homes for one hundred thousand unhoused Americans, and now as head of the Billions Institute (which helps "leaders spread solutions to the world's biggest problems"), she says, "I've spent the majority of my adult life unfucking things."

Becky has cleaned up many messes by bolstering doers rather than posers. In the early days of the 100,000 Homes Campaign, Becky's team realized that one reason they kept failing to meet interim goals was that dozens of posers were jabbering away at meetings and on calls, promising to do key work in their communities, and asking staffers for help. Yet the posers never followed through. They were adept at smart talk but allergic to grinding out the work to connect their words to action. Becky's team nicknamed these glib pretenders "hollow Easter bunnies" because "it is just like Easter when you think you are going to get a really good chocolate Easter egg and it's just a hollow Easter bunny. It's nothing." After wasting too much time on these hollow bunnies, Becky's team became adept at serving as trustees of others' time, and their own, by spotting such posers, ignoring them, and (gently) explaining to them they were hampering the campaign.

Becky's team also cranked up rewards for doers. When Becky was in the U.S. Army, if soldiers were screwing around or messing up, she or a fellow officer asked, "Who is fucking this chicken?" In other words, who was in charge? When Becky told that story to her 100,000 Homes team, they knew it would inspire doers who propelled the campaign. Becky started giving "The Chicken F'er" talk to community groups that were working to house people. And her team created the "top secret" Rooster Award. Every month, they selected ten or fifteen people who were moving the campaign forward. Each chicken f'er received a little metal rooster to recognize the person's accomplishments.

Trustees such as Becky and her team are vigilant about spotting and discouraging hollow moves that undermine rather than activate friction fixing. See our list of seven tricks that can make posers feel good about themselves and burnish their reputations but waste precious time and money when disconnected from action. Wise trustees keep an eye out for such moves and discourage others who try them.

Most of these tricks are versions of "the smart-talk trap," which is what Bob Sutton and Stanford colleague Jeff Pfeffer call eloquent, interesting, and insincere words that serve as substitutes for action (rather than to guide and inspire action). Smart but empty talk happens because it is easier to say smart things than to do smart things. And because smooth talkers get immediate kudos while dogged doers must delay gratification.

Poser Tricks
Hollow Acts That Undermine Friction Fixing

1. Promises as substitutes for action. Offering to help fix friction troubles, then behaving—and perhaps believing—that no further effort is required.
2. Holding and attending meetings to talk about friction fixing as substitutes for actually doing it.
3. Eloquent but useless talk. Spewing out impressive ideas and compelling stories about friction—which are so vague, impractical, or convoluted that no subsequent action or learning results.
4. Mission statements and lists of shared values as substitutes for friction fixing.
5. Bad-mouthing as a substitute for action. Criticizing, complaining about, and blaming people, traditions, and rules that fuel friction problems—but doing nothing to help with or encourage repairs.
6. Training as a symbolic rather substantive response to friction troubles.
7. Outsourcing friction fixing efforts to consultants and other fellow posers—so they get the blame for inaction rather than the poser.

Those hollow bunnies fooled Becky's team, at least at first, with many of the tricks on our list. They made enthusiastic promises to help with the campaign. They planned and attended meetings with campaign staffers and community members. They spewed out impressive facts, figures, and jargon about un-housed people. They said they were working to house people in their communities, but didn't follow up on their plans. In the end, their jargon was vague and impractical, and their grand promises went unkept. All they did was squander others' time and energy.

Friction fixers need to be especially wary of smart critics. Experiments by psychologist Teresa Amabile on the "brilliant but cruel" effect found that people who write nasty book reviews are seen as more intelligent and expert than people who write positive reviews. As Amabile put it, "Only pessimism sounds profound. Optimism sounds superficial." In the early days of our friction project, we focused on stories about the terrible ordeals that companies, universities, and governments imposed on people—and provided blistering critiques. Sure, there are lazy, incompetent, and cruel people—and broken systems—that deserve to be named and shamed. Yet, when we went behind the curtain to find the villains in these horror stories, we often found good people who were trying to make things better but faced onerous obstacles such as absurd rules and laws that they had to follow or be fired. Because they wrestled with the problems every day, they knew what was wrong and how to fix it.

But no one listened to them or gave them permission to change things. They didn't deserve to be bad-mouthed.

That's what Civilla cofounders Michael Brennan, Adam Selzer, and Lena Selzer found when they began working with the Michigan civil servants to redesign that convoluted forty-two-page benefits form. As Adam tells it, he had stereotyped these folks as uncaring and unimaginative. When Michael, Adam, and Lena met them, however, they found caring, conscientious, and courageous frontline employees who wrestled with and despised the terrible form, too, and senior officials who had been trying to fix it for years. Once those civil servants realized that Civilla was there to help and had the resources and patience to stick with the problem, they became imaginative, open-minded, and relentless partners throughout the redesign. As Civilla's inspiring case study of Project Re:form put it, "Rather than approach conversations with blame or accusation, we've found that giving folks the benefit of the doubt and recognizing the complexity of their jobs to be a lot more helpful in sparking partnerships and opening the door for constructive discourse."

Training is another kind of talk that substitutes for friction fixing. Organizations use it to signal that they care about challenges including diversity and inclusion, sexual harassment, innovation, and customer experiences. But their people do nothing else to implement the lessons. Leaders of such organizations also have a handy scapegoat for the lack of progress—the trainers!

We tracked a financial services firm for years as they trained thousands of employees in design thinking methods. Again and again, we asked the firm's leaders, "Which product and services have been improved by design thinking?" They told us how much employees loved the training and how it gave them tools to innovate on their jobs. But the leaders were never able to identify a single product or service that was changed by someone who took such classes, applied design thinking methods, and changed it for the better (or even made it worse!). We weren't surprised when the company abandoned this training program after a decade of such futility—and bad-mouthed faculty who taught the classes.

In contrast, the founders of Civilla were trained in design thinking methods, too. But they applied those lessons by interviewing and observing dozens of citizens and civil servants to understand their experiences with the bad old benefits form, to identify obstacles, to generate ideas for making it shorter and less confusing—and then using these lessons to redesign the benefits form.

The last trick on our list is "Outsourcing friction fixing efforts to consultants and other fellow posers—so they get the blame for inaction rather than the poser." We met one executive who moved to a new company every few years. That well-traveled fellow explained to us that he started each new job by hiring consultants from prestigious firms to develop ideas for change initiatives. Like the digital transformation plan that IT consultants developed for his last company, where he was an executive vice president. That plan helped him land his current job as a CEO because it provided a great story to tell during his job interviews. That CEO laughed as he admitted that the digital transformation effort was never implemented at his old company, and then he blamed those "blowhard" consultants for the lack of progress. We realized this savvy organizational politician had outsourced friction fixing in part because the consultants were handy scapegoats for inaction and other failures on his watch. That executive had hired high-priced consultants, so he had spent money as a substitute for action—a favorite move by rich and powerful posers.

4. Focus on Fixing Things, Not Who to Blame

When friction troubles abound, ruminating and ranting about who is to blame saps energy that is better directed at developing remedies. Leaders who blame and punish employees who raise problems, point out colleagues' mistakes, and confess their own missteps create cultures of fear—places where people are pressured to sweep problems under the rug rather than uncovering trouble and recruiting colleagues to help them make repairs.

Research by MIT's Nelson Repenning and John Sterman found that, in manufacturing and software-development companies that are riddled with inefficiency and quality problems, employees are often shunned, blamed, punished, and expelled when they identify systemic problems. In one firm, engineers were told to "never reveal a problem until you also have the solution." This penchant for shooting the messenger led engineers in another dysfunctional firm to deem their weekly review meetings "the liars' club." They felt pressured to overstate progress and to hide defects, which created big problems after their work was handed off to others.

Similar defects in Boeing's culture prompted employees to hide design and manufacturing flaws from one another, airlines that bought their planes, and pilots who flew them. That's what happened before two Boeing 737 MAX jets crashed. The first crash killed 189 passengers in Indonesia in October of 2018. The second killed 157 passengers in Ethiopia five months later. A damning 117-page trove of internal communications exchanged among Boeing employees before the crashes was released in 2020. As *The New York Times* reported, these communications exposed a "broken" culture that abandoned the company's historical focus on quality and safety. At Boeing, people had come to put revenue and stock price first even if it meant cutting corners that made their planes more likely to crash.

When Boeing insiders discussed whether the Indonesian pilots would need flight-simulator training for the new MAX, some wondered if it might be necessary "because of their own stupidity" and the "idiots" who ran the Indonesian airline that ordered the new 737 MAX—not because the new plane had design flaws that made it difficult for any pilot to fly. Despite such qualms, Boeing charged ahead and convinced regulators that a short computer-based training session was sufficient for MAX pilots. Boeing employees celebrated after that light and cheap training was approved because it meant pilots would "still be able to jump into a MAX" even if it had been thirty years since their simulator training on the original 737. One employee responded, "LOVE IT," because their marketing PowerPoint decks showed that simulator training was "a big part of the operating cost structure."

Meanwhile, other Boeing insiders who felt afraid to raise concerns about the plane with their leaders (or customers or the Federal Aviation Administration) expressed backstage reservations to one another. Including the employees who wrote, before the 2018 crash, "I honestly don't trust many people at Boeing," and "Would you put your family on a MAX simulator trained aircraft? I wouldn't." And, as Ed Pierson, a former senior manager at the plant that built 737s, told organizational psychologist Adam Grant, when employees there didn't meet production goals, they were named, shamed, and grilled in front of a hundred coworkers, so "it was a very personal, very public humiliation."

The culture of fear and secrecy, which put the almighty dollar ahead of human lives, also meant that Boeing failed to inform the FAA, airlines, and pilots about new software—the Maneuvering Characteristics Augmentation System, or MCAS—that its engineers, test pilots, and executives knew was prone to malfunction (and was eventually identified as the main culprit in the two 737 MAX crashes). According to *The New York Times,* after the MAX entered service in 2017, Boeing failed to inform airlines that "a cockpit warning light that could have helped the pilots on the Indonesia and Ethiopia flights identify an MCAS malfunction wasn't working in most planes." Instead, after the crashes, Boeing CEO Dennis Muilenburg "suggested that poorly trained foreign pilots, not the company, were to blame." But other Boeing employees blamed themselves and a culture where you were expected to shut your mouth and bury bad news so the company could move fast and make money. Including one employee who wrote, just after the two crashes, "I still haven't been forgiven by God for the covering up I did last year."

If the folks at Boeing, especially senior executives, had sustained a culture where people slowed down and fixed things, felt obligated to speak up about quality problems, and put safety before short-term profits, our opinion is that it would have saved hundreds of lives and averted employees' guilt and shame, and the company would not have taken an estimated $18 billion hit as a result of canceled, lost, and delayed 737 MAX orders.

Harvard Business School's Amy Edmondson has devoted more than twenty years to documenting the damage done by organizations like Boeing that undermine psychological safety, where people are afraid to admit mistakes or point out others' errors and missteps. Amy shows that when workplaces punish employees who reveal bad news and reward those who hide it, and employees pass flawed work down the line without warning the recipients, it damages cost and quality. And the resulting fear of speaking up can hurt or even kill people too. That's why she calls the 737 MAX fiasco a "textbook case of how the absence of psychological safety" can lead to disasters.

Organizational life doesn't have to be like that. One manager in a successful change effort studied by Nelson Repenning and John Sterman explained, "There are two theories. One says, 'There's a problem, let's fix it.' The other says, 'Someone is screwing up, let's go beat them up.' To make improvement, we could no longer embrace the second theory, we had to use the first." Amy Edmondson's research on psychological safety suggests that moving from a culture of covering up mistakes and finger-pointing to one that supports fixing and learning requires a radical shift in how we think about what constitutes "talent" in employees.

When Anita Tucker and Amy Edmondson studied 194 patient-care failures in hospitals (ranging from broken medical devices to administering the wrong drugs), they found that nurses who disguised and worked around problems without calling attention to them often caused such failures. Yet those same nurses were often deemed the *most talented* by doctors and administrators because they never complained about problems, were adept at working around broken systems, and created the impression that they rarely if ever made mistakes.

Anita and Amy concluded that hospitals would better protect and serve patients by hiring and rewarding vocal nurses who behaved in opposite ways. The implication for trustees bent on identifying and repairing friction troubles is to learn, live, and celebrate talents that will make many people squirm. Following Amy and Anita, friction fixers make it safe for "noisy complainers" who repair problems and then tell many others where the system failed. Friction fixers praise and protect "noisy troublemakers" and "self-aware error makers," who point out mistakes they and others make so people can avoid repeating such failures and improve the system.

Sure, sometimes it's easier to be quiet and compliant. But if your goal is friction fixing—rather than fueling the delusion that everything is just fine—be loud and proud about the mistakes that you and others make and flaws that you spot and fix, and reward that behavior in others. And don't stop questioning what your organization does and pressing others to figure out how to do it better.

5. Honor People Who Avert Friction Fiascoes, Not Just Firefighters

Friction fixers avert trouble before it happens—they don't just repair or remove problems that flare up. As Archbishop Desmond Tutu, the Nobel Peace Prize winner who was a powerful force in ending apartheid in South Africa, said, "There comes a point where we need to stop just pulling people out of the river. We need to go upstream and find out why they're falling in."

Unfortunately, firefighters' heroics can overshadow the invisible design and maintenance work that prevents calamities. In their research on manufacturing and software development systems, Nelson Repenning and John Sterman found that bad systems persist partly because, as an auto company engineer explained, "no one ever gets credit for problems that never happened." Nelson and John found that too many organizations celebrate saviors who develop imaginative work-arounds to compensate for broken systems that are plagued with bad handoffs, flawed information about how the system is functioning, and other coordination woes. As one project manager told them, his company rewarded "war heroes" like him, that he was promoted because "I've delivered programs under duress."

It's better to eliminate the need for such heroics. To paraphrase a conversation we had with the late Bill Moggridge, cofounder of IDEO and director of the Cooper Hewitt, Smithsonian Design Museum, the best designs—be they of products, services, or organizations—are often those that "you notice that you don't notice" because they run so smoothly or are so easy to use that you are rarely if ever jolted by confusion or ugly surprises.

It isn't just that such creations are designed and built well; you also don't notice them because they are kept in tip-top shape. Friction fixers embrace Professors Andrew Russell and Lee Vinsel's rallying cry, "Let's get excited about maintenance!" Friction fixers appreciate preventive upkeep and the people who do it. And reject the all-too-common "impoverished and immature conception of technology, one that fetishizes innovation as a kind of art and demeans upkeep as mere drudgery." When maintenance is neglected, bridges and buildings collapse, forest fires rage, drinking water becomes poisonous, and our cars, laptops, and phones don't work. Andrew and Lee point out that while engineers who invent new things get the kudos and cash, "roughly 70 percent of engineers work on maintaining and overseeing existing things rather than designing new ones." Life would be hell without their unsung heroics.

For friction fixers, artist Mierle Laderman Ukeles is the patron saint of keeping things clean, cared for, and working. Back in 1969, Ukeles wrote her *Manifesto for Maintenance Art,* which celebrates people who "keep the dust off the pure individual creation; preserve the new, sustain the change; protect progress; defend and prolong the advance; renew excitement." Her manifesto asks, "After the revolution, who's going to pick up the garbage on Monday morning?" In 1977, after the New York City Department of Sanitation got wind of Ukeles's work, they appointed her artist-in-residence—an (unpaid) position that she still holds. For her first project, *Touch Sanitation Performance,* Ukeles spent eleven months between 1979 and 1980 traveling around the city to meet, shake hands with, and thank all eighty-five hundred of New York City's sanitation workers. She told each, "Thank you for keeping New York City alive!"

Powered by Authentic Pride

Let's return to Jeremy Utley's appeal to our teaching team: "I hate wasting people's time. Let's make every minute good for them." Jeremy felt that, if we cared for those sixty executives by not wasting their time during the program, when it was over, we would deserve their respect. He never hinted that our team was so great that we were destined to run a successful program. Jeremy focused on how we could earn the right to feel proud. Not on the competitive advantage we had, say, because of traits such as smarts, creativity, or charisma.

Jeremy was driven by what psychologist Jessica Tracy and her coauthors call "authentic pride," the self-esteem gained from being a conscientious and caring person who accomplishes good things by treating others well. And who earns their admiration and respect as a result. Jessica's research also found that authentic pride has an evil twin, "hubristic pride," where people feel endowed with enduring qualities such as being *really* smart, athletic, or gorgeous that anoint them as superior to others—which unleashes their arrogance, conceit, and self-aggrandizement. Authentic pride depends on working to earn and sustain prestige over the long haul. Hubristic pride "is more immediate but fleeting and, in some cases, unwarranted." It depends more on taking shortcuts and less on doing hard work.

Authentic pride is a thread that connects our five mottos. The belief, for example, that friction fixing is like mowing the lawn means that trustees are primed to grind it out and gain self-esteem and respect for their long-term efforts—not for fleeting and flashy theatrics. The same goes for the trustees we celebrate for treating organizations as malleable prototypes, such as IDEO's cofounder David Kelley. They are confident that they can keep improving their organizations but humble because it requires dogged persistence—they know there is no "one and done" when it comes to friction fixing. The "chicken f'ers" that Becky Margiotta celebrated exemplify authentic pride, too. They gained Becky's team's respect for doing the difficult, sometimes exasperating work required to find homes for people in their communities. Those "hollow Easter bunnies" were, in contrast, felled by hubristic pride. Once Becky's team detected the posers' bullshit, they were ignored and (gently) expelled.

But beware that it can be tough to tell chicken f'ers from hollow Easter bunnies. Remember, Becky's team was initially fooled by posers. Part of the challenge is the deceptive similarity between how people look when they experience either kind of pride. That's what Jessica Tracy learned from testing an idea proposed by Charles Darwin back in 1872: "A proud man exhibits his superiority over others by holding his head and body erect. He . . . makes himself appear as large as possible; so that metaphorically he is said to be swollen or puffed up with pride." Jessica found, much as Darwin had predicted, that when people feel proud of their achievements, they display "expanded posture, slight head tilt, arms akimbo with hands on hips or raised above the head with hands in fists" (and a "low-intensity smile"). Jessica also documented that, in every culture studied, adults consistently distinguish when others express pride versus other emotions like happiness—and so do four-year-old children.

Yet these studies detected no differences in how people express authentic versus hubristic pride—both look the same. That means it is easy to be fooled, at least at first, by fake friction fixers who are puffed up by their smart talk and slogans—rather than by the pride of making the right things easier and the wrong things harder for others. And, dear reader, beware of the temptation to seek the immediate gratification that such hubris can deliver to you, too.

Friction Forensics
The Easy Way or the Hard Way?

We started the friction project because we were disgusted with organizations that make it difficult to do simple things. That overwhelm and confuse employees and customers, trigger streams of obscenities, and leave people exhausted. Our naïve early stance was that any organization that intentionally inflicted such friction on people was cruel, callous, and ineffective.

Then we thought about all the stuff we've bought at IKEA, how fondly we look back on the challenges of finding our purchases in a giant store, schlepping them to the checkout line and then home, and—despite a bit of tension with our spouses along the way—how proud we were after assembling our new bookshelves, bed frames, and file cabinets. We'd been enticed (or perhaps duped) by what Harvard Business School's Michael Norton and his colleagues call the "the IKEA effect," which happens because "labor leads to love." The upshot of their studies—building on research on cognitive dissonance that goes back to the 1950s—is that the harder we work at something, the more we will cherish it, independently of its other qualities. This happens because we humans are driven to justify our efforts to ourselves and others. We think and say, "That sure was a lot of work, but it was worth it," whether or not it is true!

That's why, in one of the experiments by Michael Norton and colleagues, "builders" who assembled an IKEA box bid 63 percent more for the same box than "nonbuilders" who inspected but didn't assemble it. IKEA also harnesses "labor leads to love" in its convoluted in-store customer experience. As Dina Chaiffetz, director of product strategy at Prolific International, says, IKEA "looked friction in the face and laughed. . . . They make you walk through the entire store to get to checkout. Along the way, you have to take notes. And then you get to play gofer, pulling your stuff from inventory yourself. And that's all before you even go home to tackle the Rubik's Cube that is your future desk."

Effort justification also explains why fraternities, sororities, and militaries subject newcomers to all sorts of exhausting and embarrassing ordeals to instill commitment and comradery. Some places take it all too far, damaging the physical and mental health of people and ruining the reputations of their organizations. Or by simply wasting too much time and money on capturing those hearts and minds. But smart leaders know—in the right doses and with proper precautions—that friction and frustration can breed enduring (if sometimes irrational) loyalty.

The bigger lesson for *The Friction Project* is that making snap judgments about what ought to be hard and what ought to be easy is risky business. Savvy trustees hit the pause button and figure out *what* to make easy, hard, or impossible before they turn to *how* to do it. They strive to get things done as quickly and cheaply as possible but keep searching for signs that it will take longer to go fast and cost more money to do things cheaply. As with everything that friction fixers do, there are no one-size-fits-all secrets. When and where you want a little friction, or a lot, requires weighing an organization's goals, values, talents, and constraints, including money, traditions, rules and laws, and power dynamics.

The First Questions

We call this the art and science of "friction forensics." We've developed eight diagnostic questions to help guide such decisions. The first two questions to ask are "Is it the right—or the wrong—thing for us to do?" and "Do we have the will and skill to do it well?

Friction Forensics
Do You Want Something to Be Easy or Hard to Do?

1. Is it the right—or wrong—thing for you to do?
2. Do you have enough skill and will to do it well—or do you need to learn how to do it or crank up your motivation?
3. Is failure cheap, safe, reversible, and instructive?
4. Is delay wasteful, cruel, or downright dangerous?
5. Are people already overloaded, exhausted, and burned out? Or do they have the bandwidth to add more to their plates?
6. Does it require people to work alone or together? To do it well, how much do different people, teams, and organizations need to coordinate (work together) and cooperate (be willing to work together)?
7. Will reducing or eliminating friction for some people result in it being heaped on others? Are you making things easier and harder in the right places? Is the redistribution of friction ethical and fair? Or is it heartless, destructive, exploitive, and cruel?
8. Are the commitment, learning, and social bonds that can result from hard work, frustration, suffering, and struggle worthwhile given the human and financial toll?

When something—be it an action, service, or creation—is safe and proven to be effective, that usually means it ought to

be quick and easy to do, use, or get. Consider the U.S. Transportation Security Administration (TSA) PreCheck program for "trusted travelers." It is prudent to keep possible terrorists, people with a history of air rage, and other criminals off commercial airline flights. And in the years since the 2001 terrorist attacks on the World Trade Center and the Pentagon, the TSA has screened millions of passengers and learned to identify passengers who pose little risk. In 2011, it created the PreCheck program, so preapproved, low-risk passengers could speed through lines where they weren't required to remove their shoes or jackets, or to take their liquids and laptops out of bags. As of December 2021, the TSA reported that 94 percent of PreCheck passengers waited less than five minutes (passengers in regular TSA lines typically wait fifteen to twenty minutes). PreCheck spares the five million or so enrolled passengers all kinds of hassle and aggravation. In *Sludge,* Cass Sunstein estimates that, if the average PreCheck customer saves twenty minutes a trip, and takes four trips a year, the program saves Americans four hundred million hours a year.

Other times, you know that something is dumb or dangerous or will never work. Then a friction fixer's job is to make it difficult or downright impossible to do. That's why driving drunk, sexual harassment, and murder are against the law. And why the Transportation Security Administration does everything it can to stop passengers from bringing loaded guns on board.

Yet, when the evidence is unclear or mixed, it is often best to wait to act until you learn more about if, when, and how to do or use something. As the quote attributed to leaders including U.S. first lady Eleanor Roosevelt and Admiral Hyman Rickover goes, "Learn from the mistakes of others. You can't live long enough to make them all yourself." By watching and learning from those brave and impatient souls who rush ahead first, you can avoid their mistakes. Sometimes, life is like a mousetrap: the first mouse gets crushed, and the second (or third or fourth) mouse gets the cheese.

Research on launching new businesses and products shows that—at best—the so-called first-mover advantage is a dangerous half-truth. When markets are treacherous and uncertainty is high, first movers often flounder because consumers aren't ready for their ideas or are put off by crummy early offerings. Companies that launch their products or services later end up as winners, in part, because they learn from the fatal missteps of eager early movers. Amazon was not the first online bookstore; the defunct Books.com and Interloc were among the earlier entrants. Netscape, the first commercially successful Web browser, was launched years before Google. Myspace was a successful social networking service before Facebook. Couchsurfing was founded before Airbnb. Being first is risky when smart fast followers can learn from your troubles and pass you by.

A study of winning contestants from the Swedish cooking show *Half Past Seven at My Place* demonstrates how this "first-mover disadvantage" can happen. Each week on the show, from Monday through Thursday night, four contestants take turns cooking one another dinner. After each dinner, the three guests rate the dinner prepared by their host—and after the dinner on Thursday, the winning "chef of the week" is revealed. Economist Ali Ahmed analyzed forty-one weeks of this reality TV show. Excluding weeks where multiple teams won because of a tie vote, Ahmed found that only 8 percent of the hosts who cooked on Monday nights were voted winners. Contestants fared better when they cooked on Tuesday nights, with 18 percent voted sole winners. And 29 percent of the contestants who cooked on Wednesday nights and 29 percent who cooked on Thursday nights were voted sole winners.

As Daniel Kahneman documents in *Thinking, Fast and Slow,* when you are in a "cognitive minefield"—when you don't know what decision is best, you are confused, things are going badly, or you haven't yet developed the skill to do something well—it is best to slow down, think, do more research, and weigh the pros and cons. Those contestants who cooked on Wednesdays and Thursdays had more time to learn and think about what worked and what didn't from their competitors—and cooked better meals as a result. As we saw in the introduction with Noam Bardin's moratorium on hiring and product development at Waze—when users kept abandoning early versions of his navigation application—pausing to figure things out can be strategic and intentional, too.

This logic also explains why creative work is and ought to be hard, frustrating, and sometimes exhausting. Skilled creators find ways to be somewhat less inefficient, for example, by generating ideas faster, testing promising ideas rather than endlessly arguing about them, and killing bad ideas fast. But piles of academic studies confirm there is no quick and easy path to creativity. Psychologist Teresa Amabile has studied creativity for more than forty years. She says, if you want to kill creativity, insist that people standardize their work methods, spend as little time as possible on every task, have as few failures as possible, and explain and justify how they spend every minute and dollar. Imaginative people, because they live in a cognitive minefield, do poor work when they are forced to be fast and efficient and to avoid mistakes. If they aren't constantly struggling, feeling confused, failing, and arguing, and trying, modifying, and rejecting new ideas, they are doing it wrong.

When the *Harvard Business Review* interviewed Jerry Seinfeld, the star and cocreator of the long-running hit comedy show *Seinfeld,* the editors asked him, "You and Larry David wrote *Seinfeld* together, without a traditional writers' room, and burnout was one reason you stopped. Was there a more sustainable way to do it? Could McKinsey or someone have helped you find a better model?" Jerry asked, "Who's McKinsey?" After learning McKinsey is a consulting firm and they aren't funny, he said, "Then I don't need them. If you're efficient, you're doing it the wrong way. The right way is the hard way."

The Friction Forensics

After deciding that you know what the right (or wrong) thing is to do, and if people have enough will and skill to do it well, then you can ask, study, and debate six additional questions to help determine whether to make something easy, hard, or impossible.

Consider a simple obstacle that Laszlo Bock imposed when he headed People Operations at Google. The company had a tradition of conducting seemingly endless rounds of interviews with job candidates before deciding whether to offer them jobs. We first heard of this tradition back in 2002 from Google co-founder Larry Page. Larry said he was making enemies among candidates because Google interviewed many ten times or more and still rejected most. Page believed that hiring people who fit Google's quirky culture and had strong leadership potential was essential for scaling the company—so it was worth devoting lots of time to interviewing candidates (and angering some).

As Google grew, this practice devolved into a sacred cow that was unnecessary for most job searches, drove away top candidates, and burdened the six, eight, ten, twelve, or fifteen Googlers who interviewed, evaluated, and discussed each candidate. Sometimes it was even worse. Laszlo told us, "People had up to twenty-five [!] interviews before being rejected."

So, he made a simple rule: if more than four interviews were to be conducted with a candidate, a request for an exception had to be approved by him. Most Googlers were hesitant to ask an executive vice president such as Laszlo for an exception, so the gauntlet disappeared for most job candidates. Laszlo added, "It was one of my first lessons in the power of hierarchy to actually do some good."

* * *

Let's assess Laszlo Bock's simple hiring rule with the eight friction forensics:

1. Laszlo had good reason to believe that endless interviews were a big problem, and this obstacle would be effective—or at least worth a try.
2. The rule was so simple that his HR team had no trouble implementing it, and Google interviewers had no trouble learning it.
3. The rule was cheap to implement. And easy to modify or reverse.
4. The rule reduced frustration and delay for eager candidates and for Google teams that wanted to hire them.
5. Most Google interviewers were already busy—burnout and exhaustion were problems in many corners of the company. This change reduced rather than increased the burden on these beleaguered people.
6. Implementing the change required little coordination or collaboration; it was simply announced, and (for the most part) Googlers gently pressed one another to follow the new rule. Coordination and collaboration were still essential for writing job descriptions, selecting and interviewing promising candidates, and deciding whom to hire. But having fewer people involved reduced such burdens.

7. The obstacle created by this rule wasn't exploitive or cruel, as it added friction in the right places and reduced it in the wrong places.

8. The old practice of endless interviews did have "labor leads to love" effects, increasing commitment and social bonds among the interviewers and candidates who survived the gauntlet. This is a potential negative effect of the rule.

Tough Trade-Offs

Laszlo's rule is elegant and instructive, and—except for the possible dimming of the labor-leads-to-love effect—appeared to help everyone affected. Organizational life is usually messier than that, and figuring out where to add and subtract friction can entail tough trade-offs. Research on electronic health records illustrates this point. As much as we admire Dr. Ashton's Getting Rid of Stupid Stuff program at Hawaii Pacific Health, adding steps to such systems that increase users' burdens can have upsides.

That's what management researchers Jillian Jaeker and Anita Tucker found when they tracked forty-two emergency-department physicians for two years. They studied some ten thousand decisions these doctors made on whether to order ultrasound scans for patients who suffered from abdominal pain. For certain types of pain, including suspected gallbladder problems, the American College of Emergency Physicians recommends ultrasounds as the most accurate test. For other complaints, including cramps, diarrhea, and vomiting blood, other diagnostic tools such as laboratory tests or a computed tomography (CT) scan provide more accurate diagnoses than an ultrasound, or an ultrasound provides no additional information.

Jillian and Anita found that heaping a bit of "process friction" on those doctors forced them to pause and think about whether patients' symptoms indicated they really needed an ultrasound—or if that test would provide little or no useful information. Patients who were spared unnecessary ultrasounds spent less time waiting in a crowded emergency department and avoided the stress and hassle of another test. Eliminating unnecessary ultrasounds also reduced patients' hospital bills and the workload on hospital radiologists, who are often busy and beleaguered.

Each of the forty-two doctors in this study worked regularly in both of two emergency departments, in hospitals less than five miles apart. Between 2009 and 2011, "General Hospital" required physicians who ordered ultrasound tests on nights and weekends to find and talk with a radiologist about whether the patient needed the test. Next, the doctor had to write a paper order justifying the decision, which was delivered to the ultrasound technician, who then did the test. This justification process required fifteen to twenty minutes of a doctor's time. In contrast, at "Flagship Hospital," during the same two years, docs who ordered ultrasound tests did so with a couple clicks in the electronic records system. It took about a minute. No conversation with a radiologist or written justification was required. Even for patients who didn't need an ultrasound because a CT scan and laboratory tests were sufficient or provided better information, physicians at Flagship often ordered all three tests because adding them was so easy.

Doctors at General Hospital were forced to stop and think if a patient really needed the ultrasound—if getting the extra information about the patient's condition (and the reduced risk of committing malpractice) was worth fifteen or twenty minutes of their time. The justification step had a big effect. At General, physicians ordered ultrasound tests for patients with abdominal pain 8 percent of the time, compared to 19.1 percent when these same physicians worked at Flagship. Jillian and Anita found this "process friction" decreased a patient's stay in the emergency department by about thirty minutes, reduced costs over those two years by about $200,000, and had no measurable negative effects on patients' health.

The broader lesson is that there is a dark side to Mark Zuckerberg's boast in 2011 that, for Facebook users, "from here on out, it's a frictionless experience," and to the nearly instant gratification enabled by Amazon, Siri, Shopify, Uber—and so many modern conveniences. As we learned from Brooke Neitzel, that six-year-old girl who ordered the $162 dollhouse from her parents' Alexa device, a bit of old-fashioned inconvenience forces us to stop and think, "Should we do this?" Not just "Can we do this?"

Another complication is that deciding if friction is good or bad depends on where you sit. The process friction at General Hospital was a win for the patients, who saved time, and for insurance companies that were on the hook to pay for tests; it was a loss for swamped docs, who were forced to justify necessary tests, and for the hospital's bottom line, given that more ultrasounds generate more revenue.

And when people weaponize friction to slow, confuse, or unnerve a foe, whether it is good or bad depends on which side you are on. Consider the *Simple Sabotage Field Manual*, which was issued to "citizen-saboteurs" during World War II by the U.S. Office of Strategic Services (OSS), the forerunner of the Central Intelligence Agency. This manual, which was declassified in 2008, is packed with advice for saboteurs in Nazi-occupied countries. It urges them to apply "purposeful stupidity" to stymie productivity and morale in the factories, offices, and transportation services where they work: "The saboteur may have to reverse his thinking, and he should be told this in so many words. Where he formerly thought of keeping his tools sharp, he should now let them grow dull; surfaces that formerly were lubricated now should be sanded; normally diligent, he should now be lazy and careless; and so on."

The manual provides hundreds of "Specific Suggestions for Simple Sabotage." Here are a few of our favorites:

- Engineers should see that trains run slow or make unscheduled stops for plausible reasons.
- Insist on doing everything through "channels." Never permit shortcuts to be taken in order to expedite decisions.
- When possible, refer all matters to committees, for "further study and consideration." Attempt to make the committee as large as possible.
- To lower morale and, with it, production, be pleasant to inefficient workers; give them undeserved promotions. Discriminate against efficient workers; complain unjustly about their work.
- Multiply the procedures and clearances involved in issuing instructions, paychecks, and so on. See that three people have to approve everything where one would do.

The destructive friction generated by such sabotage was hell for the Nazis—and exactly what the United States and its allies wanted.

The Roach Motel Problem

Friction was weaponized against the Nazis for a good cause—but beware of the temptation to harness sludge for selfish and sleazy reasons. Hordes of greedy, exploitive, and sometimes downright cruel characters and companies intentionally make it difficult, or impossible, for clients and employees to get payments, services, or information that they deserve because it saves these creeps money, time, and hassle.

The internet is packed with deceptive interfaces designed to trick, distract, overwhelm, and confuse users. Harry Brignull, a user-experience consultant in Britain, calls these manipulative methods "deceptive design" or "dark patterns." Harry created darkpatterns.org in 2010 to name and define various unsavory patterns, spread awareness about the dangers and remedies, and "to shame companies that use them." Most of us, for example, are victims of the "roach motel" or "one-way-door" problem where it is nearly frictionless to get into a situation, then is mighty hard or impossible to escape.

Greg Bensinger's 2021 editorial in *The New York Times* "Stopping the Manipulation Machines" bashes Amazon as a roach motel, for example, because "canceling a $119 Prime subscription is a labyrinthine process that requires multiple screens and clicks." Alas, Nir Eyal, a behavioral designer and author of *Hooked,* finds Bensinger's piece to be "cringeworthy" hypocrisy.

Nir documented the ordeal he endured in early 2022 to cancel his *Times* subscription. He first had to click through three screens to get to information about canceling it. Then he was required to call or have a live online chat with a representative. Nir chose the chat. "Sheila" first asked him to explain why he was canceling. Then Nir endured multiple rounds of resistance and negotiation from Sheila before she finally agreed to cancel Nir's subscription. Sheila sent him message after message with stuff like "Please think about it, honestly, this offer might not be available for the future. Please consider it. Trust me, you won't regret it." As Nir put it, "On and on the process went until I was finally allowed to leave."

Nir proposes the "regret test" for *The New York Times,* and any other company, whose leaders can bring themselves to squelch their greed and instead want to save users from a visit to the roach motel: "If people knew what it would take to cancel, would they still subscribe?" Friction fixers who take this question seriously can respect customers' time, avert hypocrisy, and possibly repair their organization's reputation. At least in California, companies including *The New York Times* now face legal friction meant to shutter their roach motels. As of July 2022, under a new California law, "Users who sign up online must be able to cancel their subscription immediately and at will by either a direct link or button on the website or a preformatted email that the consumer can send without adding additional information."

An episode in Netflix's history provides a compelling argument for shutting down roach motels even when the law allows it. And instead building a business with a competitive advantage because it is easy for customers to end subscriptions. After we noticed how easy it was to end our Netflix subscriptions (it takes just a couple clicks), we asked two former executives for the backstory: Eric Colson, former VP of data science and engineering, and Patty McCord, former chief talent officer.

Eric told us that, when he first got to Netflix, in 2006, it bothered him and his coworkers that customers had to phone a service rep to cancel their subscriptions. Then, in about 2007, CEO and cofounder Reed Hastings sent an email to the whole company that said, "The right thing to do is to make it easy to quit." So, Netflix engineers put a "cancel button" on the account page. Eric and his coworkers were proud of that change because customers wanted it and it challenged them to "make the product so good that customers don't want to cancel." They didn't want to be "a service that people are paying for and not using— such as a gym membership that sits idle, that provides no value to customers, and customers bad-mouth."

Patty was a Netflix senior executive for the company's first fourteen years and helped drive its remarkable growth through 2012. Patty believes the company's long stretch of success was fueled by this "very deliberate" strategy of "making it easy to leave and come back." Patty notes that, while "pissing off consumers" may have short-term benefits, "a subscription model creates the most profit over the long term—over years, generations." Eric, who went on to serve as chief algorithm officer at online fashion retailer Stitch Fix, added that companies that make it easy to quit get better data about how to keep customers satisfied and loyal. That's because the "time to feedback" is faster for the company and the evidence is less noisy because most customers are keeping the service because they want it, not because they are trapped in a roach motel.

Dear bosses, if all that matters to you is bolstering misleading metrics and the bottom line in the short term, go ahead and focus your friction forensics on the strategic application of such shoddy sludge. Your lawyers can probably help you steal people's time and money and deflate their dignity and spirit in ways that are all perfectly legal. But if your aims are higher and more noble, it's time to start rewarding your people for removing the noise, delays, and indignities that are baked into your business model. As Netflix demonstrates, it is possible—and perhaps more lucrative—to build a successful business based on profiting from pleasing and helping people over the long haul. Plus, as greater numbers of organizations eliminate the wrong kind of friction, the more that bad actors will stand out, be shamed and shunned as sleazy rarities, and feel pressure to change—which will help all of us lead better lives.

You Need the Gas and the Brakes

We admire teams and organizations that accomplish more, in less time, than we ever thought possible. We wrote *The Fric-*

tion Project, in part, to understand how these speed demons avoid, remove, or blast through impediments. That's why we are smitten with Patrick Collison's Fast List. Patrick is CEO and cofounder of Stripe, a San Francisco–based financial services company. He is obsessed with how to make good things happen rapidly and well everywhere, not just for Stripe's customers and employees. Patrick catalogs "examples of people quickly accomplishing ambitious things together" in companies, nonprofits, and governments. The entries on the Fast List include the team that built *The Spirit of St. Louis* in sixty days—that's the famous plane Charles Lindbergh flew in 1927 for the first nonstop flight from New York to Paris. And Disneyland: "Walt Disney's conception of 'The Happiest Place on Earth' was brought to life in 366 days."

We share Patrick's disgust with friction fiascoes that result from greed, incompetence, and ridiculous red tape. He points to a bus lane for San Francisco's Van Ness Avenue that city officials proposed in 2001 and was approved by voters in 2003. The project wasn't completed until April Fools' Day in 2022—some seventy-six hundred days after it started. City officials made lame excuses for this notoriously late project. The San Francisco Bay Area suffered from a terrible drought during most of the final decade of construction. That didn't stop a San Francisco public works spokesperson from claiming, "The project has been delayed due to an increase of wet weather since the project started."

Yet, when we dug into the entries on Patrick's Fast List, we found that many he celebrated were ultimately successful because—at key junctures—friction fixers slowed things way down and did necessary, difficult, and inefficient things. They hit the brakes to prepare for putting the pedal to the metal later, or to clean up problems caused by racing ahead too fast for too long in the past.

Consider the first item on Patrick's list: "Dee Hock was given 90 days to launch the BankAmericard card (which became the Visa card), starting from scratch. He did. In that period, he signed up more than 100,000 customers." Yes, it happened that fast in 1968. *But* that is the beginning of the story, not the end. As the late Dee Hock explains in *One from Many*, as one bank after another developed its own credit card in the late 1960s, the sprawling, cutthroat, and weakly regulated market became infected with fraud, inefficiency, and mistrust. The credit card business was on the verge of becoming untenable for customers, merchants, and banks. Dee's bosses at Bank of America supported him as he devoted two tough years to spearheading a conflict-ridden cat-herding effort to create cooperation among banks and merchants. The result was the birth of an independent entity in 1970, with Dee as founding CEO.

It's now called Visa International, and it's a decentralized membership organization composed of all financial institutions that issue Visa cards—which enables merchants to take any Visa card issued by any bank, anywhere. Participating banks use a common clearinghouse operation that assures merchants get paid for purchases, transactions are cleared between banks, and customers are billed. There are now 3.9 billion Visa cards, issued by 14,900 financial institutions, which are accepted by more than 80 million merchants, and which process more than $14 trillion in transactions each year.

Dee knew that all those banks racing ahead in different directions were hurting everyone in the credit card business. He knew it was time to inject friction—as our list of forensics suggests—because banks and merchants didn't know the right (or wrong) things to do to save the business (let alone how to do them). When they slowed down to figure out what to do, Dee and his fellow bankers realized that—because so much cooperation, coordination, and commitment were required for them to succeed—they needed to take time to develop solutions that made it easy for members to work together and hard for members to break or bend agreements to follow universal rules and business processes.

Other challenges require people to master the art and science of friction shifting, to transition constantly and instantly between hitting the gas and the brakes. This skill includes moving fast and taking risks one moment, then slowing down, reflecting, and avoiding dangerous mistakes the next. Our case study of the U.S. military's most elite team of warriors, the Navy SEALs, revealed that the extreme hardships their recruits are put through during the six months of training—notably the twenty hours a day of intense physical activity during Hell Week—aren't just to screen out those who aren't physically fit enough. Or just to use labor-leads-to-love techniques to generate extreme loyalty, trust, and bonds among the SEALs.

The 20 percent or so of recruits who make it through this six-month ordeal are selected for—and take enormous pride in—their ability to make snap judgments about when to move lightning fast, blow up buildings, bridges, and vehicles, and shoot to kill versus when to pause just long enough to avoid hurting and killing the wrong people, destroying the wrong things, and unnecessarily putting themselves in harm's way. To do so in chaotic and confusing situations where everything is going wrong. And when they are exhausted and injured, fighting for their lives, and their closest friends are dying around them.

These Navy SEALs certainly fit Patrick Collison's definition of an organization with a remarkable record of "quickly accomplishing ambitious things together"—including the raid that killed Osama bin Laden in Pakistan in 2011, the rescue of humanitarian workers Jessica Buchanan and Poul Hagen Thisted, who were kidnapped by Somali pirates in 2012 (the SEALs killed all nine captors in minutes without taking any casualties), and dozens more lightning-fast raids and rescues. The SEALs' trademark ruthless efficiency would be impossible without hitting the brakes for that six-month ordeal to select and train every SEAL. Their constant practice and rehearsal, the careful planning that goes into every mission, and the SEALs' well-honed ability to make instant judgments in the heat of battle about when to pause and assess the situation and when to commence action all result directly from that selection process and training.

How Friction Fixers Do Their Work
The Help Pyramid

"My job is part organizational design, part therapy." That's how Sandra, a CEO in one of our workshops, described her role. Proud friction fixers like Sandra taught us that their craft entails helping others in two ways. The first way to help is *prevention and cure*—implementing little and big changes in organizations to make the right things easy and the wrong things hard. That's the organizational design part, and it's the main mission of every friction fixer.

The second way is dealing with the *symptoms* of friction troubles. This work includes the "therapy" that Sandra talked about: keeping others and yourself sane and motivated so that you can survive broken systems together and be fortified with the grit and gumption to repair them. Friction fixers also help others deal with symptoms by guiding them through the best—or least bad—paths through the muck. Friction fixers serve as shock absorbers, too: doing routine chores, dealing with reasonable and unreasonable demands and interruptions, and enduring unwarranted cruelty so that others don't have to.

Once again, our message is that friction troubles wane and

do less harm when—rather than treating such troubles as someone else's problem—everybody in a team or organization does what they can, from where they are, with what they have, to make things better. No matter how little—or how much—influence you have in your organization, you can be a leader who helps clients, citizens, coworkers, or your bosses deal with the symptoms of friction troubles. Prevention and repair require wielding more power than dealing with symptoms—and, often, more patience and persistence.

This chapter unpacks our rough hierarchy of friction fixers' work. Our Help Pyramid has five levels, which are based on the amount of influence you need to help people in your cone of friction. The bottom three levels focus on ways you can dampen the wallop packed by symptoms: *reframing, navigating,* and *shielding.* The top two levels are about preventing and curing friction troubles: *neighborhood design and repair* and *system design and repair.*

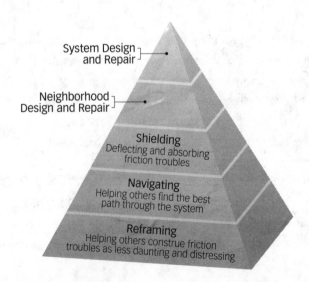

System Design and Repair

Neighborhood Design and Repair

Shielding
Deflecting and absorbing friction troubles

Navigating
Helping others find the best path through the system

Reframing
Helping others construe friction troubles as less daunting and distressing

Friction Fixing: The Help Pyramid

1. Reframing

Friction fixers' work includes shaping how people feel because so many obstacles and frustrations in organizational life are difficult or impossible to remove, at least for now. Reframing is at the bottom of our Help Pyramid because every friction fixer can comfort themselves, their colleagues, and customers in ways that bolster their mental health, maintain resolve, and strengthen social bonds—even when they are bogged down by ridiculous rules, red tape, and petty tyrants. And friction fixers can help people cope with irritation, anger, and fear triggered by necessary delays, rules, and roadblocks, too. Savvy friction fixers know that a well-designed system works better, too, and their own jobs are easier, when employees and customers who travel through it feel safe, calm, and respected—and don't feel helpless and resigned to their fate.

Friction fixers use methods akin to those of cognitive behavioral therapists, who help patients "reframe" or "reappraise" challenges and setbacks as less upsetting and threatening. Psychiatrist Aaron Beck, the father of modern cognitive behavioral therapy, began to practice and spread the word about this method in the 1950s. Since then, more than two thousand studies have documented its effectiveness for treating anxiety, depression, and other mental health challenges. Therapists teach patients to reframe difficult experiences and worries in a different and more positive light—and to behave in ways that are more constructive for themselves and others in their lives. These reappraisals include learning to identify and avoid negative and distorted thinking, such as catastrophizing (jumping to the most dire conclusions about threats and risks), focusing on the upsides of bad experiences, accepting that you aren't to blame for bad news and failures, seeing the humor and absurdity in crummy situations, and construing frustrations and setbacks as temporary troubles that won't haunt you for months or years.

Rumana Jabeen, a real estate agent based in Burlingame, California, has been among the top 1 percent in sales among agents in the United States for decades. When Rumana was Bob Sutton's agent, Bob learned how she makes masterful use of reframing to calm clients (including Bob) who are freaking out about the hassles of selling a house. Rumana says that when a client is panicking about the paperwork, home repairs, listing price, and other hassles in preparing a house for sale, she assures them that most clients are surprised because the process is easier than they feared—and that will probably be the new client's experience, too. Rumana also uses the "this too shall pass" method, or what psychologists call temporal distancing. To help clients deal with ugly surprises and frustrations that arise along the way, Rumana reminds them that in just a few months, when the house is sold, when they look back, the things that are so upsetting now will seem like no big deal. They will wonder why they got so worked-up about such little things, and everything will have turned out for the best. That's exactly what happened to Bob.

Rumana's method is supported by six intertwined studies by psychologists Emma Bruehlman-Senecal and Özlem Ayduk. Emma and Özlem found that, when bad things happen to people (e.g., the end of a long-term relationship or a lousy grade on a test), if they focus on how they will feel about such troubles in the distant future (rather than the near future), they experience less worry, fear, anxiety, anger, and guilt. Savvy friction fixers coach others to harness the human capacity for imaginary time travel. Sayings like "time heals all wounds" and "humor is tragedy plus time" might be clichés—but they can soothe our souls, too.

As our Stanford colleagues Jennifer Aaker and Naomi Bag-donas show in *Humor, Seriously,* people also suffer less emotional and physical harm when they frame distressing situations as silly, absurd, or ridiculous. Focusing on the funny side enables people to release tension and to see their troubles as less threatening. As people laugh together about the madness of it all, their bonds become stronger. Others joining the laughter affirms people aren't alone in their suffering, they aren't weak, or to blame. It is the system that sucks.

When we first started doing workshops for the friction project, we were surprised by the barrage of jokes and laughter that followed when we asked, "What makes it hard to do your job?" Now, as we touched on in the opening pages, we expect the dark humor to pour out and the room to roar with laughter as people shout, write, or type "email jail," "death by meeting," "maddeningly opaque processes," "fad surfing," "friendly fire," "blowhard bosses," "rule freaks," "management trolls," "leader-shit," "I toil in a frustration factory," "I work in the tower of no," "leadership by gobbledygook," "bullshit peddlers," and hundreds more terrible but funny terms. Such humor enables people to talk about their frustration and pain, provide one another with emotional support, and, sometimes, energize them to band together and start repairing and removing those friction troubles.

2. Navigating

The second level of the Help Pyramid entails serving as a trail guide. That means steering colleagues, friends, customers, and citizens to find the fastest, most rewarding, cheapest, least upsetting, most fun, or safest path through a system—without altering the system itself. Navigation tips from friction fixers are sometimes about how to avoid the "gunk" people that we discuss in chapter 9. These are people with a penchant for clogging up organizations, such as "workplace vigilantes."

Researchers Katy DeCelles and Karl Aquino define workplace vigilantes as people who mistrust colleagues and customers, and—even though they lack authority to do so—appoint themselves as "judge, jury, and deliverer of justice." Their surveys found that 42 percent of U.S. employees have worked with people who were on "some kind of strange power trip" and "on patrol for anyone who didn't abide 100 percent by any rules or regulations." Vigilantes take it upon themselves to call out, punish, and tattle on colleagues for imagined and real petty offenses. Like being two minutes late, having a messy desk, or, as one HR manager informed an employee, "You were observed taking a tissue from the box in the cubicle next to yours. A third party submitted a claim that you'd stolen the tissue."

Friction fixers help colleagues, customers, and citizens identify and avoid vigilantes and other gunk people. And steer them to the "grease people" we discuss in chapter 9, who pride themselves in enlightening others about how to avoid and speed through red tape and other obstacles. When we described the workplace vigilante research to executives at one tech company, several went on a rant about how they urge new employees "to avoid Sanjay at HR at all costs." They warned newcomers that Sanjay will "make your life miserable" by insisting that you follow every rule to the letter (including rules that, those execs reported, didn't exist and that Sanjay invented and inflicted on others).

The friendly DMV employee that we talked about in chapter 1 is a good example of a navigator who helps people travel through a complex and bewildering system—without changing it. That fellow helped Bob Sutton and fifty or so other visitors move more quickly, and with more predictability and control, by giving all of them the right forms so as to be ready for their transaction with the clerk, coaching them about which documents they would need at each clerk's window, telling them which of the seven windows to go to, and the best place to sit or stand as they waited to be called by the clerk. That guy explained to some visitors that if they just completed a form (which he handed them) and deposited it in the drop box, they wouldn't need to wait in line at all. For other visitors, he broke the bad news that they were wasting their time waiting. Some visitors needed additional documentation before a clerk could help them (such as the woman who didn't have a "pink slip" that proved she owned a car), others needed to wait longer before the transaction was possible (like the guy who couldn't get the title to his late mother's car yet because the required forty-day waiting period after her death wasn't over), and others wanted services that the DMV doesn't provide (including a fellow who wanted to renew his U.S. passport, which you can't do at the DMV).

Some systems are so broken that the only way to get through them is to hire a professional navigator. In San Francisco, the tangled process of getting a permit to remodel a house or a business is so burdensome that the fifty-eight-page "Getting a Permit" document warns citizens, "Obtaining a city permit can undoubtedly be one of the most confusing processes you may ever experience." It is so perplexing that even Myrna Melgar, former head of the San Francisco Planning Commission (which oversees the process), couldn't figure out how to get permission to build a gazebo in her backyard. The only hope for most San Franciscans is hire "permit expeditors," for upward of $200 an hour, who "spend their days at the department walking their client's permit applications to the right desks, making necessary changes."

This gauntlet breeds corruption: multiple San Francisco officials have been convicted of receiving bribes to speed up approvals. And it results in inequality and injustice because citizens who can't afford unlawful or lawful pay-to-play solutions can't make it through the maze. That's what happened to Jason Yu, who in 2019 hired an architect and submitted plans to remodel a storefront for an ice cream shop in the city's Mission District. By 2021, he had run up debts of over $200,000 for an architect, a lawyer, and $7,300 a month in rent. And he still faced fifteen big hurdles to get a building permit. Out of money and hope, he gave up his dream of scooping ice cream in April 2021. Jason failed, in part, because he couldn't afford to hire a permit expeditor.

Finally, mentors are essential for helping new employees navigate complicated and confusing workplaces—sometimes organizations have formal mentoring programs, and other times mentor-mentee relationships arise informally. Research on newcomers including lawyers, engineers, prison guards, and military personnel shows that when employees are tutored and supported by one or more caring and savvy insiders, the newcomers experience "greater work satisfaction and performance, higher retention, better physical health and self-esteem, positive work relationships, stronger organizational commitment, career motivation, professional competence, and career recognition and success."

A study by Brad Johnson and Gene Anderson of fifty-five officers and ninety-four senior enlisted sailors in the U.S. Navy documents the virtues of having one or, better yet, several supportive and shrewd mentors. Sailors who develop these healthy relationships are more likely to stay in the navy, feel protected and supported, and enjoy more successful careers. Their skilled mentors help with the "therapy" part of friction fixing by providing mentees with acceptance and encouragement, and emotional support and counseling. As one sailor said, "My mentor taught me to control my emotions and self-reflect." Participants in the study emphasized how effective mentors give their charges sound advice about taking the right path through the maze of career opportunities and risks in the U.S. Navy, using their influence to remove obstacles to their mentees' success (including lousy assignments and difficult peers and superiors) and creating opportunities for them to learn and advance.

An officer said, "With today's new recruits, they need to have the guidance to ensure they are directed in their careers; sailors need a 'sea daddy' to keep them on track and let them know when they have gone off it!" Another officer added, "A mentor can teach a sailor from his/her experiences therefore eliminating the trial-and-error aspect, allowing fewer mistakes and more efficient learning." The best mentors, the study found, help sailors learn to bypass the U.S. Navy's thick bureaucracy, introduce them to the right people so they can build supportive and powerful professional networks, and advocate on their behalf for plum promotions and assignments. One officer praised his mentor because she gave him "a glimpse of the road or path that I needed to take." Another explained how his mentor enabled him to learn key skills and develop a good reputation up the navy's chain of command because "when a high-visibility problem came up, he would pick me to go with him to fix it."

Shielding

Absorbing and deflecting friction so others don't have to often requires more courage and self-sacrifice than reframing and navigation. Shielding is a symptom of friction troubles and, sometimes, a prevention and cure—so we rank it above navigation on our Help Pyramid. When people need intense protection to feel safe and to concentrate on their work, it's a symptom of a bad system. But designing roles and teams to shield people so they can work unfettered by intrusions and insults is a hallmark of healthy organizations, too.

In his classic 1967 book, *Organizations in Action,* sociologist James Thompson argued that, for leaders, one of "the basic things they do because they must—or else!" is to "buffer" the people who do the organization's core work. Part of a leader's job is to take the heat, battle back, and turn murky and conflicting demands into clear expectations to protect their people from intrusions, confusion, aggravation, time sinks, and idiocy from on high so they can focus on their work.

Buffering is a routine part of management work. Henry Mintzberg's prolonged observations of senior executives revealed that they work at a relentless pace, dealing with dozens, sometimes hundreds, of planned and unplanned meetings, information requests, minor and major crises, and other intrusions day after day. They do such work so that others don't have to. As Mintzberg wrote, "Someone once defined a manager, half in jest, as someone who sees the visitors so that everyone else can get their work done."

Yet serving as a human shield sometimes goes beyond such routine efforts, which are essential in even the healthiest organizations. In "hostile and stressful" settings where priorities constantly shift "midtask on a whim," software developer and agile coach Matt Davidson deems managers who shield people from "day-to-day strife" as "shit umbrellas." In these horrid places, employees who do the core work have overlords who are clueless about what their employees need to succeed and place ridiculous demands on them. If such employees are lucky, they have "umbrella-holding" bosses who deflect and absorb the shit that rains down from above—which enables them to do the organization's work and thus protects those top dogs from suffering the consequences of their incompetence.

The foolishness that pours down in broken organizations

can provoke umbrella holders to take extreme measures. Pixar, the animated-film studio that is renowned for classics including *The Incredibles* and the *Toy Story* series, may never have existed without such protection from cofounders Ed Catmull (Pixar's president for decades) and Alvy Ray Smith (inventor of technologies that made it possible to create computer-animated films). We heard this story about ten years ago, after giving a talk at Pixar in which we argued the best bosses protect people from idiocy from on high. Veteran Pixar employee Craig Good came up afterward and told us about the time that Ed and Alvy "saved our jobs."

In 1985, Craig was working at the precursor to Pixar, the Computer Division of Lucasfilm. It was led by Ed and Alvy, who were under pressure to cut costs because Lucasfilm was having cash-flow problems. Doug Norby, then president of Lucasfilm, pressed Ed and Alvy to do deep layoffs—in part, because founder and chairman George Lucas (of *Star Wars* fame) had little faith that the animated films made by Ed and Alvy's group would ever be financially viable. Catmull pushed back, arguing that if the group was kept intact, they could create successful films, and it would maintain the group's value if Lucasfilm decided to sell it. Craig explained that Norby "was pestering Ed and Alvy for a list of names from the Computer Division to lay off, and Ed and Alvy kept blowing him off. Finally came the order: you *will* be in my office tomorrow morning at nine with a list of names."

What did Ed and Alvy do? As Craig tells it, "They showed up in his office at nine and plunked down a list. It had two names on it: Ed Catmull and Alvy Ray Smith." Norby gave up on layoffs long enough so that, a few months later, Steve Jobs bought the Computer Division for $5 million. Alvy, Ed, and Steve started

Pixar. That brave act still reverberated through Pixar decades later. Craig was proud to work for a company whose bosses had put their jobs on the line to protect people.

People further down the pecking order also protect core workers in organizations—and shield top dogs, too. That's a big part of the job for frontline workers including receptionists, executive assistants, security guards, and gate agents at airports. When sociologists Sara Arber and Lucianne Sawyer surveyed a thousand British patients about encounters with receptionists in doctors' offices, some reported dealing with grumpy and unhelpful "dragons behind the desk." But most patients found them helpful and essential—even when receptionists prevented patients from seeing a doctor immediately. Patients realized that, without receptionists deciding which patients need to see or talk on the phone to a doctor right now and which could wait, it would be impossible for doctors to do their work.

Gatekeepers also serve as flak catchers who absorb anger and abuse so that others can do their jobs. Here's how Paul Friedman defined them in his research on "hassle handlers":

> Flak catchers are an organization's lightning rods. Complainers contact them first. Part of their job is hearing about the alleged inadequacies of their unit's products or services. Some are called secretaries, some directors of customer relations, some assistant principals of schools. Whatever their official titles may be, flak catchers perform an invaluable service by taking in initial jolts sent by the dissatisfied.

Consider the flak that gate agents in airports take from pissed-off passengers—which can shield flight crews and other airline employees. Katy DeCelles, who studied those "workplace vigilantes," also dissected "fights before flights" at boarding gates. Katy and her colleagues observed 131 acts of "customer aggression" directed at gate agents before 117 flights at 35 airports. Passengers stressed by long lines, flight delays, crowding, and crying babies were more prone to sigh loudly, pound their fists, yell, and cuss. One passenger threw "a large bottle of water near (but not at) an agent who did not agree to 'hold the plane' so the passenger could return to the lounge to recover a forgotten cell phone."

The lesson for friction fixers is that, for physicians, pilots, and people in hundreds of other jobs to work efficiently and safely, gatekeepers are essential for screening out, stalling, and serving clients, citizens, and coworkers. And for doing the dirty work of absorbing the frustration and anger that such folks spew out.

Neighborhood Design and Repair

The top two levels in our Help Pyramid are about wielding your influence to put the right amounts of friction in the right places—the main mission of *The Friction Project*. Keep in mind that adding reframing, navigating, and shielding to the mix can fortify people to start and sustain local or systemic changes. You can also use these powers to reduce the harm inflicted by problems that you can't fix (at least for now)—so people have the wherewithal to fix what they can. And to dampen the adverse side effects of good organizational friction that you want to keep or crank up.

It is easier to design and repair a little part of an organization than the whole thing—especially if it's big and complicated. It's faster to make a little change, say, in one Microsoft group than to roll it out to all two hundred thousand or so employees. We saw managers make such local changes when we worked with Microsoft's learning and development team. In 2021, about a year after the COVID-19 pandemic began, we noticed our thirty-minute online meetings with the team were cut to twenty-five minutes and sixty-minute meetings were cut to fifty minutes. Josh Nicholls, a manager on the team, explained, "During the pandemic, Microsoft did research and found that virtual fatigue was very high (especially with back-to-back meetings) and a simple break of five minutes between meetings bolsters one's well-being. There is a new Outlook setting you can turn on that will automatically create meetings that start five minutes late or end five minutes early. The default becomes ten minutes if your meeting is sixty minutes or more." Josh added this wasn't a mandated companywide change but was "considered a norm in our global learning and development team."

That move by Josh's team is the kind of small win that friction fixers pile up day after day—they keep tweaking the work to make it lighter and to protect people's mental health. Others make local decisions to add obstacles. In the right hands, such burdens enable people to accomplish more and become more committed to their work.

This happens with the constructive friction that our colleagues Perry Klebahn and Jeremy Utley (whom we met in chapter 1) heap on students in their LaunchPad class, in which students "incubate and launch a real business in just ten weeks." LaunchPad is just one of fifty or so hands-on innovation classes taught each year at Stanford's Hasso Plattner Institute of Design (which everyone calls "the d.school"). And it's one of the thousands of classes taught at Stanford University each year. Perry and Jeremy impose a portfolio of obstacles on the students who apply to and join LaunchPad. These hurdles are customized to fit the class philosophy and goals, which are different from any other class in the university and are more onerous than for most classes.

To select students, Perry and Jeremy screen dozens of teams that apply each year to join LaunchPad. They interview team members multiple times and evaluate their early prototypes and pitches about their proposed company's business model and its product or service—as well as the teams' resilience and ability to update in response to these teachers' caring, but often tough, feedback. Perry and Jeremy choose a cohort of ten teams per year, each of which is required to develop and launch their business in the class. Students work on a tight schedule, constantly experimenting to develop their offering and create demand for it. Students receive candid feedback from Perry and Jeremy, visiting investors and founders as well as one another in class sessions and on the Slack platform. In week six of this ten-week class, a "trade show" is held, with 150 or so people visiting the d.school to hear pitches and talk to founders of these fledging companies—with some becoming investors or employees.

More than a hundred ventures have been founded in Launch-Pad since it was first taught in 2010—which have raised over $600 million and created thousands of jobs—and more than 50 percent are still alive in some form. Examples include Ravel Law, a search and analytics company purchased by LexisNexis. Man Crates sends gift boxes to men with macho tastes, such as the Primal Hunger Crate, with dried meats, and a Scrimshaw Knife Kit. NeuroNav assists adults with developmental disabilities to navigate through life. And Sequel is reengineering the fluid mechanics of tampons "to finally give women the leak-free menstrual experience they need to perform at their best in the boardroom, the stadium, and beyond."

In addition to the grueling screening process and hard work, students sign a ten-point pledge including "I will not miss class even once," "I will not complain about the workload," and "I will launch my product/service in the market." In most other Stanford classes, students can miss at least one or two sessions, complaints are not banned, and, while faculty may talk about what it takes to start a business, students are not required to launch one. Perry and Jeremy believe that, to build a viable start-up and a vibrant community of ten mutually supportive teams, it is essential to make the wrong things difficult to do: they are quick to call out students who break the pledge and ask those who aren't taking steps to build a business to drop the class. Perry also says that LaunchPad is so successful and beloved by students because of the massive effort required and the obstacles and failures they overcome along the way—he believes, as the research on "the IKEA effect" that we introduced in chapter 2 shows, that labor leads to love.

In spring of 2022, when Bob Sutton attended nearly every LaunchPad class and helped with the teaching a bit, Perry and Jeremy "counseled" several embarrassed but relieved students to drop the class because they weren't pulling their weight in their teams or in the class. They also disbanded two teams that failed to develop rough prototypes of their product or service that were ready for that evening trade show held the sixth week of the class. This gathering is open to the public. Silicon Valley investors, founders, executives, engineers, and other curious folks visit booths that are built and staffed by each student team, check out each fledgling business's prototypes and pitches, and ask some (often tough) questions.

We asked 2019 LaunchPad grad Greta Meyer about the impact of this gauntlet on her and Amanda Calabrese—the duo that founded Sequel. With Greta as CEO and Amanda as COO, they raised $5 million in early 2022 to reinvent the tampon. Greta was quick to say that, yes, all that work led Amanda and her to love LaunchPad—as predicted by the research on the IKEA effect. Greta added that the tough assignments and relentless (sometimes painful) feedback from Perry and Jeremy, classmates, investors, and customers caused Amanda and her to learn each other's strengths and weaknesses so well, and to create such a strong bond, that they now power through one obstacle after another together. In 2022 and 2023, they used this grit to get through the red tape and reviews required to convince the FDA that Sequel's tampon is effective and safe (so it could be sold in the United States). Their patented leak-proof tampon received FDA approval in August 2023. Greta and Amanda didn't try to bypass the grueling FDA process as CEO Elizabeth Holmes and her Theranos colleagues attempted to do—to their detriment—a decade earlier.

System Design and Repair

Other efforts are aimed at taming friction troubles in a large part or all of an organization, rather than making local changes in a small part—say, a team or department—without any intention of triggering broader change. We call this systemic design and repair work. Fixing much or all of an organization requires wielding more influence than for making local repairs, especially when the organization is big, complicated, and filled with fiefdoms. Systemic change is often instigated by commands from powerful senior executives. Drew Houston's top team implemented the "Armeetingeddon" intervention that we discussed in chapter 1 throughout Dropbox in 2013 without asking for employee input. When Steve Jobs returned to lead Apple in 1997, he fired every general manager of every business unit in the first few weeks (all in the same day). As we detail in chapter 5, within a year Steve's rebuilt senior team had discontinued all dozen or so computers that Apple was selling when he first returned—and replaced them with four new models.

Other systemic changes start at the top but are then shaped by people throughout the organization. The Getting Rid of Stupid Stuff campaign at Hawaii Pacific Health was launched by

Chief Quality Officer Dr. Melinda Ashton. But it was propelled by doctors and nurses throughout Hawaii Pacific who identified "stupid stuff"—which was, when feasible, repaired or removed by Dr. Ashton's team.

Sometimes "yes" is the best answer to the question "Should friction fixing be top-down or bottom-up?" As chapter 5 shows, the Million Hours Campaign led by Pushkala Subramanian at pharmaceutical giant AstraZeneca succeeded because it blended the two approaches to free up employees' time. Top-down changes included adding steps before employees could "reply all" to more than twenty-five email recipients—users had to pause, read a warning, and do an extra click. That little speed bump saved employees from thousands of unnecessary emails. The estimated two million hours that AstraZeneca had saved by 2017 from this effort also resulted from work by local "simpli-fication champions" throughout this sprawling company—such as the meeting-free days implemented by businesses in Taiwan and Thailand.

Some friction fixing efforts should require implementing the same steps in the same way everywhere in the system, par-ticularly when straying from a prespecified sequence violates laws, creates destructive confusion and disorder, or puts lives at risk. Consider the standardized preflight checklists used by airplane pilots throughout the world. These checklists were de-veloped in the 1930s after a fatal crash of a B-17 bomber. The crash happened because a veteran pilot forgot to disengage the control lock, a device that holds the flight controls in place so that they are immovable. Using an identical checklist for every pilot who flies, say, a Boeing 787 Dreamliner assures that none will miss any such critical steps. Checklists also facilitate coor-dination and communication among pilots, copilots, and flight attendants, who, even when flying together for the first time, know who ought to do what and when each person ought to do it—so when a teammate misses a step it can instantly be spotted.

Other systemic repairs work best when, although driven by shared principles and goals, teams and locations are allowed to customize lingo, tools, and guidelines to fit local needs and sensibilities. Joe McCannon learned this lesson when he managed the 100,000 Lives Campaign between 2004 and 2006—which saved approximately 122,000 patients from preventable deaths. The campaign, led by the Boston-based Institute for Healthcare Improvement, spread evidence-based practices to more than 70 percent of U.S. hospitals, including rapid response teams, "experts who could be called upon when an unexpected deterioration in a patient's condition was observed." Joe found, rather than thinking of their strategy as distributing sheet music, it's often better for leaders who want to unleash large-scale change to encourage people to "play jazz," to adapt to circumstances and try new things "without ever entirely abandoning the original theme."

Joe adds the best change agents are "almost playful" about "finding many ways there." That means, he says, they look for signs their "sheet music" isn't working. That it's time to "play jazz" by experimenting with different messages, tools, people, and partnerships—and to keep tweaking the mix. They resist locking in to a single theory or method. No matter how well things are going right now, they know that "what got us here won't get us there."

A study by Northwestern University's Jillian Chown of a big Canadian hospital found that, when top executives and change agents tried to implement the same prepackaged daily prep meeting in six outpatient clinics, they were saved from their own rigidity because, rather than following the sheet music, staffers in each outpatient clinic played jazz instead. The executives were smitten with this rigid practice because it had proven so effective for improving coordination and communication when inpatient wards implemented it throughout the hospital. As Jillian explains, this "mandated control mechanism required employees in each [outpatient] clinic to meet for fifteen minutes each morning with their manager to discuss the upcoming day. The discussion was supposed to be standardized and highly structured, following a series of questions listed on their daily prep sheet." Every outpatient team was required to answer identical questions, such as, "What known or anticipated safety risks for patients, families, or staff worry you the most today?" "Who or what should we celebrate today?" and "What is (+) or (-) impacting our financials today?"

When hospital change agents trained healthcare workers, administrators, and managers in those six outpatient clinics in this method and pressed them to implement it, members pushed back. Those staffers identified plenty of troubles in response to questions from change agents: "What bogs you down?" "What are the stresses?" "What are you running around looking for all day?" and "Where are the fires that you're trying to put out?" But staffers argued that the daily standardized prep meeting wasn't right for tackling their clinic's particular problems. That their work was different because patients come and go throughout the day—rather than stay overnight and often for many days.

So, the staff in all six outpatient clinics resisted the standardized change that their leaders tried to impose. But the interesting lesson from Jillian's study is that the staff of each clinic responded by developing a new local, customized solution that was even better for their work—they rejected the sheet music and improvised instead.

Trial and error led the staff in three of those outpatient clinics to develop a customized daily prep meeting: Each group implemented homegrown guidelines about who led and attended their daily meeting, the questions they addressed, and the decisions they made. The other three clinics rejected the new process entirely. They saw it as unfit for their work. Of those, two clinics switched to weekly meetings because a daily meeting would steal too much time from patients. A clinician explained, "The [week preview] meeting on Friday is about looking forward and backwards to see what the main issues are and talking about how we will manage issues if they come up again."

The third clinic abandoned meetings completely. So many different staff members moved in and out of that clinic every day and throughout the week that it was impractical to a find a time when all or most could meet. Instead, to facilitate communication and coordination, that clinic developed a "Popsicle stick" system. On arrival, patients were given multiple Popsicle sticks, each with the name of a different provider they needed to see during their visit. Each provider collected the stick with the provider's name on it when seeing the patient. Patients were instructed to leave when they ran out of sticks.

The Five Traps: On-Ramps for Finding and Fixing Troubles

The Friction Project is about how to make the organizations in your life a little—or a lot—better for everyone they touch. We all face obstacles and aggravations that aren't our fault and we will never defeat. Some of us have a modest cone of friction, others a massive one. Some of us wield a little influence, others a lot.

Sure, friction fixing is easier if you are a powerful top dog and can use your authority and resources to help design systems that hum along rather than hammer employees and customers—and to get the incentives right to attract top talent and shower them with cash, promotions, and kudos. Yet, we've repeatedly been surprised by the frustrations that even the most seemingly powerful CEOs express to us about how limited their influence is over their companies—with obstacles such as middle management "trolls" who clog up the works, the inability to attract and keep great talent, major customers who are impossible to satisfy, competing companies that keep eating their lunch, and laws and regulations that stymie performance. And compared to these captains of industry, most of us have far less influence over the organizations in our lives.

Our Help Pyramid shows that such obstacles are no excuse for doing nothing. We all can do some good. Rather than fretting over and feeling defeated by what they don't have, friction fixers start where they are with what they do have.

Each of the next five chapters focuses on a friction trap and provides ingredients for you to select and blend to fix friction troubles. And to add and subtract stuff as you adjust the recipe along the way. Each trap is an on-ramp, or intervention point, where you can concentrate your efforts. We provide tactics, tools, exercises, and rituals to help you wrangle each bundle of afflictions.

Chapter 4, "Oblivious Leaders," shows how power and privilege can render bigwigs clueless to ways they make the right things too hard, the wrong things too easy, and drive people crazy. We detail how leaders can avert and dampen the damage. And how they can avoid falling prey to such power poisoning— and prevent waste, frustration, and disgust and the associated blame and bad-mouthing.

Chapter 5, "Addition Sickness," documents how the human penchant for solving problems by adding rather subtracting complexity triggers ugly ripple effects in organizations, including pointless rules, red tape, administrative bloat, and exasperating ordeals for employees, customers, and citizens. We show how such addition sickness is amplified by rewards that organizations heap on employees. Our antidote is to learn and live the subtraction mindset—we provide friction fixers a menu of subtraction tools, including rituals and games, subtraction specialists, simple rules, purges, and movements.

Chapter 6, "Broken Connections," details the causes and antidotes for destructive conflict, wicked internal competition, and debilitating coordination snafus. Our remedies include telling good stories, onboarding people so they understand how their job fits into the organization, building roles and jobs dedicated to weaving together different activities, and fixing handoffs.

Chapter 7, "Jargon Monoxide," focuses on the (mostly) destructive jargon spewed out in organizations. We show how to dampen and banish the convoluted crap, meaningless bullshit, in-group lingo, and mishmash of jargon from varied experts that clogs up our workplaces and our minds.

In chapter 8, "Fast and Frenzied," we detail the damage done when leaders create too little friction, including mounting technical and organizational debt, which, similar to when people borrow so much money that they can never repay it, drags down and sometimes destroys companies. We show when to race ahead and when to slow down or stop. The remedies in chapter 8 include pausing to get off to the right start, asking questions that make people think, doing a team reset, harnessing the rhythms and cadence of organizational life, and taking time to end things right.

As a friction fixer, your job is to figure out where each on-ramp will take your team and organization. To uncover which paths will help you most and enable you to fix the right things in the right order. We suggest starting with traps that are most damaging right now (or will soon be) *and* that you have the power to change for the better (even in small ways). Don't worry about traps that annoy people but are less menacing. And try to avoid the all-too-human temptation to tilt at windmills that are impossible to topple no matter how much time, energy, and goodwill you squander.

Part III

THE FRICTION TRAPS

INTERVENTION POINTS FOR FRICTION FIXERS

Oblivious Leaders
Overcoming Power Poisoning

Buying a new car is an ugly experience for many Americans. Our experiences at car dealers have been time-consuming, frustrating, and downright insulting. The high-pressure salespeople, the long waits, the rip-offs, and the lies about features, inventory, prices, and service seem inescapable.

We've had conversations with General Motors executives over the years about why they don't fix this wretched ordeal. They acknowledge that it sucks. Then they blame the independent dealers who sell their cars and emphasize GM's limited legal and financial powers over them. But that's just part of the story. Another reason it's been so bad for so long are the privileges granted to leaders of traditional American auto manufacturers—including Ford, Chrysler, and General Motors—going back at least fifty years. They've been spared paying the real cost for a new car and from the often-ugly negotiations over the price of a new car or the trade-in value of an old one. Plus, at least at GM, their gas and maintenance has been paid for, too.

We first learned of such perks when we visited GM middle managers and senior executives in Michigan nearly twenty years ago. They told us that, every six months, they were given a different new GM car to drive—and it cost them an "administra-tive fee" of just $250 a month. This Product Evaluation Program (PEP) enabled them to choose among varied GM cars, SUVs, and trucks—with senior executives given the added privilege of selecting expensive rides such as Cadillacs and Corvettes. The new cars were delivered to their workplace. And lest they have to deal with the headache of selling it, their "old" GM car was taken away.

The program persisted for decades despite complaints from critics including former General Motors strategist Rob Kleinbaum—who admitted he found the program "fun," loved the free gas and that nice "Chevy Suburban with ten-way ad-justable, heated leather seats." In 2009, he pointed out that eight thousand white-collar employees continued to get deeply dis-counted company cars and free gas even after U.S. taxpayers spent $50 billion to bail out the failing company—after it lost $30 billion in 2008. Kleinbaum argued that GM should have ended the program years earlier, even when it was making piles of money, because it reinforced the company's infamous insu-larity. He said ending it "would drive everybody in the company to be much closer to the marketplace and so they kind of feel the same things their customers feel."

As of late 2022, a version of the PEP still existed, and buying a new car at most GM dealers still sucked (and from most of their competitors, too). When we fact-checked this section, a former GM executive who recently left the company told us that managers and executives not only still got free cars, but they also still got free gas and maintenance, too. He added that most big GM offices have free gas pumps and maintenance opera-tions on-site—so managers and executives are spared high gas prices and the hassles of visiting gas stations and dealership ser-vice departments.

This former executive, like Rob Kleinbaum, admitted to enjoying the cheap and convenient car and free gas when he worked at GM. But he, too, believed the PEP had done "terrible damage to the company" over the years, as it relieved decision-makers from wrestling with the burdens of buying and owning a GM car and from experiencing the (often superior) vehicles and dealership experiences offered by competitors.

By making things too easy on themselves, GM prevented leaders from coming to grips with the bad friction that their system imposed on customers—and with other drawbacks of their offerings.

Power Poisoning: The Symptoms

If you are more powerful than your colleagues or customers, you are at risk of being clueless about their friction troubles, and of how you add to their misery. Beware of three symptoms of such power poisoning.

The first symptom is privilege that spares you from the hassles, humiliations, and barriers heaped on everyone else. Privilege, as psychologist and former National Basketball Association player John Amaechi explains, provides an "absence of inconvenience" from obstacles and challenges that others cannot escape. People with privilege often don't notice they have it and are clueless about the trials and tribulations faced by those who lack it.

GM's Product Evaluation Program is a textbook example of such privilege; the company has struggled with foreign competition for decades, and especially in recent years from Tesla, the upstart electric-car company that doesn't have any franchised dealerships (only company-owned showrooms; customers have to buy cars online). Yet, for decades, the PEP spared the most powerful people from the inconveniences of buying and owning a GM vehicle.

Similarly, Comcast, our internet and TV provider, protects a privileged few from the complicated phone tree, long hold times, and useless text chats with virtual and human assistants that ordinary customers cannot escape. In early 2021, Bob Sutton called Comcast five times one week because the company shut off his service, failed to restore it, and made multiple billing errors. Bob learned about this privilege after a Comcast executive and a board member saw Bob's tweets that complained about his ordeal. Bob soon received an apologetic email from "Rich" from the "The Office of Tom Karinshak" (executive vice president and chief customer experience officer), and then "Dan" called and gave Bob a special phone number and email address for a VIP lounge of sorts.

When Bob called the special number, "Kimberly" answered after two rings and provided fast, friendly, and excellent service. Kimberly explained she was on a small "personal service representatives" team in Arizona that (it seems) exists to spare VIPs (and, apparently, critics the company wants to cool out) from the inconveniences imposed on regular customers.

That privilege felt mighty good. But using it to protect Comcast's leaders from inconveniences heaped on other customers is a bad idea, especially as the company struggles to overcome its reputation for terrible service. In 2014, the company was ranked "at the very bottom of the American Consumer Satisfaction Index, underperforming even the rest of the cable industry." The company continues to face bad press for lousy service, including the litany of "Comcast debacles" that dominated the 2022 "horror stories" reported in *Ars Technica* by Jon Brodkin about internet service providers.

We believe that Tom Karinshak ought to disband that VIP lounge: feeling the sting just like ordinary customers would provide motivation and information to help execs fix the system.

Leaders at the top of the organizational pecking order are also spared numerous inconveniences that employees in the middle and at the bottom of the hierarchy cannot avoid. CEOs of big companies get elaborate perks like private limousines and personal use of the corporate plane, while their underlings are required to drive their own cars and to buy the least expensive airline tickets when traveling on company business. And the leaders enjoy other protections from encounters with the unwashed masses, such as the private elevators in Manhattan skyscrapers that were reserved for Jimmy Cayne when he was CEO of Bear Stearns and Richard Fuld when he was CEO of Lehman Brothers—until both investment banks were brought down by the 2008 financial meltdown.

In our visits with senior executives over the years, we've also been struck by the relentless relief that their privilege provides from little hassles heaped on other employees. Such as the chief technology officer who was spared from waiting in line in the company cafeteria because his assistant fetched his lunch. The COO who had her own permanently reserved conference room, which was empty most of the time, just in case she needed it. Meanwhile, engineers and marketers in her company sometimes had to wait days for meetings because conference rooms were in such short supply, or to schedule them early in the morning or late in the afternoon. Or the CEO who is provided a "concierge" doctor who visits her at the office and at home, so she is spared the inconvenience of office visits.

Sure, time is a precious commodity for most senior leaders, perhaps more so than for other employees as the leaders' actions and decisions have stronger impact than their underlings'. Yet, as John Amaechi suggests, the problem with such privilege is that leaders are at risk of becoming oblivious to, or downplaying, the emotional and financial costs that their actions and organizational designs inflict on the multitudes of employees and customers who can't escape such inconveniences.

The second symptom of power poisoning is the belief that, because you are powerful and a connected insider, you automatically know everything that matters about your organization. Academics call this the fallacy of centrality. It was uncovered by Ron Westrum in a study of why pediatricians did such a lousy job of diagnosing child abuse in the 1950s and 1960s. The limited self-awareness of these experts, their failure to see through parents' lies, and the silence of terrified children led the doctors to conclude, wrongly, "If parents were abusing their children, I would know about it; since I don't know, it isn't happening."

Similarly, prestigious leaders who spend their days interacting with colleagues and clients, reading internal reports, and studying spreadsheets, conclude, "It is my organization, I spend my days learning about the details, I know everything important that is going on here." Yet they often don't know, or they reach the wrong conclusions, about what is (and ought to be) harder and easier in their organizations—and cling to their flawed beliefs.

Like leaders who are convinced the only way to be a star performer in their company is to work harder than their colleagues, and who believe that—since they are the boss and get all the best information—they can distinguish the slackers from the hardworking stars. Yet, in one prestigious consulting firm, although leaders were *sure* that working long hours (and neglecting one's family) was the path to success, and they *knew* who worked like dogs and who didn't, they turned out to be wrong on both counts. After conducting more than a hundred interviews at this firm, Erin Reid of McMaster University concluded that leaders did penalize consultants who admitted to putting in less time—especially women who sought permission to reduce work hours. But Erin also found that leaders couldn't distinguish consultants who actually worked long hours from the (mostly male) consultants who only said they did. The firm's leaders believed that the ideal employee put in sixty to eighty hours a week. Yet they were fooled by underlings who made "small, under-the-radar changes to their work that allowed them to pull back, while still 'passing' as the work-devoted superheroes the firm valued." One consultant rarely worked more than forty hours a week, yet leaders believed he was among their hardest-working stars. The week that Erin interviewed him, he said, "I took calls in the morning and in the evening, but I was able to be there for my son when he needed me to be, and I was able to ski five days in a row."

The third symptom of power poisoning is selfishness. People who are puffed up with self-importance are prone to devote little attention to the burdens they inflict on others, and to care little about the plight of people with less privilege. In *The Power Paradox,* Dacher Keltner from the University of California at Berkeley shows that, in numerous studies—on everything from donating money, to teasing, to how much people talk, to ne-gotiation strategies, to sharing cookies—when people lord over others or feel powerful and prestigious, they (1) focus more on satisfying their own needs, (2) focus less on others' needs and behaviors, and (3) act as if the rules don't apply to them.

Consider the studies of rude motorists by Dacher and his col-leagues. Their research assistants stood (discreetly) at a busy in-tersection on the Berkeley campus and rated approaching cars on a five-point measure of prestige (e.g., one point for an old Dodge Colt and five points for a new Mercedes). Eight percent of mo-torists in the least prestigious cars cut off fellow drivers without waiting their turn; 30 percent of those in the fanciest cars did so. Next, the researchers stood at a busy pedestrian crosswalk. They recorded if drivers allowed waiting pedestrians to cross or, in violation of California law, cut in front of them. Not a single driver in those old Dodge Colts and such cut off a pedestrian; 46 percent of drivers in Mercedes and the like did. A similar study of driver behavior in Las Vegas found that, for every $1,000 increase in their car's value, drivers were 3 percent less likely to stop for pedestrians who had the right-of-way at a crosswalk.

In short, if you wield influence over others or just feel powerful, you may become oblivious of "inconveniences" that you heap on the people below you and that your organization heaps on customers and clients. You may suffer from the delusion that you know everything that matters about your organization, even though you are oblivious to what ought to be—and is—hard and easy. Finally, you may act like a self-centered jerk, who behaves like rules apply to "the little people" but not you—and not even realize it.

The bad news is that this toxic trio can render leaders ignorant about the causes and remedies for the friction troubles that plague their organizations—especially about ways that they unwittingly fuel such problems. The good news is that there are effective countermeasures for coming to grips with, avoiding, and overcoming such power poisoning. The chapter digs into six consequences of such obliviousness and shows how, by fixing themselves, leaders can fix their organizations.

Consequences of Cluelessness

1. Executive Magnification

Leaders often lament that followers resist change—such as the CEO who complained to us that his company's innovation efforts were undermined by middle management "trolls." Yet as organizational theorist James March observed, leaders rarely notice the opposite problem: when employees pursue their leaders' instructions "more forcefully than was intended" or inaccurately infer their bosses will be pleased by moves that never occurred to their bossses (and their bosses may not want). When that happens, the result is often unnecessary friction because employees squander their money and time and impose obstacles on customers and clients that the boss never wanted in the first place.

One executive told us about the magnification that ensued after his CEO commented that no blueberry muffins were served at a breakfast meeting. That CEO wasn't especially fond of such muffins; it was just small talk. After that, his staff gave advance instructions to hosts about their boss's strong preference for these goodies. It took him years to discover why piles of blueberry muffins appeared every place he went.

In all primate groups, members direct attention up the hierarchy rather than down. We humans are a lot like baboons and chimpanzees, who check every twenty or thirty seconds to see what the alpha male in their troop is doing. This lopsided attention is adaptive because more powerful creatures dispense rewards and punishments. Human bosses often don't realize how closely underlings monitor their every word and deed—and are oblivious of the gyrations that subordinates go through to protect themselves from and please those at the top of the pecking order. As anthropologist David Graeber explained, "The powerless not only end up doing most of the actual, physical labor required to keep society running, they also do most of the interpretative labor as well."

We saw some ridiculous consequences of executive magnification years ago when we studied 7-Eleven stores. The company launched a multimillion-dollar campaign to improve courtesy in its seven thousand U.S. convenience stores. The goal was to get clerks to offer greetings, smiles, eye contact, and thanks to customers—assessed by an army of "mystery shoppers" who observed clerks' behavior. The program included training for managers and employees, performance metrics, and feedback systems. The incentives ranged from $25 bonuses for clerks "caught" being courteous to the Thanks a Million contest, which culminated with Debra Wilson, a lucky store manager from Plano, Texas, winning a million bucks at a heavily hyped media event hosted by Monty Hall of *Let's Make a Deal* fame.

This campaign was launched after the company's CEO complained about a rude clerk that he'd encountered at a 7-Eleven. His underlings inferred that he wanted them to work on improving employee courtesy and would be pleased with this expensive program.

In fact, the CEO soon forgot about his rant. A couple of years later, he was dismayed to learn about the campaign, which he saw as a colossal waste of money. He ordered his team to end it. The company's research supported his decision. Most 7-Eleven customers didn't care about smiles and such—they just wanted to get out of the store fast. Courtesy had no impact on customers' satisfaction, loyalty, or spending.

Executive magnification also strikes in smaller ways. Like when bosses send out emails at night or on weekends. Eight experiments by Laura Giurge and Vanessa Bohns on "email urgency bias" show that when people receive emails outside of work hours, they *overestimate* how fast the sender expects a reply—and feeling such pressure triggers stress and burnout. The problem is pervasive. More than 50 percent of U.S. employees send or respond to work emails outside of work hours, and

76 percent of email recipients routinely respond within the hour. This pressure is especially pronounced when emails come from powerful people. Dozens of employees have told us, no matter how disturbed they are by their bosses' emails, they feel compelled to answer right away—a pattern supported by studies of power, status, and online behavior. The good news, however, is that once bosses are aware of urgency bias, they can dampen it. Laura and Vanessa found that when senders write, "This is not an urgent matter so you can get to it whenever you can," receivers answer more slowly and feel less distress.

Wise leaders keep reminding themselves that their charges are wired to respond to their words more strongly than they intend—and their privilege can render them clueless to such magnification. When they make offhand comments, write missives with unfinished ideas, or get pissed off, they pause to add, "Please do *nothing*, I was just thinking out loud."

2. Multiplication Madness

Power poisoning can render leaders oblivious to the compound effects of the small (and unnecessary) burdens that they heap on employees and customers—especially when their cone of friction includes many people they can influence over long stretches of time. Leaders are often clueless about, downplay, or just don't care about the cumulative toll that burdening, annoying, and alienating all those people has on their organizations and reputations. We call this multiplication madness.

In the opening pages of *The Friction Project*, we illustrated such madness with the 1,266-word email with a 7,266-word attachment that a Stanford vice-provost sent to more than two thousand professors—including us! That email could have been at least five hundred words shorter, and the attachment thousands of words shorter, if that leader—or her staff—had thought of themselves as trustees of our time. This episode is a microcosm of what happens in too many workplaces. Power and privilege blind people to small actions that have a big cumulative impact—and even when confronted with evidence about the burdens they heap on others, leaders blame their victims. If more leaders lived the trustees' mindset that Winston Churchill advocated in his "Brevity" memo and that Dr. Melinda Ashton implemented in Hawaii Pacific's Getting Rid of Stupid Stuff program, employees, customers, and community members would get more done, feel less frustrated and alienated, and respect their leaders more.

That's what happened at Distributed, a British software company, when they cut most meetings to fifteen minutes. Co-founder Callum Anderson explained, "When you do the maths and realize that a one-hour meeting for eight people equals one full business day, along with serious costs associated with that for a business, these shorter, more focused meetings are a no-brainer."

3. Decision Amnesia

We once worked with a Fortune 100 company in which the CEO had a habit of revisiting and reversing tough decisions made by the management team—even though members had studied it, debated it, and believed it was final. As an example, the team made the decision in one meeting to put the company name on the products they sold—a decision that most members were certain had been made in a past meeting. The CEO then rehashed that same decision during several subsequent meetings. He acted as if the prior discussion and decision were unfinished. He asked for more data, opinions, and debate. Then, one more time, the team decided it was the right choice.

Such amnesia wastes time as people travel down the same

old road again and again; it damages confidence in leaders' judgment and undermines implementation. People learn that, when they are instructed to act, their bosses don't really mean it. So, they stall, claim that planning is taking longer than anticipated, or do a half-assed job at implementation because—after all—their bosses will ask them to redo or scrap it anyway. At that big company, the heads of engineering and manufacturing didn't believe the CEO would stick to the decision, so they slow-walked the rollout, and it took at least five years before the company name and logo were stamped on most products.

One reason that leaders keep revisiting decisions is that they lack confidence in themselves, their team, and their organization. Rather than accepting it's impossible to make decisions that please everyone or can be rolled out without a few ugly surprises, such speed bumps prompt insecure leaders to reconsider decisions too early and too often. The CEO of that Fortune 100 company was infamous for overreacting to bits of bad news and for ever-shifting positions that were shaped by "the last person he talked to" rather than sticking to the consistent and repetitive messages that are hallmarks of successful change efforts.

Another reason for such amnesia was that the company rewarded empty talk rather than action. The top jobs were packed with the corporate equivalent of those hollow Easter bunnies that plagued the 100,000 Homes Campaign, as we saw in chapter 1. After all, it's far easier to make decisions that sound smart than to do the work required to implement them across a big company. Such hollow talk also protected executives from the finger-pointing that ensues when decisions that sound great in theory turn out to be terrible in practice.

If your organization is plagued with decision amnesia and other symptoms of the smart talk trap, the long-term solution is to recruit, reward, and promote doers rather than posers. As the

100,000 Homes team did when they banished the bunnies and celebrated chicken f'ers. Sure, making such systemic changes are easier for us to talk about than for leaders to do—especially in large and entrenched organizations. Yet, all friction fixers can chip away at empty words by starting where they are with what they have. Our first tip is to remember, talk, and act as if *a decision by itself changes nothing*. A decision has no impact unless people agree it's been made, it is communicated to and accepted by people who have sufficient will, skill, and resources to implement it. In other words, remind yourself and press others to act as if making a decision is the beginning rather than the end of your work.

Our second tip is tactical: *make sure that before a meeting ends, everyone is on the same page about if a decision was made, what it is, and who will implement it, then follow up with notes confirming what was decided.* Many leaders fail to follow this obvious advice, which results in differing memories about what was decided, the arguments made for and against the decision, and how it was meant to be implemented.

Here's how one master of the obvious did it. When we interviewed Patty McCord, Netflix's chief talent officer from 1998 to 2012, she explained, "The most important role I played at Netflix was, at the end of every executive meeting, to say, 'Have we made any decisions in the room today, and if we have, how are we going to communicate them?'" Again and again, Patty found that executives had wildly varying memories of decisions—which would have stymied progress if she hadn't asked these questions, taken notes, and reminded people at key moments:

Someone would say, "Well, we decided to spend fifty million dollars on this." I'm like, "No, no, no, no. We decided to consider spending fifty million dollars on that." They say, "But if we don't tell them, we're not being honest." I respond,

"Tell them that we haven't decided. We can tell them that. If they want to know why we haven't decided, tell them we think there's more that we need to find out before making the decision."

We call these Patty's Parting Questions. Asking them averts confusion, wasted effort, and embarrassment down the road.

4. Cookie Licking

The term *cookie licking* is inspired by sneaky children who lick all the cookies to deter their friends and family from eating them. Urban Dictionary defines it as "the act of calling 'dibs' on something long before you actually intend to do it." Cookie lickers take resources, projects, and decisions away from others, even when they have less expertise, time, or interest in such things. As former Microsoft technical assistant Steven Sinofsky explained, this classic "Microspeak" reflects one reason the company stalled again and again under CEO Steve Ballmer's reign "when one group would lay claim to innovate in an area by simply preemptively announcing (via slides in some deck at some meeting) ownership of an initiative," which blocked others from working on it—even if the cookie lickers never got around to it. Steven explained, "The basic idea is that teams wanted to keep features to themselves by declaration or fiat, almost always independent of a schedule, resources, design, or any concrete steps."

Cookie licking is pervasive in organizational life, doing minor harm when people reserve conference rooms they never use or take slices of cake they never eat. Putting up one of these no-trespassing signs does more damage when leaders insist on doing work or being involved in decisions but are so busy or put such chores so low on their priority list that their inaction slows progress and drives people crazy. Beware of deluding yourself into believing that *only you* can do the job right, calling dibs and jamming up the works.

It made sense, for example, for one CEO we know to interview every job candidate when her company had twenty-five employees. But not when it grew to over five hundred. Yet she still insisted on interviewing every candidate before an offer was made. Fitting interviews into her packed schedule placed enormous burdens on her assistant and HR staffers. And top prospects kept accepting jobs elsewhere before interviews with this cookie licker could be scheduled. A year too late, the CEO announced she was too busy to interview every candidate. She remained oblivious to how her cookie licking had created a bottleneck.

5. Sham Participation

Most leaders believe, or at least say, they should ask stakeholders for input—because it improves decisions and motivates people to help with implementation. But some leaders just pretend the input matters—while ignoring those supposedly welcomed ideas from employees, customers, or citizens. Such sham participation wastes people's time, dulls their initiative, and is usually painfully obvious—at least to the victims. It communicates that leaders are oblivious to or just don't care about how people feel or can make the organization a better place.

Some leaders use sham participation in hopes of fooling others into rubber-stamping decisions. Others see it as a necessary if empty ritual given local traditions and procedures. And some believe that, even when people realize their input doesn't count, the mere opportunity to voice their opinions somehow makes them feel better about their leaders and workplaces. Yet research on organizational justice suggests the deception and disrespect that define sham participation will alienate and anger employees and other stakeholders. Here's how it can backfire.

A few years back, our Stanford colleague Steve Barley joined a committee formed by administrators to get input from faculty, students, and staff on the design of a new building that would house his department. Steve resigned from the committee in frustration a few months later. He was annoyed because the administrators and architects decided most occupants would sit in open offices—and those in closed offices would have minimal visual and sound privacy. This happened even though users interviewed by design consultants listed privacy as their top priority—because their work required intense concentration. Steve reinforced the design consultant's findings by assembling studies showing that open offices dampen productivity, satisfaction, and social interaction—and facilitate the spread of contagious diseases, too. He wrote us, "I feel so used. Not one thing I said or argued for the whole time mattered. Not one thing the consulting company who did the early study of our needs for space mattered." Nearly all building and office design decisions were made before this committee ever met.

This happened years ago, but Steve is still angry about his wasted effort and by how the open office makes it tough for people to concentrate. Steve left Stanford for another university a few years later. This experience wasn't the main reason that he left, but he says it made the decision easier.

The lesson from Steve's story is that leaders who believe they can get away with such deception are living in a fool's paradise. People will see through their bullshit. And the lost trust makes their jobs tougher to do.

6. Hurting by Trying to Help

In contrast to disingenuous moves like sham participation, too often leaders are oblivious to how their sincere efforts to fix friction troubles can backfire. As the Dalai Lama said, "If you can help, by all means do so. If not, don't make it worse."

Unfortunately, for clueless people with expertise and power, the road to hell is often paved with good intentions. In medicine, *iatrogenesis* refers to treatments that cause more harm than benefit. George Washington's death is a famous example of iatrogenesis. His demise was hastened, or perhaps caused, by well-meaning doctors who—following best practices back in 1799—drained at least five pints of blood to treat his bacterial infection.

Research on "management by walking around," or MBWA, suggests that, a bit like bloodletting two hundred years ago, this much-ballyhooed practice sometimes does more harm than good. MBWA sounds like a great idea—leaders visit employees where they work, ask about challenges they face, and try to make things better. Management guru Tom Peters, coauthor of the 1982 business blockbuster *In Search of Excellence,* still urges bosses to embrace this practice. In 2019, former HP executive John Doyle wrote us that he invented the phrase MBWA in 1963 after watching founders Bill Hewlett and Dave Packard walk around a manufacturing facility in England and talk to frontline employees. John had become concerned that HP manufacturing systems were being ruined by all the MBAs hired by the company who believed that, if they couldn't count something in a cold, detached, and quantitative way, it didn't matter. John saw Bill and Dave's behavior as an antidote. The acronym caught on when, at the annual HP management meeting, John proclaimed, "We need less of the MBA perspective and more MBWA, management by wandering around, action."

Yet when researchers Anita Tucker and Sara Singer conducted an eighteen-month experiment on the impact of
MBWA on fifty-six healthcare teams in nineteen hospitals, they
found, on average, it undermined performance improvement
efforts. MBWA did improve performance when leaders used it
for problems that were easy to solve (e.g., moving nurses who
prepared medications to a less cramped room). MBWA back-
fired, however, when leaders used it for more difficult problems
(e.g., lab results that came back too slowly). Nurses reported that
these regular chats with the boss about big recalcitrant problems wasted their time, rarely led to improvements, and drew
attention to leaders' failings. Nurses complained that, instead
of blabbering and wasting staff's time, bosses ought to focus on
fixing the broken parts of their organizations.

Anita and Sara explain that their findings don't mean that
leaders should stop using MBWA. Rather, as that silly saying
goes, it means "problems are like dinosaurs. They're easy to
handle when they're small, but if you let them go, they'll grow
up to be big and nasty." Research on everything from improving
quality in manufacturing settings, to avoiding terrible accidents
such as nuclear power plant meltdowns, to reducing surgical
errors suggests that most big problems are explained by the
Swiss Cheese Theory: an "unpredictable combination of small
magnitude problems rather than from a single large magnitude
problem." Anita and Sara point to research on patients who were
harmed during heart surgery that "found that adverse events
were more likely to be caused by multiple, simultaneous 'minor'
issues than by a single, 'major' issue."

That's why this duo believes that MBWA worked for solving
small but not big problems. More broadly, they argue that "an
easy-to-solve prioritization approach" is more likely to lead
to long-term improvements because it is easier to nip small

problems in the bud and because many, perhaps most, big problems result from a complex and hard-to-predict combination of a bunch of little problems. So, by chipping away at the little troubles, friction fixers can eliminate those pesky little annoyances and reduce the chances of big, overwhelming problems that are difficult or impossible to repair.

Antidotes to Cluelessness

Less Transmission, More Reception

When we teach people about power poisoning, we say, "If you are the HIPPO, don't be a hippo, be an elephant." HIPPO is (sort of) an acronym for "highest paid person," the most powerful one around. Hippopotamuses, with their giant mouths and tiny ears, are an apt metaphor for the blabbering triggered by wielding influence and feeling powerful. When people (especially men) gain power, they hog airtime and interrupt others. Unfortunately, the more leaders blab, the less they learn about what to make hard and easy, what drives people crazy, what works, and how to fix things.

We suggest taking inspiration from the elephant's giant ears and small mouth—and stifling your inner HIPPO. Like the vice president who kept his talking in check by making his phone's background picture a hippopotamus with its giant mouth wide open.

We help leaders uncover and repair HIPPO problems by measuring two key behaviors. The first is talking time, how much the leader talks (versus other members). The second is the ratio of the questions the leader asks to the statements the leader makes. We worked with our Stanford colleague Kathryn Velcich to develop a "meeting audit," which our students used to assess all-hands meetings at five early-stage start-ups. Between six and eighteen employees attended these daily or weekly meetings. Our students measured these two behaviors and estimated people's energy levels as these meetings unfolded.

One first-time CEO was surprised to learn that, during an eleven-minute stand-up meeting with eight employees, he talked 50 percent time, made ten statements, and asked only two questions. He was disturbed by the team's low energy (which perked up after he asked questions) and that his employees told our students (anonymously) that these stand-ups were a waste of time. This feedback helped that rookie boss to talk less and ask more questions—and to devote more attention to the five employees who talked the least.

Ride Along, Help, and Do the Work

Leaders use the "ride-along" or "shadowing" method when they watch, follow, and question employees, customers, and citizens. This usually means going deeper than MBWA, which entails strolling around and having brief chats with people about their troubles. Taking the time to watch, talk to, and follow people as they try to do their work and struggle with the broken parts of an organization can shatter a leader's delusions about the causes, costs, and cures for friction troubles.

We met a New York City high school principal who blamed students for being late to class—until she spent a week shadowing them. One girl she followed had a class in the basement and, after it ended, had five minutes to climb the stairs to the top floor of the six-story building for her next class. That student could make it on time if she left just as class ended and sprinted up the stairs. But if the teacher kept students for a few minutes after the bell, which he often did, it was impossible. And when the girl was having her monthly period, she sometimes had to stop in a crowded bathroom to change her tampon between classes.

That principal learned she was blaming tardy students too much. She realized her power and privilege had blinded her to the "inconveniences" heaped upon students. To her credit, she began holding teachers accountable for ending classes on time and changed the schedule so that students had eight minutes rather than five minutes between classes.

Leaders can gain even deeper understanding of friction troubles and remedies by helping employees do their work and, when feasible, doing employees' jobs for short stretches. At Disney Resorts and Parks, executives do regular "cross-utilization" shifts, where they work frontline jobs (especially on busy days). Like Dan Cockerell, who started his twenty-six-year Disney career as a parking attendant at Disney World and retired as the vice president in charge of the Magic Kingdom in Florida (and its twelve thousand employees)—where his shifts included dressing as Disney characters and taking pictures with guests. In an earlier role, when Dan ran Disney's All-Star Resort, he discovered big differences between the best housekeepers and the rest—which mattered a lot because the All-Star has almost six thousand rooms. Dan spent two weeks with the most skilled housekeepers, especially "Blanca," watching her work, helping her make beds and clean rooms, and talking with Blanca and fellow housekeepers during breaks. He figured out the best housekeepers devised their own system: "Mondays was mirrors. Tuesdays was baseboards. Wednesdays were fans. They had a rotation." Dan and his colleagues rolled it out to other housekeepers at the All-Star—and sold them on the idea by asking, "Hey, do you want your job to be easier?"

Downward Deference

Researchers Tsedal Neeley and Sebastian Reiche tracked 115 senior leaders in a global technology consulting company who were responsible for selling and implementing projects in countries where they had limited prior experience. Tsedal and Sebastian found that leaders who were rated as top performers and got more promotions practiced "downward deference." They reduced "social distance" and gained employees' trust by taking time to learn about their lives and working "side by side"—rather than lording over them. Such leaders yielded to subordinates' technical and cultural expertise by deferring to their judgment and delegating authority. Like the Brazilian leader who told his Singapore team, "Let's invert the jobs here, right? You don't work for me. I work for you."

An American-born leader of the Southeast Asian operation reported he had limited understanding of "nuances between Philippines, Singapore, Thailand, Malaysia," and did not know the key players. Yet sales in his territories boomed because he won the trust of teams in each country and did as they suggested. Another U.S.-based leader described how, after a client in China who agreed to sign a major deal left for a vacation, she insisted her team track him down and press him to sign the paperwork right away (as she would do with American clients). Her China team pushed back, arguing the client would see such pushiness as violating his personal privacy. They asked, "Please, trust us." Her instincts screamed, "This is a terrible plan." But she listened to her team, and the client signed the deal when he returned.

In contrast, the worst-performing leaders lacked respect for their subordinates' expertise. Such as the American boss who was sent home from China after a year because he didn't trust his local team, talked too much, and conveyed, "OK, I'm the expert because I have led so many things."

"Flex" the Hierarchy

The lesson, and perhaps the irony, of Tsedal and Sebastian's study is that executives who deferred to subordinates moved up the pecking order faster than those who refused to bend to their underlings' will and wisdom: Leaders were granted more power because they gave it away. Yet deference and "flattening" the hierarchy aren't always the right moves. The University of Michigan's Lindy Greer shows that the best leaders are adept at "flexing" the hierarchy. They know when to delegate, defer, and get out of the way. And when to bark out orders, make decisions, and signal to subordinates to do as they are told without debate or discussion. Lindy points to the U.S. Navy SEALs: "When they're on the ground, there's a clear chain of command. If their commander says, 'Get out now,' there's no playing devil's advocate—no one argues. You listen and you fall into rank. But once they go back to the base to debrief, Navy SEALs literally take their stripes off at the door. When they sit down, everybody's equal and has a voice."

After Lindy's team analyzed more than a hundred hours of observations and sixty interviews from ten start-ups, they found the best CEOs shifted between accentuating and flattening the hierarchy—and the worst ones treated the hierarchy as static. When one CEO was asked if her team was flat or hierarchical, she explained, "You have to have both. If you don't have that flat piece where you're taking everyone's input, you're dropping expertise on the table, and if you don't have a hierarchical piece, then you're just heading in all different directions." The best leaders "activated" their authority to squelch destructive conflict, when discussion and debate became repetitive, and time pressure necessitated immediate decisions. These flexible leaders "flattened" the hierarchy when creativity, problem-solving, and buy-in were top priorities.

Another lesson from Lindy's research is that to avoid confusion and missteps, leaders and teams ought make explicit when to activate or flatten the hierarchy. Navy SEALs take off their stripes. In one start-up Lindy's team studied, when the CEO wanted everyone to speak, he passed around a football, and "whoever has the ball has the right to speak and everyone needs to listen to them."

Hierarchy Is Inevitable and Useful; Clueless Leaders Are Avoidable and Destructive

While it's preventable, people at the top of the pecking order are at risk of turning clueless, overconfident, and selfish. Hierarchies suck when they have too many levels and are hobbled by ridiculous rules and traditions, and when the leaders behave as if power differences are fixed rather flexible.

Perhaps that's why so many authors and consultants argue that, if we could just abolish power differences and banish hierarchies—or at least massively "flatten" and "de-layer" every organization—then efficiency, innovation, and happiness would spread throughout the land. Like management guru Gary Hamel, who preaches that "bureaucracy must die" and that "you can't endorse a top-down authority structure and be serious about enhancing adaptability, innovation, or engagement."

Yet evidence is overwhelming that, when any group of creatures comes together, hierarchy is inevitable and useful, and that fewer levels and smaller power differences aren't always better.

As psychologists Deb Gruenfeld and Lara Tiedens document, although the forms that hierarchy takes vary wildly, it is impossible to find groups or organizations where all members have roughly equal prestige and power. Whether researchers study people, dogs, or baboons, hierarchies are evident after just minutes of observation. When strangers meet, a hierarchy of leaders and followers immediately begins to emerge. And while some organizations do dampen power differences between members and have fewer levels, Deb and Lara found that "when scholars attempt to find an organization that is not characterized by hierarchy, they cannot." Take the New York–based chamber orchestra Orpheus, which is renowned for having no conductor. Orpheus appoints a different member as "concert master" for each piece of music played. And Julian Fifer, who founded Orpheus and led it for twenty-six years, had "full control over the nature of the program, including what set of pieces are played."

Deb and Lara also found that when efforts are made to eliminate hierarchy, or the pecking order is unclear, members are less committed to groups and less productive, dysfunctional competition for status emerges, and coordination and cooperation suffer. Too few hierarchical levels and too little top-down control is as toxic as too much. That's what Google cofounder Larry Page discovered in 2001 when the company grew to about four hundred people. Larry longed for the good old days when Google wasn't filled with middle managers. So, he got rid of them. As we wrote in *Scaling Up Excellence*, "More than one hundred engineers reported to a single overwhelmed executive. Frustration and confusion were rampant. Without those middle managers, it was nearly impossible for engineers to do their work and for executives to grasp and influence what happened at Google." Page soon brought all those managers back. Google's Project Oxygen later confirmed—just like hundreds of prior studies—that skilled managers are essential to successful employees and teams.

The answer, then, isn't to get rid of hierarchy, or even to assume that a flatter structure is always better. As a friction fixer, your job is to build and operate the most effective pecking order you can—and to use your power to bring out the best in those you can influence. Mark Templeton, former CEO of the software firm Citrix, makes a lovely argument about the difference between the need for hierarchy versus how people ought to be treated:

> You have to make sure you never confuse the hierarchy that you need for managing complexity with the respect that people deserve. Because that's where a lot of organizations go off track, confusing respect and hierarchy, and thinking that low on hierarchy means low respect; high on the hierarchy means high respect. So hierarchy is a necessary evil of managing complexity, but it in no way has anything to do with respect that is owed an individual.

If you are a top dog on your team or organization, remember the advice that teenage Peter Parker got from his uncle Ben in the 2002 *Spider-Man* film: "With great power comes great responsibility." Use the influence granted to you—by virtue of your position, expertise, and reputation—to operate a hierarchy that dampens and destroys power poisoning and enables people to do their work well and feel respected. That way, you can understand how your cone of friction affects others. And recognize when to defer to—and when to impose your will on—others.

Addition Sickness
Putting the Subtraction Mindset to Work

As the late great comedian George Carlin put it, "My shit is stuff. Your stuff is shit." That line explains much about why we humans can't resist adding more and more stuff to our workplaces: staff, space, gizmos, software, meetings, emails, Slack threads, rules, training, the latest management fad. We are wired to see stuff we add as righteous and essential. And to see stuff that others add as annoying and unnecessary.

Such "self-serving biases," as psychologists call them, make it easy to justify—indeed glorify—creating that new procedure, form, or rule that makes your job easier (and everyone else's harder), using your favorite app to schedule a meeting (even though no one else uses it), hiring another person for your team (even though it's too big already), or calling that extra meeting about your pet project (even though no one else cares about it).

To make matters worse, humans default to asking, "What can I add here?" Not "What can I get rid of?" As we touched on in the introduction, twenty studies by Gabrielle Adams and her colleagues show that "addition bias" shapes the solutions that people generate to improve universities, edit their own writing, edit others' writing, modify vegetable soup recipes, plan trips, and build LEGO creations. When a university president asked students, faculty, and staff for suggestions about how to improve the university, only 11 percent entailed subtraction solutions. For one design problem, participants were challenged to modify "a sandwich-like structure made from LEGOs so that it was strong enough and high enough to hold a masonry brick above the head of a storm trooper figurine." The best solution was to remove a brick. Yet most participants added several bricks—even though they were charged ten cents for each additional brick.

As Leidy Klotz says—he's the author of *Subtract*—we are wired to neglect subtraction and use addition as a substitute for thinking.

Organizations accentuate addition sickness by rewarding it with promotions, prestige, and money. And ignoring—or even punishing—people who subtract. Leaders who start big programs are celebrated, not those who disband bad ones.

A study of 137 U.S. public universities by economist Robert E. Martin found that, in 1987, there was a one-to-one ratio of administrators to tenure-track faculty. By 2008, there were two administrators for every faculty member. Robert explained, "Those who hold the purse strings have a natural incentive to hire more employees like themselves." A 2021 study of 117 universities in the United Kingdom by Alison Wolf and Andrew Jenkins found that such administrative bloat keeps getting worse—and growth is especially rampant among the most highly paid managers, professionals, and executives. Recent studies in the United States, Germany, France, and Australia show that their universities suffer from the same disease. Alison Wolf concludes that administrators are added at a higher rate, in part, because there is "far less scrutiny of nonacademic than academic hiring."

All those administrators aren't just expensive. Like most of us, they feel the need to justify their existence. Many of the organizational changes they understand, value, and implement entail heaping rules, processes, forms, training, and metrics on faculty, fellow administrators, and students. Timothy Devinney, chair of international business at Alliance Manchester Business School, says, as a result, "Universities are basically strangling the capabilities of the people within them." The road to such hell is paved with good intentions—administrators who add friction believe they are improving universities. But the cumulative impact can be stifling—and ridiculous. Timothy described "his horror when he was shown a sprawling spreadsheet of the 'key performance indicators' for the university department where he once worked. It included 110 targets, each with staff assigned to monitor them."

This syndrome reminds us of "The Tragedy of the Commons," a famous article by economist Garrett Hardin. He uses the analogy of a pasture that is open to all "herdsmen." Hardin argues that, even after a group of herdsmen have added so many animals that the collective good is declining, each herdsman still has individual incentives for adding more of his own animals:

Each man is locked into a system that compels him to increase his herd without limit—in a world that is limited. Ruin is the destination toward which all men rush, each pursuing his own best interest in a society that believes in the freedom of the commons.

Similarly, organizations often provide potent incentives for individuals—including prestige, money, and interesting work—for adding burdens that inflict collective harm. And weak incentives for resisting such temptations.

That's the bad news. The good news is that friction fixers can counteract such addition sickness. It starts with activating the subtraction mindset. Gabrielle Adams's team found that when people paused to think about solutions or were reminded to consider subtraction, they were less prone to default to addition. Venture capitalist Michael Dearing fires up this way of thinking by urging leaders to act as "editor in chief" of their organizations. When Michael was a guest on our *Friction* podcast, he argued, much like skilled text and film editors, the best leaders are relentless about eliminating or repairing things that distract, bore, bewilder, or exhaust people.

Good Riddance Reviews

You've got to decide what to subtract before you remove it. Smart friction fixers do "good riddance reviews" or, as Harvard's Cass Sunstein calls them, sludge audits. These are quantitative and qualitative methods that expose the location and levels of destructive friction and resulting damage. We list seven such methods to help you identify subtraction targets. Remember, you are wasting time if you measure all that ugly stuff but don't use it to guide some subtraction action.

Good Riddance Reviews
Methods for Finding Subtraction Targets

1. **Identify "stupid stuff."** Lisa Bodell, CEO of FutureThink, asks, "If you could kill all the rules that frustrate you or slow down your efficiency, what would they be?" A similar spirit propelled the Getting Rid of Stupid Stuff effort at Hawaii Pacific Health. Dr. Melinda Ashton asked healthcare workers to nominate anything in the electronic patient records system that "was poorly designed, unnecessary, or just plain stupid"—which generated 188 subtraction targets.

2. **Figure out the value and cost of your meetings.** In their Meeting Reset, sixty Asana employees rated each of their standing meetings. They identified more than five hundred meetings that were of low value. And don't forget the time that people spend getting ready for meetings. Bain, the management consulting firm, calculated that one company devoted three hundred thousand hours a year preparing for a weekly executive team meeting.

3. **Measure the burdens imposed by performance measurement.** Are you spending so much time evaluating one another that you don't have time to do your work? Deloitte's leaders were appalled after they "tallied the number of hours the organization was spending on performance management— and found that completing the forms, holding the meetings, and creating the ratings consumed close to *two million hours a year.*"

4. **Catalog sources of email overload.** The average employee spends 28 percent of their time dealing with emails. Is this true at your company (or is it worse)? Review the number, length, recipients, and timing of the emails that people send and receive. What can you subtract? Perhaps an email policy like that used at the consulting firm Vynamic will help. They call it zzzMail, as in catching some z's: "team members are to refrain from sending emails to other team members between 10pm and 6am Monday through Friday, all day Saturday and Sunday, and all Vynamic holidays. In urgent matters, a call or text is preferred over email."

5. **Observe and interview users.** To identify unnecessary and confusing questions in a benefits form completed by more than two million Michigan residents each year, Civilla researchers conducted over 250 hours of interviews with residents and civil servants—and observed them as they filled out and explained the form. Civilla identified dozens of obstacles that jeopardized residents' ability to get benefits.

6. **Build a journey map.** Diagram the stages that customers or clients travel through as they try to get information, obtain services, or buy products from an organization—and how they,

and employees, feel along the way. Our students Elizabeth Woodson and Saul Gurdus used interviews and observations to map the slow and bewildering process imposed on families of disabled children who sought services from the Golden Gate Regional Center, a social services agency in the San Francisco area. They identified numerous bottlenecks that marred clients' journeys—especially botched handoffs between silos.

7. **Try a perfectionism audit.** In *The Systems Bible,* John Gall proposed the Perfectionist's Paradox: in complex systems, "striving for perfection is a serious imperfection." Pressures for perfection cause needless effort and delay, interfere with learning from imperfect prototypes, and provoke despair. Many things that are worth doing—or are required by others—aren't worth doing well. Or, as Gall preaches, ought to be done poorly. In that spirit, ask people to identify tasks where the standards are too narrow or too high, or that are enforced with too much zeal.

Rebecca Hinds's journey at the software firm Asana shows how a dogged friction fixer applies such methods and, as we will see later in this chapter, helps her colleagues remove unnecessary stuff. We met Rebecca when she was a master's student at Stanford more than a decade ago and have worked with her since. Rebecca has been a research assistant on our friction project, a coauthor and a Stanford Ph.D. student, and, now, we're advisers to Asana's Work Innovation Lab—a think tank that Rebecca heads to develop actionable research.

Rebecca got interested in bad meetings when she worked at Dropbox and learned about the Armeetingeddon intervention that we described in chapter 1. Rebecca and Bob Sutton wrote a piece for *Inc.* in 2015 about how Dropbox's leaders removed most standing meetings from employees' calendars and made it impossible for them to add new ones for a couple weeks.

When Rebecca launched Asana Labs in 2022, she was inspired

by Armeetingeddon to recruit a small group of colleagues for a pilot program called Meeting Doomsday.

All participants started by removing all standing meetings with five or fewer people from their calendars for forty-eight hours. They used the break to think about which meetings were valuable, deciding which to subtract, modify, or keep. As we detail later in this chapter, this prototype "meeting repair and removal" tool showed much promise. We worked with Rebecca to scale lessons from Meeting Doomsday to sixty employees who participated in the subsequent Meeting Reset program. We learned that people wanted a fine-grained but simple way to assess meetings. We asked them to use a three-point scale to rate how much effort each meeting required and its value for helping them achieve goals. Of over 1,100 standing meetings, those Asana employees rated more than 50 percent as low value and identified more than 150 that required great effort and had low value.

Rebecca is not only uncovering meetings, rules, and traditions that frustrate people and squander time. As we show below, she also is developing tools for removing such obstacles and convincing her colleagues to use them to make experiences with Asana (and its products) better for themselves and customers.

Turning such knowledge into action isn't easy. Cass Sunstein has been railing against "sludge" since he was an adviser to former president Barack Obama from 2009 to 2012. Cass reports that the 1995 Paperwork Reduction Act (PRA) federal guidelines stipulate, "The benefits of paperwork burdens must justify their costs." In his book *Sludge*, Cass tells us, as of 2021, the U.S. government had, unfortunately, made no systematic effort to see which paperwork burdens pass this test. This is even though a 2017 report by the Office of Management and Budget (OMB) found that "Americans spend 11.4 billion hours on federal paperwork" per year. Cass calculates that if all 2.7 million Chicago residents devoted forty hours per week to such paperwork, after a year they wouldn't be close to completing it.

Yet there is a promising new effort to chip away at this red tape. In April 2022, Director Shalanda Young and Deputy Administrator Dominic Mancini of the Office of Management and Budget (OMB) introduced guidelines in a memo that spells out how U.S. government agencies ought to identify the harmful burdens they impose on citizens. The memo puts some teeth into the much-maligned Paperwork Reduction Act by detailing how agencies can ease such burdens.

Cass praised this promising memo on Twitter. As did Don Moynihan and Pamela Herd in a nuanced Substack memo. Don and Pamela, who study the administrative burdens that governments inflict on people, offered kudos because the memo not only instructs agencies to measure how long it takes to complete forms, it also urges agencies to calculate the time that people fritter away gathering information to complete forms, traveling to agencies, waiting in line or on hold, and figuring out if they are eligible for programs. Don and Pamela were especially impressed that the memo encouraged agencies to assess "the cognitive load, discomfort, stress, or anxiety a respondent may experience as a result of attempting to comply with a specific aspect of an information collection." As they wrote, "This new guidance is a remarkable expansion in the recognition of the burdens government imposes on the public."

The OMB memo outlines more than forty solutions for civil servants to reduce administrative burdens on the public. Most are tried-and-true. Such as providing "navigators" to support the public throughout applications—the solution we discussed in chapter 3 for helping people travel through complex systems and get what they deserve. Others are simple rules, including "shift in-person interview requirements to telephone or video-teleconference," "eliminate ink signature requirements where not required by statute," and "lengthen time between recertifications." Each of these solutions targets something to subtract—in-person interviews, signing with a pen, and the frequency that people must reapply for benefits.

Of course, just listing solutions isn't enough. People need to implement them, or it is all just hollow talk.

Subtraction Tools

Here are seven tools to help you live the subtraction mindset and spread it to others. We offer this summary (with details below) to help you mix and match tools and experiment with different blends so you can assemble—and constantly tweak—the right portfolio for tackling your friction troubles.

Subtraction Tools
Means for Spotting and Removing Destructive Organizational Friction

1. **Simple subtraction rules.** Building on Don Sull and Kathy Eisenhardt's **Simple Rules,** these are simple shortcuts and crisp constraints that help people focus their attention on what ought to be removed from their organizations.

2. **Subtraction rituals.** These are scripted actions that people take to mark routine or rare changes when they remove or lose people, places, and practices that have been part of their work lives. These choreographed packages of words and deeds can be simple or elaborate, are imbued with meaning for the people who practice them, and can provide comfort, guidance, and stronger social bonds.

3. **Subtraction specialists.** People or teams charged with keeping life as simple, easy, delightful, and cheap as possible in the

organization and have the authority, skill, time, and money to subtract (or add) as they fit.

4. **Subtraction games.** Exercises in which people begin with solo brainstorming about organizational obstacles that slow their work and drive them crazy. Then they meet to share "subtraction targets," select one or a few to remove, and outline implementation plans. Subtraction games can be as short as thirty minutes or extend for months when people are determined to remove destructive friction.

5. **Meeting repair and removal tools.** These are methods to help people identify and eliminate bad meetings. For meetings that remain, these methods help people make them shorter and less frequent, with fewer attendees, and give people permission to decline invitations and leave meetings that are a poor use of their time.

6. **Purges.** Deep, focused, rapid, and sometimes downright authoritarian efforts to remove an organization's broken parts.

7. **Subtraction movements.** These are enduring, participative, and multipronged efforts to spread the subtraction mindset throughout an organization, to teach people and reward them for making systemwide and local changes that, taken together, eliminate unnecessary burdens inflicted on employees, customers, partners, and community members.

   P.S. Celebrate people who don't add unnecessary stuff in the first place. Don't forget those precious people who abhor and resist adding needless stuff, which averts the need for subtraction.

Simple Subtraction Rules

In *Simple Rules*, Don Sull and Kathy Eisenhardt document how many leaders and workplaces benefit from "shortcut strategies that save time and effort by focusing our attention and simplifying the way that we process information." Those rules in the

OMB memo about eliminating in-person interviews and ink signatures are examples of such shortcuts: they are easy to grasp and apply and can improve the lives of so many people.

Another simple subtraction rule is, when you write or revise the core values for your organization, don't list more than four. *And* use vivid imagery to describe each value. If you are running a nonprofit, for example, don't talk about "excellence in fund-raising." Instead, talk about donors who tell friends and neighbors that their gift was "among the best decisions they have ever made." A short list of vivid values triggers a shared sense of purpose in employees, customers, and other stakeholders, which in turn fuels effort and coordination.

That's what University of Pennsylvania's Andrew Carton and his coauthors concluded after studying patients treated for heart attacks in 151 California hospitals. When a hospital had four or fewer values and used vivid imagery, patients were far less likely to be readmitted for further treatment within thirty days—a key indicator of the quality of care. Carton's team found similar results in an experiment where they assembled sixty-two virtual teams to design new toys. Before designing the toy, team members learned their "company's" values—and were instructed that their design should be "congruent" with the values. An "expert panel" of seven children was more enthusiastic about playing with toys designed by teams in companies with short lists of vivid values.

"The rule of halves" is one of our favorite simple rules. We learned it from Leidy Klotz, author of *Subtract*. Use it as a thought experiment. Look at your work. Your meetings and emails. Those letters and reports you write. Imagine you eliminated 50 percent of them, and those that remained were 50 percent shorter. Bob, in an article with Leidy, urged academic leaders to apply this rule to their own institutions. For example, when hiring and promoting faculty members, most universities require at least ten reference letters from prestigious experts and students—and sometimes twenty-five or more. Leidy and Bob argued, in this case, the rule of halves doesn't go far enough: "Five is plenty—and limit each to five hundred words." These constraints wouldn't harm the decisions, but would save letter writers, readers, and administrators who nag people to finish these things thousands of hours each year.

Subtraction Rituals

Birthday celebrations. Daily prayers. Sunday family dinners. Funerals. These are all rituals. Actions that people do repeatedly, or to mark major transitions, that follow a script, are imbued with meaning for people who practice them, and can provide comfort, direction, and strengthened social bonds.

We've worked with interaction designer Kursat Ozenc over the years to help students and executives learn and invent rituals, including subtraction rituals. In *Rituals at Work,* Kursat and Margaret Hagan outline the "smashing the old ways" ritual to "break from a previous strategy or dysfunctional practice." The car-sharing company Zipcar used this ritual for abandoning desktop computers and adopting a "mobile-first" strategy. Employees used sledgehammers to smash old desktop computers—which made an abstract management mandate mighty visceral.

When a difficult colleague gets fired, even if coworkers feel relief, it's still jarring. Kursat and Margaret created the "mourning for the recently left" ritual for such occasions. The team gathers and writes notes about everything they *won't* miss about their departed colleague. Then they write notes about everything they *will* miss. Each member claims one of those good things and commits to doing it. Then both lists are destroyed—burned, shredded, or, if generated online, deleted.

Annette Kyle made masterful use of subtraction rituals back in the 1990s when she banished bad old traditions at the Celanese Corporation's Bayport Terminal in Seabrook, Texas. Annette is one of the heroes in Jeff Pfeffer and Bob Sutton's book *The Knowing-Doing Gap*—which describes the "revolution" she led after being put in charge of the terminal, which loaded and unloaded three billion tons of chemicals each year from ships, barges, trucks, and railroad cars. When Annette took charge, Bayport was plagued with delays, poor planning, and despondent employees who weren't proud of their crummy performance. Bayport was paying millions of dollars of fees each year because, when a ship arrived to load or unload, and employees weren't ready, up to $10,000 an hour in "demurrage fees" were assessed while the ship waited.

Annette's "revolution" at Bayport changed metrics, brought in new tools, improved workflow, and eliminated unnecessary positions. She staged dramatic rituals to help people come to grips with abandoning their bad old ways—and to understand and embrace new beliefs and actions. To reinforce that "there should be no corner-office mentality" among management, Annette gathered all sixty employees one morning, who watched as Bayport's supervisor's office—where her leadership team had worked—was demolished by a bulldozer. Annette auctioned off her big green desk from the building for $60 because "I shouldn't be sitting behind a big desk. I should be contributing to our team goals whenever possible." To underline that bad practices were dead, Kyle put items in a pine coffin, including a SHIPS HAPPEN sign from the demolished office—which reflected the old philosophy that the arrival of ships (and barges, trucks, and railroad cars) wasn't something to plan for in advance.

In less than a year, there were marked improvements. Demurrage fees plummeted from $2.5 million in 1994 to less than

$10,000 in the first half of 1996. Before Kyle's revolution, it took employees an average of three hours to load a truck after it arrived; afterward, 90 percent were loaded within an hour.

Subtraction Specialists

Michael Dearing's advice that leaders act like editors doesn't mean they've got to do it alone. They can recruit people and give them the authority, staff, and money to make changes.

Here's how Hootsuite CEO Ryan Holmes did it. In 2015, when the company's director of technology, Noel Pullen, tried to send a customer a $15 company T-shirt, so many approvals were required that Noel calculated it cost $200 to send the single shirt. Noel hounded people in finance and marketing to scrap this ordeal and trust employees to send T-shirts. As Ryan put it, "Worst-case scenario? A few extra Hootsuite T-shirts find their way into the world."

Ryan liked what Noel did with those T-shirts so much that Ryan appointed him "czar of bad systems." The czar is an antidote to treating friction as an orphan problem, which, as we showed in the introduction, plagues many workplaces. As Ryan put it, bad processes "often lurk in a power vacuum; frontline employees don't have the authority to make changes, while senior leaders overlook these issues or assume they're someone else's problem."

Instead, at Hootsuite, when employees struggled with a broken process that they or their bosses couldn't fix, Noel was the go-to person to help them work across people and departments. Noel created a Bad Systems @ Hootsuite group to track bad policies and bottlenecks. Ryan explained, "We triage efforts based on a rudimentary points system: the number of people impacted by a bad process is weighed against the estimated time needed to fix it." As a result, Hootsuite wasted less of employees' and customers' time and left fewer confused and cursing at the company's processes.

Ryan recruited his colleagues to help identify bad systems, review suggestions, and select problems to fix. That's what savvy subtraction specialists do. They create or join networks or teams of subtraction specialists—rather than going it alone. That's what happened in Dr. Melinda Ashton's Getting Rid of Stupid Stuff campaign at Hawaii Pacific, when Civilla mobilized civil servants in Michigan to help revise that terrible benefits form, and, as we discuss later in this chapter, how Pushkala Subramanian's team scaled simplicity at AstraZeneca.

Subtraction Games

In the research for our last book, *Scaling Up Excellence,* we learned that well-run organizations are relentless about removing obstacles that waste time, squander money, and drive people crazy. To help people apply this lesson, we've run the Subtraction Game with at least a hundred organizations, including: the top eight executives at Bloom Energy;100 credit union executives; 150 Netflix film postproduction employees; 300 partners in a big law firm; 400 Microsoft executives; and 60 Stanford staffers at a "Help Center" workshop.

We ask people to start with solo brainstorming, to "think about how your organization operates. What adds needless frustration? What scatters your attention? What was once useful, but is now in the way?" For some organizations, we add, "Identify impediments that are within your sphere of influence and that are systemic at your company." Next, people meet in small groups or online rooms for ten minutes or so, discuss the impediments each member generated, and brainstorm more potential subtraction targets. Then, to focus their attention, they select a couple of targets and outline rough implementation plans—who would lead the charge to eliminate these obstacles, whose support they would need along the way, and which people and teams might push back against the change.

If multiple groups are participating in the game, each group picks a spokesperson, who shares their selected targets and implementation plans. When the CEO or other powerful leaders are in the room, we ask them to speak last or not to participate. On a couple of occasions, savvy senior executives have decided—without our prompting—to leave the room during the game to avoid stifling frank conversation.

Based on our prompts, some groups pick a practical idea (e.g., the CEO who vowed to keep his emails under five hundred words) and a crazy one (e.g., the engineers who proposed disbanding HR). Others select a target that is easy to remove (e.g., the managers who decided to get rid of the unused telephones in their offices) and a tough one (the top team that agreed their company would run better, and their mental health would improve, if they removed two micromanagers from their board of directors).

Some groups act on the spot. While we were running the game with twenty-five managers at a software firm, a vice president sent emails to disband a troubled project and to change his weekly team meeting to every other week. Another time, as we described in the introduction, the CEO of a financial services company stood up and told his top eighty people that, in a week, he wanted an email from each with two subtraction targets. Within a month, he wanted proof the changes were implemented—and offered each a $5,000 bonus for doing so. Those managers made hundreds of changes, including ending poorly performing product lines, eliminating meetings, and terminating contracts with unreliable vendors.

At one large global healthcare company, the general counsel

(top lawyer) reported that nearly a hundred different parental and family-leave policies were on the books, which confused managers, employees, and those in HR charged with implementing the policies. A year later, he told us that the Subtraction Game had inspired him and the head of human resources to review and combine policies—and they had trimmed the list by about 50 percent.

Some groups talk about subtraction but never do it—they enjoy the conversation and opportunity to complain but don't have the bandwidth, power, or incentives to implement their ideas. Others identify trivial and vague targets, especially in workplaces with little psychological safety where people fear that speaking the truth about problems will trigger reprimands, demotions, and firings from above. As the aim of the game is to identify as many subtraction targets as possible, and then to focus on a few feasible ones, many proposed targets—even in the healthiest organizations—are ignored and forgotten.

Meeting Repair and Removal Tools

Rob Cross from Babson College reports that collaborative work such as attending meetings and sending emails has ballooned by at least 50 percent over the past two decades. After the COVID pandemic hit in 2020 this overload—especially attending remote and hybrid meetings—got worse. A Harvard Business School study of 3.1 million employees found they attended 13 percent more meetings after the onset of the pandemic.

Some organizations fight back with strategic subtraction. Like the monthlong Meeting Doomsday pilot program that Rebecca Hinds at Asana ran with that small group of marketing employees. As we explained above under "Good Riddance Reviews," the first stage was a meeting audit, where employees studied their calendars and identified recurring meetings that lacked value. The second stage was the Meeting Doomsday part, in which employees removed all of the standing meetings with less than five people from their calendars for forty-eight hours. Then, as Rebecca put it, after people lived "with their newly cleansed calendars" for a couple days, they repopulated them "only with those meetings that are valuable—according to their own meeting audit."

Employees eliminated some meetings, reduced the frequency of others, and made many shorter—cutting thirty-minute meetings to fifteen minutes, and sixty-minute meetings to forty-five minutes. Meeting Doomsday packed a wallop. Rebecca reports participants saved an average of eleven hours per month. One Asana employee, Francesca, in the marketing group, believed her calendar was already in "top shape" before participating in the pilot. But she turned out to be the Doomsday "all-star," saving thirty-two hours a month.

We worked with Rebecca on a follow-up Meeting Reset program for sixty Asana marketing employees, which resulted in each employee saving an average of five hours per month. Canceling meetings had the biggest impact (37 percent of total minutes saved). But the combined impact of scheduling meetings less often, making them shorter, and relying more on written communication and less on presentations and conversations was even bigger (63 percent of total minutes saved). When we asked Rebecca if there were any drawbacks to the reset, she said, "Although most participants embraced the program and the resulting time savings, a few expressed reservations about eliminating lower-value meetings because they saw them as important for building relationships with their colleagues."

Other ways to repair and eliminate meetings might work better for you—or inspire homegrown solutions. In a classic study by Harvard's Leslie Perlow, she embedded herself in a software company in which engineers met and interrupted one another so much that they felt compelled to work nights and weekends to finish projects. Leslie nudged them to experiment with "quiet time": two periods each day when interruptions were banned, 8:00 A.M. to 11:00 A.M. and 3:00 P.M. to 5:00 P.M. Leslie found productivity increased 59 percent during the morning quiet time and 65 percent during the afternoon break.

Or you might be inspired by Salesforce's experiments with "async week" in 2021 and 2022. More than ten thousand employees tried going meeting-free for a week. There were drawbacks: 13 percent of employees reported working longer hours overall because meetings were more efficient for the kinds of work they did or for their work styles, and 16 percent reported an increase in "digital" interruptions made their work harder. Other async-week participants struggled with misunderstandings because relying solely on written communication caused them to miss key nuances. Salesforce folks learned to avert such problems through careful planning, communicating expectations explicitly, and encouraging exceptions when people believe a meeting is essential. By June of 2022, several big Salesforce divisions decided to implement a quarterly async week: everyone from senior executives to individual contributors was encouraged to cancel all meetings that week—except for training, critical business issues, and customer meetings.

Purges

A purge happens when powerful leaders spearhead a deep and focused effort to remove broken parts of an organization. Purges were part of the renowned turnarounds by Lou Gerstner when he led IBM from 1993 to 2002 and by Steve Jobs when he returned to lead Apple in 1997. One of Lou's first moves was to hire Abby Kohnstamm to head corporate marketing.

Abby inherited a mess. Every big IBM business had its own advertising agency, budget, slogans, logos, and strategy—which confused customers and wasted money. Lou brought IBM's top thirty-five executives into a room where the walls were adorned with "advertising, packaging, and marketing collateral of all our agencies." After Abby reviewed this "train wreck of brand and product positioning," Gerstner asked, "Does anyone doubt we can do this better?" Abby soon fired all those agencies, got rid of most of their work, and hired Ogilvy & Mather to develop one voice for the IBM brand.

When Steve Jobs returned to Apple in 1997 (after being forced out in 1985), he spent his first weeks investigating its vast, unprofitable, and confusing product lineup. He discovered that few insiders (let alone customers) understood the differences among the array of Macintosh computers, including the Performa 3400, 4400, and 5400. Most other Apple products were losing money, too, including the Newton (a handheld device) and Pippin (a gaming system). Within a year, Jobs eliminated every product he inherited. The new lineup consisted of just four new Macintoshes: a business desktop and laptop, and a consumer desktop and laptop.

IBM's marketing train wreck and Apple's bewildering product lineup were fueled by a similar cause: decentralized businesses each had enough power to add stuff, but not enough to stop others from doing so, too. This is a twist on Hardin's tragedy of the commons. Each business had incentives for adding yet another campaign or product, but each addition hurt IBM and Apple by confusing customers and wasting money. Although management gurus often bad-mouth leaders who exercise "command and control," as Lou Gerstner and Steve Jobs did, sometimes that's just what a broken organization needs.

Subtraction Movements

A subtraction movement is an enduring effort that involves many, or all, people in an organization. Our Stanford case study on how pharmaceutical giant AstraZeneca scaled simplicity shows how one such movement blended an array of subtraction tools. It was led by Pushkala Subramanian, who launched the company's Center for Simplification Excellence in 2015. The center launched the "million-hour challenge" to give back thirty minutes a week to each employee—to free up time for clinical trials and serving patients. By mid-2017, the center calculated that AstraZeneca's sixty thousand employees had saved over two million hours in less than two years.

Pushkala's team knew that top-down approaches like those used by Lou Gerstner and Steve Jobs would backfire in this company as, unlike IBM and Apple, AstraZeneca wasn't in crisis—although revenue and profits fell between 2011 and 2016. AstraZeneca is also a decentralized company, in which local leaders have substantial authority to accept, modify, or ignore orders from on high. So, rather than telling people what to do, Pushkala's team took "a player-coach" approach. They implemented some key companywide efforts, but believed their success hinged on the cumulative impact of small systemwide and local changes. Most employees would join the effort because they wanted to, not because they had to. And the team believed that many of the best solutions would be tailored for tackling distinct local problems. As Pushkala put it, "Let us not solve world hunger; let us start eating the elephant in small chunks."

In many parts of AstraZeneca, it took days for new employees to get their company laptops. This reduced productivity and planted early seeds of doubt and cynicism. Pushkala's team worked with human resources, hiring managers, and IT leaders to launch a program to ensure that, on the first day, every employee in every country had a functioning laptop and access to instant technical support. Her team also led another company-wide effort that saved thousands of hours: the default meeting length on Outlook software was changed from thirty to fifteen minutes.

Pushkala's team provided websites, workshops, and coaches to help employees throughout the company identify what frustrated them and their customers, and to imagine and implement local repairs. Hundreds of local improvements followed. The Mexico IT team cut paperwork in half, saving 690 hours a year. Meeting-free days were introduced in Taiwan and Thailand. Each employee in Japan simplified one thing, saving fifty thousand hours per year. On May 17, 2017, the company held World Simplification Day to celebrate saving two million hours in less than two years and to spread time-saving practices throughout the company.

In December 2017, Pushkala and AstraZeneca's senior executives made another subtraction decision: to disband the Center for Simplification Excellence. From the start, Pushkala's goal was to work herself out of a job. Her team members were also burned-out from their intensive effort and ready to move on to other adventures. Pushkala worried the movement would lose momentum. But she believed it was up to the firm's leaders, businesses, and employees to sustain it.

P.S. Celebrate People Who Don't Add Unnecessary Stuff in the First Place

As the Chinese philosopher Lao-tzu put it, "Do nothing, and everything will be done." Smart friction fixers never forget that, if they add nothing unnecessary, excessive, or destructive, then no subtraction will be needed.

Our Stanford colleagues Perry Klebahn and Jeremy Utley

made the "add nothing unnecessary" philosophy a cornerstone of their ten-week LaunchPad class. As we said in chapter 3, more than a hundred companies have been founded by Launch-Pad students since 2010, and more than 50 percent are still alive in some form. Perry says each founding team is taught to experiment with one or a few narrow prototypes at a time and to assume they won't be able to predict which offerings customers will want. That means most teams will need to keep abandoning and changing offerings before creating an offering that customers want and will pay for—and will generate enough revenue over the long haul to build a company.

As a result, Perry and Jeremy teach students not to take or to delay, many steps that other entrepreneurial classes and investors preach as essential for starting a company. For example, many start-up experts recommend writing a detailed business plan to help founders flesh out and explain their product or service, financial model, target market, and backgrounds. Perry and Jeremy do teach students to keep iterating a three-to-five-minute pitch, because potential investors, employees, and customers will want to know what your company does. Perry and Jeremy also coach strategic inaction, because they believe that writing a detailed business plan is useless or worse. That's because the company's offering (and target customers) will almost certainly keep changing. Founders who work hard on writing a perfect plan, Perry and Jeremy argue, waste time that is better spent prototyping, iterating, and learning. And—since labor leads to love—all that effort can cause founders to become irrationally attached to bad early ideas.

Perry and Jeremy aren't alone in their dim view of business plans. A study of seven hundred start-ups led by David Kirsch of the University of Maryland found no relationship between the quality of business plans and whether start-ups received venture-capital funding. Carl Schramm, economist and author of *Burn the Business Plan,* argues that Amazon, Apple, Facebook, and Microsoft never had business plans, and "empirically, it appears as if you don't need a business plan."

In short, before you heap some burden on people and eventually figure out that it wastes their time (or worse), slow down and ask, "Suppose we did nothing?"

Clearing the Way for the **Right** Hard and Inefficient Stuff

When we started this friction adventure, we believed that nearly everything in organizational life ought to be as quick and easy as possible. We were wrong. We now believe that subtraction is beautiful because it clears our minds and gives us time to focus on what ought to be hard, inefficient, complex, and frustrating.

Subtracting unnecessary distractions and burdens creates time to develop the deep relationships that are essential for doing great work—and living a fulfilling life. Yes, teams of strangers who are well trained and understand their roles can develop swift "cognitive trust" that enables them to do good work—such as flight crews on commercial airlines and teams of doctors and nurses in emergency departments who have never before met but know their roles so well they can perform complicated tasks together. Yet, the best work happens after collaborators develop deep "emotional trust," which requires working, talking, and failing and succeeding together over long stretches of time.

That's why teams and networks of people that start new companies, develop products, do surgery, and put on Broadway musicals perform better when they've worked together repeatedly and developed emotional trust. Sure, old teams can become stale and need an injection of fresh blood. But it takes years before that is necessary. And some enduring relationships never lose their spark. The "Oracle of Omaha," Warren Buffett, and fellow investor Charlie Munger of Berkshire Hathaway began working together in 1965 and produced a remarkable record of financial performance for nearly sixty years.

Subtraction also clears the way for the necessary, time-consuming, and inevitable failure, confusion, and messiness that are the hallmarks of creative work. That's why, as we noted in chapter 2, comedian Jerry Seinfeld told the *Harvard Business Review* that, to practice his craft, "If you're efficient, you're doing it the wrong way. The right way is the hard way." There are some ways to make creativity less inefficient—such as by pulling the plug on bad ideas faster. But Seinfeld's belief that streamlining creativity can kill it is bolstered by piles of studies—especially the folly of trying to reduce your team's or organization's failure rate. As psychologist Dean Keith Simonton documents, the most creative people don't succeed at a higher rate than others. Renowned geniuses including Picasso, da Vinci, and physicist Richard Feynman had far more successes *and failures* than their unheralded colleagues. In every occupation Simonton studied, from composers, artists, and poets to inventors and scientists, the story is the same: "The most successful creators tend to be those with the most failures!"

Subtraction also gives people time to slow down and create good rather than bad rules. Research on effective rules, or "green tape," reveals that the best rules aren't always the simplest and shortest. A study by Leisha DeHart-Davis in four Midwestern U.S. cities showed that civil servants and citizens found rules to be most effective when they were written down explicitly, with the nuances and key details spelled out, rather than being informal guidelines subject to bureaucrats' whims. More explicit and comprehensive rules were seen as fair because they left less room for exceptions or alternative interpretations. A public works secretary explained that her city's detailed snow-removal policy, which listed which streets were to be plowed first, was helpful in dealing with people angry that their street had not yet been plowed because "I can refer citizens to our procedures and show they are not being picked on."

Leisha's study found that another hallmark of green tape is that city employees who enforce such rules slow down and take the time to explain to citizens why the resulting hassles and expenses are necessary. Like the building official who worked hard to explain regulations to disgruntled residents because "if people understand that having a fence around a pool in the backyard is important because so many kids die per year drowning in pools, they understand."

The upshot—as our friction forensics in chapter 2 suggest—is that knowing what to add, when to slow down, where complexity is useful, and what to make impossible is as important as knowing what to subtract, when to go faster, and what to make easier. That means our last suggestion in this chapter is the opposite of what we offered at the outset. You and your fellow friction fixers need a "good friction review" to go along with your "good riddance review." You might ask, "What is too simple, easy, fast, and cheap around here?"

Broken Connections
On Preventing Coordination Snafus

- A cancer patient asked her oncologist to treat her strained bowel movements and upset digestive system and expressed deep anxiety over her abnormal brain scan (which wasn't related to the cancer he was treating). That doctor gave her no help and offered little sympathy. Afterward, he commented to his team, "Nothing really wrong with her; her tumor is doing great."

  That oncologist, the residents he mentored, and the nurses and administrators on his team viewed their job as curing her cancer. Not treating the whole patient (including treating side effects from the chemotherapy they prescribed). They left it to this sick and upset woman to find and schedule treatment for problems outside their specialty.
- Another cancer patient couldn't get two departments in the hospital to schedule and share information about her appointments. Out of desperation, she took a painful walk back and forth between the two departments to make it happen—while dressed in her hospital gown with tears streaming down her cheeks.

- After fourteen harrowing weeks in the hospital getting aggressive chemotherapy, a patient was discharged for outpatient treatment. He hugged his young son for the first time since being admitted. After a few minutes of joy, his wife asked, "Okay, now where to?" They realized that no one had told them about the next steps or whom to contact. It was up to his wife to organize his treatment.

These are just a few troubling stories from Melissa Valentine's three-year study of the birth of a state-of-the art cancer hospital—a "Cancer Center" that hired the best specialists, built state-of-the art facilities, and bought the latest and greatest technologies to deliver "patient-centered care."

The center's inability to achieve its patient-centered mission reveals much about a set of friction troubles that plague many organizations, even those staffed by skilled people with good intentions: *coordination problems. These are failures of communication, collaboration, and integration of action among the different parts of organizations.* Failures that ruin products when engineers "throw the design over the wall" to manufacturing without working with those folks to make sure the thing can actually be built. That create mayhem for travelers when the operation that cancels flights takes hours to get the message to frontline employees and passengers. And that provoke the aggravation you feel when, after ordering your favorite dish at a restaurant, it takes forty-five minutes before the kitchen staff informs your server that it's sold out for the night.

This chapter is about the causes of and remedies for such failures to weave together knowledge and action in organizations. Coordination troubles, like other kinds of destructive friction, are often orphan problems that everyone knows about, but no one feels accountable for fixing. As those cancer patients above learned the hard way, coordinating patients' visits and treatments across specialists and departments wasn't anyone's job at the Cancer Center. It fell to patients and their families to wrestle with a complex system, which provided them little help and lousy information as they struggled to figure out the cast of healthcare providers they needed, and to find other essential services including transportation and financial assistance. And to do nearly all the work themselves to orchestrate when and where it all happened.

One patient at the center, for example, described how it fell to him to contact, schedule appointments with, and convey messages about his condition and the treatment he needed with at least fifty healthcare professionals during his treatment. That included "thirteen different doctors, and that's not counting anesthesiologists." He said each doctor was great as an individual provider, but coordinating his care was a full-time job, and he felt "scattered" as he tried to keep track of all the specialists, the information they needed about past treatments, side effects, and insurance, the different medicines they prescribed, and his schedule of appointments.

The patient activists, who ultimately persuaded the center to reduce these burdens, called this demanding unpaid work the cancer tax. The Cancer Center suffered from two hallmarks of organizations that are plagued with coordination snafus.

First, powerful people ignore, dismiss, denigrate, and even undermine people and groups they need to mesh their work with. Oncologists saw themselves as being at the top of the pecking order at the center and the work of other specialists as secondary, trivial, or downright useless. They dismissed side effects, including fatigue, diarrhea, and cramps, caused by chemotherapy that they prescribed as "normal" and left it to patients to find specialists to treat such problems.

Second, powerful people devote little attention to solutions for coordination problems. Executives, consultants, and physicians who launched the center gave lip service to collaboration across silos. Yet they focused on building strong teams and departments in areas such as brain tumors, breast cancer, and skin cancer—and ignored how to help the units work together. They gave even less thought to specialists outside the center that patients needed, including social workers, hospice caregivers, and cardiologists and radiologists who treated side effects of cancer treatments and patients' other health issues.

The center's leaders prepared a road map that spelled out their mission. It emphasized that patients would get the best care because their treatments would be based on the latest cancer research, and the center would lead the way in conducting scientific research to discover new and better cancer treatments. The road map, Melissa tells us, never mentioned facilitating "patients' and families' administrative work for coordinating their care across multiple medical and nonmedical specialists."

People in different center roles and departments lacked the shared knowledge and will to collaborate, and with nobody in place to knit their roles and responsibilities together, basic coordination didn't happen for patients. The Cancer Center isn't unique. Similar friction problems plague many workplaces because of baked-in human biases, the ways that organizations are designed, and the kinds of behaviors that are rewarded (and punished).

Why People Neglect Coordination

The people who led the Cancer Center were smart and hardworking and cared deeply about patients and their families. How could they create a system that seemed designed to inflict the cancer tax on the very people they wanted to help? And why do so many other organizations suffer from coordination troubles?

Part of the answer stems from how people are wired, from a common cognitive bias. Stanford's Chip Heath and the late Nancy Staudenmayer showed that people are prone to suffer from *coordination neglect:* they fixate on parts of organizations and ignore how the parts ought to work together.

Chip and Nancy distinguish between two modes of coordination neglect. The first mode is *component focus,* where people in a team or silo devote too much attention to their own work and too little to how it will shape and be shaped by others' work. Like the Ford Motor Company engineer who admitted his group was so fixated on designing car chassis that "when I saw a car driving down the road, all the rest [other than the chassis] disappeared. All I could see were the suspension arms going up and down." In his mind, the rest of the car—and the people at Ford who made it—barely existed. The Cancer Center, too, was stymied by component focus. Like that oncologist who viewed his patient's tumor as the only pertinent element of her health.

As Chip and Nancy put it, for people afflicted with component focus, "wholes are not the 'sum of their parts,' they are a function of one part."

The deeper a person's expertise, the worse this narrow focus gets. Chip and Nancy show how "the curse of knowledge" accentuates the coordination troubles caused by component focus: Experts wrongly assume that—because a subject comes so easily to them after learning about it for years—what they know is obvious and can quickly be grasped by others. Experts unwittingly create coordination snafus by failing to pass along essential information to people in other positions and fields because they assume it is self-evident. Or, when they try to pass information along, experts provide explanations they believe are easy to understand but are incomprehensible to people who aren't indoctrinated into their circle. Such as the "technical people" studied by organizational theorist Deborah Dougherty. These technical people provided vague and jargon-laden specifications for building computer disk drives that they assumed would be easy for manufacturing colleagues to implement—based on designs they believed reflected exactly what the company's customers would want. But when those technical people and their customers saw the final product, so much knowledge had been lost in translation that both said, "Oh my God! We didn't want that!"

Specialists are also prone to overconfidence, to believe their narrow knowledge makes them experts in all other areas. They overestimate their understanding of others' work, oversimplify it, and denigrate the dedication and skill of people outside their area. Overconfidence is another reason that the technical people Deborah studied designed flawed products. They were sure their narrow technical knowledge was all that was required to design great products—and believed that talking to and listening to manufacturing people, salespeople, or customers was a waste of time. They assumed their designs would be easy to manufacture when, in fact, doing so was difficult. And rather than considering pricing and market size, they assumed if the product was packed with the latest technology, commercial success was a sure thing.

Partition focus, the second mode of coordination neglect, happens when decision-makers devote too much attention to assembling an organization with great parts—and too little attention to how the pieces ought to work together. That's what happened when Cancer Center leaders fixated on assembling the best specialists in the world and supporting them with excellent staff and technologies—and thought little about linking their work with that of other departments and specialists. Partition focus also afflicted U.S. Navy leaders in the early days of World War II. In *Military Misfortunes,* historians Eliot Cohen and John Hooch describe how the United States tried to stem U-boat attacks by imitating British solutions, including using sonar and destroyer escorts, which were operated by specialists. But what worked well for the Brits failed for the U.S. Navy, whose ships continued to be sunk at a far higher rate than British ships.

What was the difference between the performance of the two countries? U.S. leaders failed to take the additional step of adopting the British solution of integrating people, equipment, and information: an intelligence center that tracked ships and planes, gathered photographs and prisoner interviews, and intercepted German messages. This hub was linked to all British ships and quickly informed them about routes for avoiding German attacks and tactics for finding and sinking U-boats. After months of failure, the U.S. Navy created the Tenth Fleet to play this integration role in submarine warfare. *Military Misfortunes* reports, "In the eighteen months before the creation of the Tenth Fleet, the U.S. Navy sank thirty-six U-boats. In the six months after, it sank seventy-five."

The lesson from the British and U.S. navies, and, as we will see later, from the Cancer Center, too, is that savvy leaders can avert and repair coordination neglect. Friction fixers set the stage for coordination by building organizations that reward people to help their colleagues do great work—rather than undermining and double-crossing them.

The Foundation: Don't Treat Friends like Enemies

It's impossible to operate an organization of any size without breaking it into smaller pieces. Organizations can't function without

sorting people into roles, teams, locations, shifts, and departments. Even tiny organizations need such "differentiation."

That's what founders Akshay Kothari and Ankit Gupta
learned when building Pulse News, a start-up that developed a
news application for phones and tablets. Akshay and Ankit told
us that after Pulse grew from three to eight employees—who all
worked in one room—communication breakdowns began to
occur, with an attendant rise in bickering and confusion. They
responded by dividing the group into three small teams. This
division enabled each team to focus on its work without being
interrupted and distracted. To help with communication and coordination across teams, "each team maintained a bulletin board
that captured their current work to help everyone at Pulse follow
what they were doing." Also, at three thirty each afternoon, "each
team also gave a short talk to the company about what they were
working on and where they needed help." Almost immediately,
the turmoil subsided, and the little company started produc-
ing better software and doing it faster. Pulse kept growing until
LinkedIn bought it for $90 million in 2013.

Yet the same divisions that enabled Pulse News to grow can
wreak havoc in bad organizations and cause nasty side effects
in even the best. That's because of the all-too-human tendency
to see "the other" team, department, or role as a threat and
competitor. Experiments show that trivial differences such as
wearing different-color shirts or believing a hot dog is or isn't a
sandwich trigger beliefs that our own kind is superior, provoke
us to treat those in different categories as competitors, and un-
fairly favor "our people" when dispensing rewards.

Organizations amplify such dynamics by creating "I win,
you lose" competitions for money and prestige—rewarding
employees who ignore, demonize, and refuse to cooperate with
coworkers, and punishing those who help colleagues succeed.

The culture and resulting incentive system that Steve Ballmer created at Microsoft during his reign as CEO from 2000 to 2014 was infamous for rewarding employees who ignored, bad-mouthed, and backstabbed colleagues. As one Microsoft engineer put it, "Staffers were rewarded not just for doing well but for making sure their colleagues failed."

When we visited Microsoft in 2014, just after CEO Satya Nadella took over, insiders were open about the damage wrought by Ballmer's culture and reward system. During our speech to some three hundred managers, we showed a slide quoting Paul Purcell, then the CEO of Baird (a financial services firm), who defined assholes as people who "put their needs ahead of customers, coworkers, and the company." A woman in the back shouted, "That describes most of our current executives, except Satya." The room broke into applause. We asked for examples. A manager explained the Microsoft operating system worked better with the Apple iPhone than the recently discontinued Microsoft phone because "we see each other as the enemy, not Apple."

A Diagnostic Question

To help assess if an organization suffers from destructive competition and conflict—and to figure out how to fix it—we ask, "Who are the superstars here?" Followed by "Do people get ahead by doing great work *and* helping others succeed? Or doing great work while ignoring and even undermining colleagues?" When people are rewarded for helping others, many of the ugly dynamics that infected Microsoft—and so many other places—disappear.

The difference between the two dynamics is illustrated by a story we heard U.S. soccer legend Brandi Chastain tell at a gathering of the Girl Scouts of Northern California. Brandi is famous for scoring the winning goal for the U.S. soccer team at the Women's World Cup in 1999 and throwing off her jersey in celebration. Brandi credited her grandfather for teaching her to be a good soccer player and person. This included his reward system, in which he paid Brandi $1 for scoring a goal but $1.50 for an assist. Because, as Brandi put it, "it is better to give than receive."

Reward Collaboration and Coordination

When Satya took over Microsoft in 2014, the system he inherited from Ballmer saw employees pitted against one another with a "stack ranking" performance system. All the employees in the company were ranked from best to worst, with the top 20 percent getting the lion's share of rewards and—no matter what—the bottom 10 percent were rated "poor." A manager explained, "It's management by character assassination."

One of Satya's first moves was to abolish stack ranking. He worked to reverse the traditional emphasis on rewarding the smartest person in the room, who dominates and pushes around others. He encouraged people to ask questions and listen—to be "learn-it-alls" not know-it-alls. He pressed people to live the One Microsoft philosophy, that the company is not to be "a confederation of fiefdoms" because "innovation and competition don't respect our silos, so we need to transcend those barriers." To support this new culture, Satya changed the reward system so that the superstars were people who worked across silos and teams to build products and services with pieces that meshed together well. *And* so that people deemed as superstars were those who helped others succeed in their careers. The backstabbers who'd flourished under Ballmer changed their ways, left the company voluntarily, or were shown the door.

These changes, and many others by Satya's leadership team,

seem to have spurred cooperation and coordination through-out the company—and led to a marked turnaround. In 2019, the Reputation Institute reported that, while reputations of tech giants including Facebook and Google had plummeted, Micro-soft was the most improved company on their list because of its better products, services, and leadership. In 2018, according to surveys by Glassdoor, 95 percent of Microsoft's employees ap-proved of Satya's performance, a marked change from Ballmer's 46 percent rating in 2012. Finally, after Satya took over in 2014, the company's market capitalization rose from about $300 bil-lion to more than $2.5 trillion in autumn of 2023.

Flex the Hierarchy to Squelch Bad Behavior

Friction fixers don't just rely on bold statements and rewards to discourage people from treating friends like enemies—they exercise influence as events unfold. As we saw in chapter 4, Lindy Greer found that savvy leaders know how and when to shift between flattening and activating the hierarchy. In Lindy's research, she found that skilled CEOs signaled when everyone was expected to add ideas, argue, or criticize. At one health-care company that Lindy worked with, "the CEO kicked off a monthly meeting with his eleven-person executive team with a few inspiring reminders of the bigger vision the company was seeking to realize. Then he passed the baton to the chief mar-keting officer, who shared her goal for the discussion: making a final decision about the new brand logo. She then invited all in the room to speak their minds—which prompted a barrage of facts, recommendations, and concerns." That CEO "minimized his power" by moving to the to the back of the room and speak-ing last.

Yet when interactions turned nasty or wasted time, the best CEOs that Lindy studied exercised authority. One CEO, for example, "would come back in and take charge" when "there's a disagreement that I fear is getting either personal or it's distracting us from progress." In the hands of a savvy leader, moves like that help assure that—in the moment—people understand how to behave and what the ground rules are for coordinating their actions.

On the Same Page: The Power of a Hot Cause

Once people are motivated to play well with others, the question is where to direct that constructive energy. People coordinate better when they understand and agree on the direction they are heading. Friction fixers energize people by turning such goals into emotionally "hot causes," especially goals that crank up shared anger and pride, which they use to fuel the creation and implementation of "cool solutions"—concrete and coordinated actions. That's what happened with the cancer tax. Once patient activists convinced Cancer Center leaders that they were heaping debilitating burdens on the people they wanted to help, the upset and determined hospital staffers began working with patients and their families to fix such problems.

Staffers began by asking patient activists to talk about their ordeals to groups throughout the center. Those stories got center employees fired up about the cancer tax, which motivated them to develop cool solutions. One task force met each week to redesign "the oncologist clinic team structure to be more patient-centered." At first, physicians resisted being distracted from seeking funding, doing research, and practicing their specialties. Such as the oncologist who said he didn't care about improving patient flow between clinics and didn't think it mattered. After recalcitrant physicians like him heard patients' stories, got to know patients and their families, and read research on "care coordination," they changed their tune. Ten months later, that same oncologist insisted that the problem "comes down to coordination," that "too much is put onto the patient," and the system had to be revamped to help physicians across departments "talk to each other to exchange information and plans" about patients.

The Nitty-Gritty: Ways to Prevent and Repair Coordination Snafus

As a friction fixer, to dampen coordination troubles, your job is to find and test new solutions, teach them to others, and keep updating your tool kit. Here are six solutions that might work for you.

1. Onboard People to the Organization, Not Just the Job

Friction fixers who are intent on building a culture of coordination go beyond training newcomers to perform their narrow job responsibilities. They teach newbies how their work meshes with that of others, how the organization functions, and how to use the system to help them do their work. This saves a lot of trouble down the road.

That's what studies of new software developers show—whether they worked for a big company like Google or volunteer for a loosely structured open-source software project. Developers who stuck around and contributed valuable code had mentors who made them feel welcomed, explained who does what, and showed them how their work fit into the larger mission. And they had mentors who taught them to use the right tools and follow local norms so they could work well with fellow developers.

Well-designed onboarding is critical when people join an organization that requires nuanced coordination with a big cast of coworkers and customers. Like the onboarding at Harvard Business School (HBS) for new faculty members. Although we are Stanford professors, we believe HBS teaches the best MBA classes in the world. HBS faculty are masterful at teaching cases ranging from "Tesla and Elon Musk," to "Oprah," to "Maersk: Betting on Blockchain." In most classes, faculty use pointed questions and "cold calls" to press students to go beyond the obvious facts of a case and analyze subtle forces and opportunities. Faculty weave students' points together on the spot (usually by writing them on the board) and guide students toward key takeaways—often a nuanced appreciation of the tough choices they would face, for example, if they were in Elon Musk's or Oprah's shoes.

During visits to HBS classes, we've been impressed by how the room vibrates as the professor orchestrates action among the ninety or so students. All students are on full alert because they want to make comments that earn their classmates' respect. Our friends who graduated from HBS decades ago still talk about classmates who were smart and funny (or not) in class. Students are also motivated because every comment is evaluated by the professor—often 50 percent of their grade is based on class participation.

HBS students and faculty don't work in walled-off silos. They have carefully coordinated roles that help ensure that everyone gets the most out of the courses. Students work late into the night in study groups to dissect each case. For classes that are required of all nine hundred or so MBAs who come to HBS each year—including Finance and Leadership & Organizational Behavior—students are divided into ten sections, and each section takes each required class together. The five or six faculty who lead the ten sections of each required class coordinate tightly. Each professor teaches the same cases in the same order. They meet to discuss how to teach each class—questions to ask, student comments to expect, and how to organize their "boards" (summaries of students' comments that faculty write on the whiteboards). Faculty also meet with students regularly, especially elected "section officers," who celebrate the good and voice concerns and make suggestions on behalf of classmates.

Veteran HBS faculty and administrators run an onboarding experience to help new faculty learn the ropes. Each year, every new faculty member takes the immersive three-day START class with their cohort of fifteen or so new HBS professors—you take it, and need it, whether you are a rookie with no teaching experience or were a star classroom teacher at another business school. We talked with an HBS professor who attended START twenty years ago as a new faculty member, and again recently as a veteran who helped teach in the START program. That professor was "wowed" in both roles because START is so well crafted to help newcomers navigate the complex HBS culture and system.

START includes talks from administrators on how the school is structured, how it earns and spends money, and the numerous staff at the ready to help faculty and students. Veteran HBS teachers explain the cast of characters that faculty are expected to meet with and how to learn from them—with an emphasis on listening to student feedback. During the first two days, new faculty play the role of students. They break into small groups to prepare for case discussions. Then they're taught cases by HBS faculty—cold calls and all—to get a taste of the student experience. On the third day, new faculty do practice teaching stints that are videotaped and critiqued by experienced faculty. For the rest of the academic year, the START cohort meets every month to dig into topics including using student feedback, teaching executives, and juggling demands on their time.

We aren't suggesting that every business school do such intense onboarding; the coordination demands aren't as strong elsewhere, including at Stanford. But if your organization is plagued with coordination snafus, take a critical look at on-boarding. Figure out what happens during employees' first weeks on the job, ask them what sucks, and shadow a few. You might discover that newcomers and old-timers keep dropping balls because no one ever taught them whom to work with or how pieces of the system fit together.

2. Get Up Close and Personal with People Who Make the System Tick

Michael Lewis has cranked out bestsellers for decades, includ-ing *Liar's Poker*, on the inner workings of investment banks, *The Big Short*, on the 2007 financial meltdown, and *The Premoni-tion*, on public health experts who sounded the alarm about the COVID-19 pandemic months before the U.S. Centers for Disease Control. To understand how big and complicated orga-nizations function, Michael downplays what senior leaders say and talks to people in the middle and on the front lines. He says folks six levels down from the top are the real experts who make things tick and know why things go wrong. Michael calls this the "L6 strategy," a term he learned from Todd Park, a former software executive who served as chief technology officer for the U.S. Department of Health and Human Services during the Obama administration.

On Michael's *Against the Rules* podcast, Todd talked about how he helped reverse the botched launch of Obamacare, the administration's signature health insurance legislation. The HealthCare.gov website that went live in October of 2013 was intended to enable millions of Americans to find and sign up for health insurance. The site kept crashing and was plagued with glitches—it took eight seconds to respond to each mouse click. After Todd volunteered to lead the effort to fix HealthCare .gov, he discovered that the people who were supposed to be in charge didn't know why it crashed, let alone how to repair it. Todd used the L6 strategy, which he had learned as cofounder of Athenahealth, an information technology company. Six levels down, he found government contractors who had worked on HealthCare.gov for months and knew why it sucked because they had produced the individual features of the website, "the security protocols, the accessibility requirements, and hundreds of other details."

But the problem was that none of the contractors had "dealt with overall performance issues, like the speed at which the website should respond to a user's input." It was a classic orphan coordination problem: "No contractor was responsible for even making sure the site was operational."

Todd linked those contractors to a team of Presidential Innovation Fellows, Silicon Valley technologists who were serving six-month stints in the Obama administration. Those Fellows and the lifer bureaucrats and government contractors had plenty of conflicts. Yet, as *Wired* reported, they developed grudging respect for one another. Together, they patched HealthCare.gov by bringing "order to the site through careful monitoring, automated testing, and a *collaborative,* methodical, commonsense approach to bug fixing."

There is nothing sacred about L6. Elsewhere, traveling down three or four levels is plenty. The key is locating the people—such as employees, customers, or vendors—who understand how a system works and why it doesn't. Carl Liebert is one of our favorite practitioners of this strategy. He's served as CEO of 24 Hour Fitness (when it was the largest U.S. chain of fitness clubs), COO of USAA (an insurance company and bank that serves more than thirteen million past and current U.S. armed forces members and their families), CEO of AutoNation (the largest U.S. auto retailer), and CEO of KWx (parent company of Keller Williams, the largest U.S. real estate company).

Carl, too, believes that to lead a big company effectively you've got to bypass the hierarchy and go to where "the real experts" work. Carl developed this penchant as a twenty-three-year-old supply officer on a U.S. Navy ship. Part of his job was to procure what his shipmates ate from the navy's supply chain. Meals for officers and noncommissioned officers were cooked separately, and they got the best stuff. But Carl and every other officer knew the morale and operation of the ship depended on serving good food at "crew's mess," where enlisted sailors ate. Those sailors were quick to remind Carl it was his job to know the food and drinks they wanted (and didn't) and to figure out how to get that good stuff. Carl took to eating most of his meals at the crew's mess rather than with fellow officers. As Carl told us, that way he could hear the sailors' complaints, compliments, and suggestions and taste the food himself—so he could work to procure what the sailors really wanted.

Carl brought that philosophy to Home Depot in 2002 when he was hired as executive vice president of stores and charged with modernizing the supply chain—which procured and distributed inventory to some two thousand home improvement stores. Carl's motto was, "You can't learn what you need to know at corporate headquarters, you've got to go to the stores." For Carl, visiting stores and talking to employees wasn't enough. One of the main bottlenecks occurred in stores during the early-morning hours when trucks delivered inventory. When new goods arrived, they were logged into a computer system, unpacked, and stacked and shelved. That work happened between midnight and 7:00 A.M. Once a month for eighteen months, Carl and a couple of his engineers reported to a store at midnight, put on Home Depot's orange aprons, and clocked a seven-hour shift alongside store employees.

Working those graveyard shifts helped Carl's team identify causes and cures for troubles, including delivery snafus, slow stocking of shelves, and high labor costs. For example, about 20 percent of Home Depot's suppliers consistently sent stores boxes of tools, paint, and such with missing items—a box labeled as containing twelve cans of paint might have ten. Store managers were evaluated and paid, in large part, for reducing "shrink," lost and stolen inventory. They didn't want to be dinged for missing stuff that wasn't their fault. So, workers spent hours opening boxes, counting the contents, and updating the inventory system when they found discrepancies—a bottleneck that execs at corporate HQ hadn't known was clogging up the system.

As Carl said, the six thousand or so Home Depot employees who did such work were squandering time and money. And merchandise that customers wanted was left unstocked. That discovery spurred changes throughout the supply chain to assure the contents of boxes were accurately recorded before getting to stores, to hold suppliers accountable for errors, and to build an inventory system that managers and workers had faith in—so they didn't have to open all those boxes and count the stuff inside.

3. Good Stories Stoke Coordination

Paleoanthropologist Ian Tattersall argues that storytelling is what makes us distinctively human and gave us an evolutionary edge over other primates because stories are such efficient and nuanced means for capturing and sharing group knowledge. Similarly, research on some three hundred members of Agta, a hunter-gatherer tribe in the Philippines, found that "camps" with the best storytellers had a competitive advantage because numerous specialists inside and outside the center, as the cancer tax is especially tough on such patients and their families.

Center leaders also recognize that the CarePoint program isn't a "one and done" repair—they know that battling the cancer tax is like playing a never-ending game of Whac-A-Mole. Executives, administrators, doctors, and nurses still meet with the Patient and Family Advisory Council each month to develop solutions to new and pesky old obstacles.

People who do such integration work are often generalists in a sea of specialists. CarePoint nurses have broad knowledge about every department in the Cancer Center—including whom to count on for help and whom to avoid. Employees who have held multiple roles in an organization are especially adept at fitting the pieces together. Bob Sutton once visited the Operations Control Center for Bay Area Rapid Transit (BART), a train system in the San Francisco Bay Area. His guide was Chief Transportation Officer Rudy Crespo, who had worked at BART for over thirty years. Rudy explained how the dozen or so people in that nerve center coordinated the work of employees in the field. Their jobs included managing train movement, security, power management, and emergency response, with Rudy as boss of the operation. Bob asked Rudy how many of those jobs he had held. Rudy answered, "All of them."

5. Fix Handoffs

Bungled information exchanges between people in different roles, silos, shifts, and time zones are among the most potent causes of coordination snafus. As we saw at the Cancer Center, clients can face terrible ordeals when handoffs between roles and silos are broken. But when employees from different silos get together and learn about what each does and needs to succeed, they can fix handoffs.

"stories appear to coordinate group behavior and facilitate cooperation by providing individuals with social information about the norms, rules, and expectations."

Anthropologist Daniel Smith's team examined eighty-nine stories that Agta elders tell, including the "Sun and the Moon": "There is a dispute between the sun (male) and the moon (female) to illuminate the sky. After a fight, where the moon proves to be as strong as the sun, they agree in sharing the duty—one during the day and the other during the night." Daniel and his colleagues found the main themes in Agta stories are cooperation, coordination, and fairness for the greater good. The sun and the moon stopped fighting, divided up their labor, and scheduled their work to be fair and benefit all—and the story conveys equality between men and women.

Daniel's team asked tribe members to nominate the best storytellers; they rated 125 fellow members as skilled storytellers (60 percent women, 40 percent men) and 199 as unskilled (45 percent women, 55 percent men). Then, the team did an experiment where members of eighteen Agta camps were each given rice (enough for a meal) as a gift and could keep it or share it with a campmate. In camps populated with more skilled storytellers, more members shared their rice. When the researchers asked members which fellow Agtas they would want to live in their camps, skilled storytellers were overwhelming favorites. Skilled storytellers also had more children on average than unskilled storytellers, bolstering anthropologists' arguments that they have an evolutionary advantage.

Good stories trigger effort, cooperation, and coordination in modern corporations, too. Consider the stories that CEO Hubert Joly told when he led a turnaround at Best Buy. In 2012, when Hubert took charge, sales and profits were plunging, and pundits were writing obituaries for this electronics chain. Under

Hubert's leadership, Best Buy had five consecutive years of sales growth, increased shareholder returns by over 250 percent, and doubled online sales.

Hubert believes the stories that he told strengthened connections between Best Buy employees and customers, and employees and management. Like the one about Jordan, a three-year-old in Florida who loved his *T. rex* toy and called it his "dino baby." When dino's head snapped off, Jordan was heartbroken. Jordan's mother found the same *T. rex* at Best Buy, ordered it online, and drove Jordan to a store to pick it up. She told the Best Buy associate that they needed a "dinosaur doctor." The associate, T, recruited a colleague, Stephanie, and they took Jordan's headless dinosaur to "surgery" behind the counter out of Jordan's view. "Just a few more stitches," the pair said as they replaced the broken *T. rex* with the new one. When they handed Jordan the "cured" dinosaur, he squealed with joy.

Neuroeconomist Paul Zak explains that such stories spotlight attention on desirable and sometimes heroic actions and create tension that engages listeners and transports them into the character's world—so they experience the same emotions. The brain waves of storytellers and listeners sync up as a good story unfolds. When Hubert told the *T. rex* story to other Best Buy Associates, they were hooked by it and felt the same desire to help Jordan that T and Stephanie did. They felt connected to Hubert and the characters and relived the emotions experienced by T, Stephanie, Jordan, and Jordan's mom. They realized that, like T and Stephanie, they could work together to create magic for customers, too.

Good stories like this activate "help muscles"—rather than selfish "me, me, me" behavior—which are essential for collaboration and coordination. And such stories spell out what work looks like when people combine their efforts.

4. Build Roles and Teams Dedicated to Integration

The idea here is to create specialists in your organizatic are charged with integrating the once-disconnected ro los, and action. The Cancer Center created a centralized Point program to reduce the cancer tax for patients anc families. CarePoint administrators use their knowledg relationships to smooth patient journeys, and when pro arise, patients and families have a place to turn for help. I how the center's medical director described the program:

> CarePoint is a new single-point-of-contact program th connects patients to many services and programs at [th Cancer Center] such as Palliative Medicine, Integrative Mec icine, Pain Management, Cancer Supportive Care, Adoles cent and Young Adult Program, Survivorship, Social Work Psycho-Oncology, Neuropsychology, Nutrition, Spiritua Care, Financial Counseling, Resource Library with transla tion services, Ostomy/Wound care, Genetics and Genomics, to name a few.

Melissa explained to us that the CarePoint program does reduce the cancer tax as much as patient activists had hope because administrators have limited influence over schedulir patients' appointments with units that provide direct oncolog care (i.e., the specialists that provide cancer treatments). Th leaders of these powerful departments balked at giving admin istrators authority over their actions. CarePoint administrators do reduce the cancer tax by "informing, referring, scheduling, and coordinating" numerous other "auxiliary services" for pa tients. The CarePoint team also takes special effort to directly coordinate complex patient cases that require support from

The organizational psychologist Karl Weick describes the rules and routines used by the U.S. Forest Service to help firefighters overcome the overload and confusion they face when a crew that is battling a fire is relieved by a new one. One rule is "never hand over a fire in the heat of the day." Firefighters learned this lesson from the Dude Fire in Payson, Arizona, in 1990. Six firefighters were burned to death after a botched handoff, which occurred at "1:00 P.M. on a hot, windy day with temperatures in the high nineties while the fire was making spectacular runs." Crews now do handoffs at night, when it is easier to see fires and "low winds, high humidity, and cool temperatures stabilize the fire."

Crew chiefs use a briefing for such handoffs to help pass along the "big story," steps that could by adopted by friction fixers in other settings. During a forest fire, the outgoing chief goes through five steps during a conversation with the incoming chief:

1. Here's what I think we face.
2. Here's what I think we should do.
3. Here's why.
4. Here's what I think we should keep an eye on.
5. Now talk to me (i.e., tell me if you (a) don't understand, (b) cannot do it, (c) see something that I do not).

That last step places responsibility on both chiefs to assure that messages are received and to resolve clashing perceptions.

A study in *The New England Journal of Medicine* of 875 pediatric residents in nine medical centers focused on improving handoffs during shift changes. Each newly minted doctor took a three-hour class to help them communicate patient information to fellow healthcare workers during shift changes. Residents learned the I-PASS method; I-PASS stands for *"illness* severity, *patient* summary, *action* list, *situational* awareness and contingency planning, and *synthesis* by the receiver." Then they used role plays to practice the method. Over the next six months, residents were monitored and coached during shift changes to remind them to apply I-PASS and were given small rewards such as cookies and gift cards for providing data about their behavior to the researchers.

The study tracked 10,740 pediatric patients who were admitted during the six months after the I-PASS training at each center. The I-PASS intervention was linked to a drop in preventable medical errors, mistakes like forgetting to give patients a drug such as insulin, or administering the wrong drug or dosage. These weren't near misses or harmless mistakes. These were errors that hurt kids—causing complications that required more treatment or lengthened hospital stays. Overall, such preventable injuries decreased by 30 percent—from 4.7 to 3.3 errors per 100 admissions.

6. Coordinate on the Fly

Friction fixers are of two minds. First, they labor to prevent unpleasant surprises. To build workplaces where people aren't exhausted by one emergency after another and don't live in fear of system failure. Second, they know, as Beatle John Lennon put it, that "life is what happens to you while you're busy making other plans."

Management professors Beth Bechky and Gerardo Okhuysen studied how, as complex work unfolds, teams start with "sheet music" but shift to "playing jazz" when surprises arise. Beth did in-depth interviews and observations on location for two movies, a commercial, and a music video—and worked as a production assistant on three of these projects. Gerardo interviewed and observed eighteen officers on a SWAT team (a heavily armed police unit that uses military tactics for high-risk searches, hostage rescues, active shooters, and dangerous crowds).

Film crews and SWAT teams faced so many surprises that "they expected the unexpected" and took pride in improvising and recombining what they "already had at hand" and "returning to the task quickly." Film crews were temporary teams, composed mostly of strangers or acquaintances who worked together on each project for a few weeks or months. These gig workers performed roles including director, camera operator, wardrobe supervisor, or, like Beth, production assistant. SWAT teams worked and practiced together for years and had completed dozens of dangerous missions together. Yet both used similar strategies to craft fast and imaginative responses to unforeseen jolts.

These teams started with a provisional plan, the "sheet music." Film crews had a detailed daily schedule. The SWAT team outlined a plan for each mission—which specified, for example, who would cover the exits of a house, where snipers would be stationed, and when officers would bust down the door. *But* when things didn't go as expected, because people understood one another's roles so well and how their roles fit together, teams were adept at revising their plan on the spot.

Role shifting helped them make such rapid adjustments. It happens when a surprise leaves a critical role empty and someone else fills in. Beth was on location when a specialist who operated the aerial camera didn't show up for work. The cinematographer gathered the five remaining camera operators, and it took them just a few minutes to figure out who else could operate the aerial camera, and to shift two other operators to different cameras to fill his vacant role.

Reorganizing routines is another improvisational practice. It's triggered when a surprise reveals that the planned sequence or methods aren't working and something different ought to be done. On one SWAT mission, involving a hostage held at gunpoint, the plan was that a sharpshooter on the team would kill the hostage-taker with a single shot. But the sharpshooter missed and hit the doorframe next to the hostage-taker, who "was instantly alerted that the team was trying to kill him." The team shifted gears in seconds. As Gerardo tells it, "without taking time for a conversation," the "break-in team" executed a violent and well-choreographed "dynamic entry."

The implication for friction fixers is, yes, start with a plan when possible. It helps you weave the work together (play sheet music) and recognize when to improvise because that plan isn't working (play jazz). Beth's and Gerardo's studies also suggest, to hone your organization's capacity to coordinate on the fly, you should nudge and nurture people so that they don't play the blame game when things go wrong. Instead, take advantage of what SWAT officers call their "box of toys" instead. That means mastering the craft of rummaging through, choosing, and blending the roles, tactics, and tools on hand to nip ugly surprises in the bud.

P.S. If People Don't Need to Coordinate, You Won't Have Snafus!

We've focused on what to do when coordination is crucial, complex, and challenging. A complementary path is to reduce the need for coordination. Here are a couple tried-and-true strategies.

We Don't Need You, You Don't Need Us

This strategy is to design organizations to rely on less exacting forms of "interdependence" between people and parts. In "stories appear to coordinate group behavior and facilitate co-operation by providing individuals with social information about the norms, rules, and expectations."

Anthropologist Daniel Smith's team examined eighty-nine stories that Agta elders tell, including the "Sun and the Moon": "There is a dispute between the sun (male) and the moon (fe-male) to illuminate the sky. After a fight, where the moon proves to be as strong as the sun, they agree in sharing the duty—one during the day and the other during the night." Daniel and his colleagues found the main themes in Agta stories are coopera-tion, coordination, and fairness for the greater good. The sun and the moon stopped fighting, divided up their labor, and scheduled their work to be fair and benefit all—and the story conveys equality between men and women.

Daniel's team asked tribe members to nominate the best storytellers; they rated 125 fellow members as skilled story-tellers (60 percent women, 40 percent men) and 199 as unskilled (45 percent women, 55 percent men). Then, the team did an experiment where members of eighteen Agta camps were each given rice (enough for a meal) as a gift and could keep it or share it with a campmate. In camps populated with more skilled story-tellers, more members shared their rice. When the researchers asked members which fellow Agtas they would want to live in their camps, skilled storytellers were overwhelming favorites. Skilled storytellers also had more children on average than un-skilled storytellers, bolstering anthropologists' arguments that they have an evolutionary advantage.

Good stories trigger effort, cooperation, and coordination in modern corporations, too. Consider the stories that CEO Hubert Joly told when he led a turnaround at Best Buy. In 2012, when Hubert took charge, sales and profits were plunging, and pun-dits were writing obituaries for this electronics chain. Under

Hubert's leadership, Best Buy had five consecutive years of sales growth, increased shareholder returns by over 250 percent, and doubled online sales.

Hubert believes the stories that he told strengthened connections between Best Buy employees and customers, and employees and management. Like the one about Jordan, a three-year-old in Florida who loved his *T. rex* toy and called it his "dino baby." When dino's head snapped off, Jordan was heartbroken. Jordan's mother found the same *T. rex* at Best Buy, ordered it online, and drove Jordan to a store to pick it up. She told the Best Buy associate that they needed a "dinosaur doctor." The associate, T, recruited a colleague, Stephanie, and they took Jordan's headless dinosaur to "surgery" behind the counter out of Jordan's view. "Just a few more stitches," the pair said as they replaced the broken *T. rex* with the new one. When they handed Jordan the "cured" dinosaur, he squealed with joy.

Neuroeconomist Paul Zak explains that such stories spotlight attention on desirable and sometimes heroic actions and create tension that engages listeners and transports them into the character's world—so they experience the same emotions. The brain waves of storytellers and listeners sync up as a good story unfolds. When Hubert told the *T. rex* story to other Best Buy Associates, they were hooked by it and felt the same desire to help Jordan that T and Stephanie did. They felt connected to Hubert and the characters and relived the emotions experienced by T, Stephanie, Jordan, and Jordan's mom. They realized that, like T and Stephanie, they could work together to create magic for customers, too.

Good stories like this activate "help muscles"—rather than selfish "me, me, me" behavior—which are essential for collaboration and coordination. And such stories spell out what work looks like when people combine their efforts.

4. Build Roles and Teams Dedicated to Integration

The idea here is to create specialists in your organization who are charged with integrating the once-disconnected roles, silos, and action. The Cancer Center created a centralized Care-Point program to reduce the cancer tax for patients and their families. CarePoint administrators use their knowledge and relationships to smooth patient journeys, and when problems arise, patients and families have a place to turn for help. Here's how the center's medical director described the program:

> CarePoint is a new single-point-of-contact program that connects patients to many services and programs at [the Cancer Center] such as Palliative Medicine, Integrative Medicine, Pain Management, Cancer Supportive Care, Adolescent and Young Adult Program, Survivorship, Social Work, Psycho-Oncology, Neuropsychology, Nutrition, Spiritual Care, Financial Counseling, Resource Library with translation services, Ostomy/Wound care, Genetics and Genomics, to name a few.

Melissa explained to us that the CarePoint program doesn't reduce the cancer tax as much as patient activists had hoped because administrators have limited influence over scheduling patients' appointments with units that provide direct oncology care (i.e., the specialists that provide cancer treatments). The leaders of these powerful departments balked at giving administrators authority over their actions. CarePoint administrators do reduce the cancer tax by "informing, referring, scheduling, and coordinating" numerous other "auxiliary services" for patients. The CarePoint team also takes special effort to directly coordinate complex patient cases that require support from numerous specialists inside and outside the center, as the cancer tax is especially tough on such patients and their families.

Center leaders also recognize that the CarePoint program isn't a "one and done" repair—they know that battling the cancer tax is like playing a never-ending game of Whac-A-Mole. Executives, administrators, doctors, and nurses still meet with the Patient and Family Advisory Council each month to develop solutions to new and pesky old obstacles.

People who do such integration work are often generalists in a sea of specialists. CarePoint nurses have broad knowledge about every department in the Cancer Center—including whom to count on for help and whom to avoid. Employees who have held multiple roles in an organization are especially adept at fitting the pieces together. Bob Sutton once visited the Operations Control Center for Bay Area Rapid Transit (BART), a train system in the San Francisco Bay Area. His guide was Chief Transportation Officer Rudy Crespo, who had worked at BART for over thirty years. Rudy explained how the dozen or so people in that nerve center coordinated the work of employees in the field. Their jobs included managing train movement, security, power management, and emergency response, with Rudy as boss of the operation. Bob asked Rudy how many of those jobs he had held. Rudy answered, "All of them."

5. Fix Handoffs

Bungled information exchanges between people in different roles, silos, shifts, and time zones are among the most potent causes of coordination snafus. As we saw at the Cancer Center, clients can face terrible ordeals when handoffs between roles and silos are broken. But when employees from different silos get together and learn about what each does and needs to succeed, they can fix handoffs.

terviewed and observed eighteen officers on a SWAT team (a heavily armed police unit that uses military tactics for high-risk searches, hostage rescues, active shooters, and dangerous crowds).

Film crews and SWAT teams faced so many surprises that "they expected the unexpected" and took pride in improvising and recombining what they "already had at hand" and "returning to the task quickly." Film crews were temporary teams, composed mostly of strangers or acquaintances who worked together on each project for a few weeks or months. These gig workers performed roles including director, camera operator, wardrobe supervisor, or, like Beth, production assistant. SWAT teams worked and practiced together for years and had completed dozens of dangerous missions together. Yet both used similar strategies to craft fast and imaginative responses to unforeseen jolts.

These teams started with a provisional plan, the "sheet music." Film crews had a detailed daily schedule. The SWAT team outlined a plan for each mission—which specified, for example, who would cover the exits of a house, where snipers would be stationed, and when officers would bust down the door. *But* when things didn't go as expected, because people understood one another's roles so well and how their roles fit together, teams were adept at revising their plan on the spot.

Role shifting helped them make such rapid adjustments. It happens when a surprise leaves a critical role empty and someone else fills in. Beth was on location when a specialist who operated the aerial camera didn't show up for work. The cinematographer gathered the five remaining camera operators, and it took them just a few minutes to figure out who else could operate the aerial camera, and to shift two other operators to different cameras to fill his vacant role.

Reorganizing routines is another improvisational practice. It's triggered when a surprise reveals that the planned sequence or methods aren't working and something different ought to be done. On one SWAT mission, involving a hostage held at gunpoint, the plan was that a sharpshooter on the team would kill the hostage-taker with a single shot. But the sharpshooter missed and hit the doorframe next to the hostage-taker, who "was instantly alerted that the team was trying to kill him." The team shifted gears in seconds. As Gerardo tells it, "without taking time for a conversation," the "break-in team" executed a violent and well-choreographed "dynamic entry."

The implication for friction fixers is, yes, start with a plan when possible. It helps you weave the work together (play sheet music) and recognize when to improvise because that plan isn't working (play jazz). Beth's and Gerardo's studies also suggest, to hone your organization's capacity to coordinate on the fly, you should nudge and nurture people so that they don't play the blame game when things go wrong. Instead, take advantage of what SWAT officers call their "box of toys" instead. That means mastering the craft of rummaging through, choosing, and blending the roles, tactics, and tools on hand to nip ugly surprises in the bud.

P.S. If People Don't Need to Coordinate, You Won't Have Snafus!

We've focused on what to do when coordination is crucial, complex, and challenging. A complementary path is to reduce the need for coordination. Here are a couple tried-and-true strategies.

We Don't Need You, You Don't Need Us

This strategy is to design organizations to rely on less exacting forms of "interdependence" between people and parts. In

James Thompson's classic 1967 book, *Organizations in Action*, he shows that *reciprocal interdependence* is most demanding. That's when people, teams, silos, and such must constantly adjust back and forth in response to one another as the work unfolds. Football (aka soccer) is a great example. Players constantly change what they do in response to passes and shots from teammates and competitors—who, in turn, constantly adjust to others' passes and shots.

Pooled interdependence is least demanding. That's when organizations combine, or "roll up," the separate and independent efforts of people or parts. They have little need—or it is impossible—for them to communicate or collaborate. Think of the team gymnastics competition at the Olympics. Teammates give one another advice and support. But team performance is based solely on adding up individual scores on the floor exercise, parallel bars, and such. Similarly, as consultant Roger Schwarz explains in the *Harvard Business Review,* "Your sales team is designed with pooled interdependence if you and others sell individually and combine your monthly individual sales numbers to get the team result."

Sometimes, it's best to structure jobs or units this way, to provide each with the resources, incentives, and freedom to charge ahead independently. So that each can operate as an island. That's what happened at an emergency department that Melissa Valentine and her mentor Amy Edmondson studied. It was composed of four six-person "pods," each designed to be staffed by three doctors and three nurses. Before the pods, the twenty-five or so nurses and doctors who staffed the department twenty-four hours a day operated as a discombobulated mob. Confusion reigned, in part, because the cast of characters was in constant flux. Doctors and nurses worked four-to-twelve-hour shifts and had flexible schedules. In the bad old days, an administrator assigned each patient a nurse or two, a resident, and an attending physician from the twenty-five or so folks on hand. Doctors often forgot which nurses were working on which cases. Doctors and patients were rarely updated when a nurse who started on a case was replaced by another—in part, because administrators were overloaded and overwhelmed, too.

Then executives split the department into four pods, which created reciprocal interdependence within each pod and pooled interdependence among the four pods. Each pod had a dedicated location with computers, supplies, beds, and "crash rooms" to work on patients. Each patient was assigned to a pod for the patient's entire stay. Each pod was set up for three nurses, two residents, and an attending physician. When doctors or nurses arrived at work, they were assigned to whatever pod needed them. Melissa and Amy's analysis of 160,000 patient visits showed that the new design meant the average patient visit lasted five hours rather than eight—because communication and collaboration were less complicated and baffling.

Collaboration, information sharing, and transparency are often portrayed as purely good. But when people feel obliged—or tempted—to weigh in on others' work too much and to assemble a bigger group of collaborators than necessary, they are plagued with interruptions and distractions.

Apple employees are spared such intrusions because they are "scared silent." As Adam Lashinsky reports in *Inside Apple*, employees know that revealing company secrets will get them fired on the spot. This penchant for secrecy means the small teams that do most of the work at Apple are given only the slivers of information that executives believe they need. A few years ago, we talked to a senior Apple executive who speculated—but, of course, didn't know—that CEO Tim Cook might be the only person who knew all the major features of the next iPhone.

Sharing information with other teams, or asking them for help without permission from executives, is so taboo that even veterans who have worked at Apple for decades tell us they always eat lunch with just the folks on their team. They aren't allowed to talk to anyone else!

The Apple system isn't for every organization; few require that level of secrecy. Devotees of transparency and trust may howl at the isolation and fear, and it makes us squirm, too. But the pooled interdependence at Apple means that employees work with fewer distractions compared to places where people feel compelled to understand everyone else's work, and to spend their days giving and asking for help.

Fewer Parts, Fewer Snafus

The fewer people and units that you need to weave together, the fewer opportunities for botched communication and collaboration. Simpler systems also overload people less, so they have more bandwidth to focus on their work and coordinate when necessary.

It is best to resist adding too many people and units in the first place. When it's too late for that, building on chapter 5, it's time for subtraction. That's what Rob Cross and his colleagues learned from studying collaboration overload. They found, when employees are connected to and mutually reliant on too many others, they are pummeled by the double whammy of "surges" and "the slow burn." Their shabby, late, and incomplete work disappoints colleagues; and if nothing changes, they crumple in exhaustion and defeat.

In *Beyond Collaboration Overload*, Rob describes Scott, an executive on the verge of being fired. Scott was "flying up the hierarchy" of a large company until he took charge of three big units—some five thousand people. Scott had just a few direct reports in his past roles; but added sixteen this time. He wanted to be "less hierarchical" and "send a signal that rank doesn't matter to me." Scott was proud of his open-door policy and urged people "to bring him problems and concerns or to include him in discussions."

When Rob was called in to help, he found Scott was "strung out, wrung out," and had designed a job that was impossible to do. Scott worked sixteen hours a day, seven days a week, and was racked with anxiety, and his marriage was falling apart. Part of the trouble was—in a move opposite of the pod redesign— Scott had merged numerous small groups into larger groups. This "delayering" effort was meant to increase "agility." Instead, it fueled overload throughout this five-thousand-person organization because members had more connections to tend to, which made communication more important and more difficult, and coordination snafus followed.

When Rob examined the networks of the top ten thousand people in the company, Scott "was the Number 1 most overloaded person." More than 118 people came to Scott every day for information from the three units he ran. Rob learned in one unit "78 people—some 50 percent—of the 150 top managers in that one unit felt they couldn't hit their business goals unless they got more of Scott's time."

Rob worked with Scott on a subtraction and delegation campaign that salvaged his job and reputation. Scott cut back his direct reports, meetings, and emails by about 50 percent. It worked. His direct reports felt more empowered (and less overloaded) because they could make more decisions without constantly checking and coordinating with Scott. Because Scott had fewer people to deal with—and resisted jumping into every decision—his unit operated more efficiently. Scott worked fewer hours, his health improved, and he saved his marriage, too.

Scott's story shows that, when it comes to the coordination snafus that plague so many organizations, trying to help yourself and others cope with and navigate a broken system might ease sting. Yet, a more effective and enduring remedy is to redesign your job and organization to create fewer and better connections. That's why, as we say in chapter 1 and demonstrate throughout this chapter, the best leaders treat their organizations as malleable prototypes. They use their influence to keep tinkering with, replacing, and removing rules, structures, and responsibilities. So, it's the best they can do, for now, and the system keeps getting better.

Jargon Monoxide

On the Drawbacks and (Limited) Virtues of Hollow and Impenetrable Babble

We first heard the phrase *jargon monoxide* from Polly LaBarre some fifteen years ago when she talked to our Stanford class about her bestseller, *Mavericks at Work*. The students howled at Polly's term for the convoluted, soulless, and meaningless language used by too many leaders, consultants, and gurus. We thought of that funny and cutting phrase again and again throughout our friction project because so many organizations are infected with language that fuels misunderstanding and confusion and gums up the works.

We have no idea what leaders mean by "let's leverage our core competencies to create synergies that move the needle." When you ask them to explain what it means for how people ought to act, it becomes clear they have no idea what they are talking about either. We also don't know what consultants from places such as McKinsey mean by "the helix organization," "squad-to-squad meetings," or "fit-for-purpose accountable cells." Of course, professors are not immune from such crimes against clarity—many of us take perverse pride in baffling our students and colleagues with highfalutin language. As Columbia University's Zachariah Brown and his colleagues asked, "Why do academics describe their research as elucidating the antecedents of upright striding vertical bipedality on horizontal terrestrial substrates by non-human primates instead of describing why primates walk on the ground?"

This chapter shows how jargon monoxide leaves people bewildered about what to do and how to do it. We break down the major types of jargon monoxide. We dig into how such pretentious and overly complex language makes it tough for people in organizations to work together and hold one another accountable. And we explore how rewarding people for spewing out impressive talk can undermine the will and skill required for turning knowledge into organizational action.

Types of Jargon Monoxide

We love how *jargon monoxide* captures the silliness, cynicism, and befuddlement generated by empty and opaque talk of all kinds. But a bit more precision is helpful for designing targeted remedies. We've sorted jargon monoxide into four categories. We'll introduce the nuances of each of these overlapping types, explain why they fuel destructive friction, show how to avoid and repair each, and, sometimes, suggest how to use such language to your advantage.

Friction fixers use a trio of solutions to combat all four types. First, they just stop; they abandon their crummy talk. No matter how much time and money they've wasted learning and advocating for the monoxide in the past, they force themselves and their colleagues to flush the old language and start from scratch.

Second, building on chapter 5, friction fixers who battle jargon monoxide embrace venture capitalist Michael Dearing's advice to embrace the "editor in chief" role. They are relentless, stubborn, and sometimes downright annoying as they revise language that

confuses, distracts, or overwhelms people both inside and outside their team.

Third, friction fixers build workplaces that reward people
who use constructive language and discourage those who use
hollow and impenetrable babble. Fiction fixers don't fall prey
to the smart talk trap that we discussed in chapter 1. They deliver kudos and cash to people who use talk that spurs concrete remedies and repairs—and ignore, punish, and banish
the blowhards.

Types of Jargon Monoxide

Type	Definition
Convoluted Crap	Using far too many words, longer and more complicated words, and more twisted explanations than is necessary.
Meaningless Bullshit	Empty and misleading communication that is meaningless to both bullshitter and bullshittee.
In-Group Lingo	Specialized, technical, and well-defined lingo that facilitates communication and feelings of belonging among insiders. But undermines communication and coordination with outsiders, who can't decipher what people in the club are talking about.
Jargon Mishmash Syndrome	When a label or phrase means so many different things to so many different people that it has devolved into a random scatter of ideas.

Convoluted Crap

Convoluted crap is the use of too many words, unnecessarily
long and complicated words, or unduly elaborate explanations.

Because this type of jargon monoxide is so wordy, impenetrable, or both, it can fuel commitment to an organization, to a
cause, or among comrades in confusion. As we saw in chapter 2,

labor leads to love. This IKEA effect compels people to justify all that effort to themselves and others—which means that people who struggle to comprehend and act on long and intricate communications may place excessive and irrational value on the fruits of their labors.

There are also handsome rewards for administrators, consultants, lobbyists, and lawyers who produce mountains of perplexing language—they get paid for explaining, teaching, coaching, and guiding people who need to understand those bewildering words to do their jobs, get benefits, or stay out of trouble. And there are rewards for specialists who punish and defend people who run afoul of traditions, rules, and laws they can't understand. The more convoluted the crap, the more work there is for such folks—including billable hours for consultants and their ilk.

We rail against needless words in this book's opening paragraph and in chapter 5, "Addition Sickness." But if you write or blab on and on, you might be judged as more creative than if you abide by Shakespeare's advice that "brevity is the soul of wit." In studies by marketing researchers Laura Kornish and Sharaya Jones, consumers evaluated descriptions of new products, including cake frostings, smartphone applications, and insurance offerings. Consumers consistently rated products with longer descriptions as more creative than those with shorter descriptions, even when longer ones provided no additional meaningful information.

Laura and Sharaya conclude that length triggers two instant judgments that help explain this persuasive power. First, people see ideas with more parts as more useful because they enable us to do more things—and even when a long explanation contains no more parts, they assume more words mean more features! Second, the longer the description, the more work it is to digest.

Because new ideas require us to slow down to understand them, and familiar ideas do not, we judge them—and people who produce them—as more creative.

Yet the virtues of convoluted crap rarely offset the damage—especially if your aim is to enable people to get something done rather than to baffle and perhaps dazzle them with an onslaught of words and complicated ideas. Such language forces people to squander massive amounts of time deciphering documents, websites, speeches, or spoken instructions. And makes it tough to explain to others what you are doing, what they ought to do, and to coordinate their work with yours.

The hazards of convoluted crap are illustrated by Holacracy, a complex system of rules, roles, and intertwined groups called "circles" that eliminates formal management positions. This governance system is supposed to create fluid structures in which the "golden rule of Holacracy" is that "you have the full authority to make any decision or take any action, as long as there's no rule against it."

Holacracy is best known for being implemented in 2014 by Zappos, the online shoe company started and led by the late Tony Hsieh (who died in a fire in 2020).

The Holacracy.org website reports, as of early 2023, that 227 organizations in thirty-five countries were "practicing Holacracy." Most were small; 168 had fifty or fewer employees. Only 12 had more than five hundred employees (Zappos was listed, but seems to have stopped practicing it).

After trying repeatedly to write an accurate brief summary of Holacracy, we realized the problem wasn't just our limitations—it's the convoluted crap, too. We've spent a good hundred hours trying to understand the fundamentals. We are still confused and are not alone. Holacracy evangelist Diederick Janse, a consultant who helps companies adopt the system, says that people "either love it or hate it" and admits there is some truth to critiques that it is "rigid, complex, and inhuman." Diederick explains that the key to operating this rule-based system is understanding and adhering to the detailed Holacracy Constitution. That's because "when organizations adopt Holacracy, they 'ratify' (sign) that same set of rules, regardless of size, industry, culture, purpose, etc."

Unfortunately, after trying to grasp the over seven thousand words in the Holacracy Constitution v2.1 back in 2015 and, again, the over eight thousand words in the updated version 5.0 in 2022, we can't figure out if we love or hate Holacracy or are somewhere in between. Both versions are so badly written that we can't understand how the system works. We get lost in the complex rules, roles, and specialized lingo. Exhibit A: "Notwithstanding the foregoing, a Person serving as a Circle Member of a Circle by virtue of appointment or election by such Circle's Super-Circle or Sub-Circle, as specified in this Section 2.2, may not be removed except through due-process or due-authority within such Circle's Super-Circle or Sub-Circle, as the case may be."

In the words of George Orwell, this sentence and many others in the constitution "anesthetizes a portion of one's brain."

Devoting the time to comprehend and comply with this Byzantine rulebook seems to be worth the trouble for Convert, a small California software company. The cofounders committed to the Holacratic model in 2016 and hired Morgan Legge as their "Holacracy Bootstrapper" to help translate and implement this thicket of practices among their forty employees. By doing so, they've followed advice in the preamble to the constitution: "We do not recommend reading the Constitution as a way to learn Holacracy practice. The metaphor Holacracy Coaches often use is that it's like trying to learn to play football (soccer) by reading the FIFA Laws of the Game handbook."

Yet the complexity of the system and the burden the constitution imposes drove heavily coached companies, including Buffer and Medium, to abandon Holacracy. As Medium's Andy Doyle wrote in 2016, "For us, Holacracy was getting in the way of the work" because all the "record keeping and governance" took too much time, and "we found that the act of codifying responsibilities in explicit detail hindered a proactive attitude and sense of communal ownership." Zappos also struggled with the constitution's complexity. Jordan Sams, a former trainer on the Zappos Holacracy team, told *Business Insider* that the company was so hamstrung by "the nuances and complications of the Holacracy Constitution" that, by 2017, they shifted to "Holacracy lite, a system that incorporates its values and guiding principles without relying on its rigid constitution and governance structures."

In 2022, we talked with knowledgeable insiders (who prefer to stay anonymous) about the history of Holacracy at Zappos. They reported that many employees relished the freedom to do their work as they saw fit, the ability to influence decisions, and the absence of a fixed hierarchy of managers enabled by this new form of organization. Yet, even at the height of the Holacracy implementation in 2015 and 2016, the insiders and consultants who guided the movement didn't follow the system to the letter. Some rules were too harsh for Zappos's warm culture—including ruthlessly crushing "out of process behavior" by shushing people who speak out of turn, as Holacracy coinventor Brian Robertson advises. A Zappos insider added that, even in its heyday, too many employees only paid lip service to Holacracy principles—because Tony Hsieh and other leaders expected them to use the system. Yet they still behaved as if they worked in the old manager-led traditional system. Their attitude was, "Like, yeah, we're playing Holacracy. It's fun. It's cute. But really, we have shit to do."

In 2022, that fellow explained that pieces of the system were "still baked into the fabric of the organization," but "I personally wouldn't say that we operate as a Holacracy anymore." He said Zappos newcomers no longer learn about Holacracy, or much about the history of the company, during onboarding. So, if an old-timer like him mentions the constitution, or elements such as "circles" and "roles" that are still used in parts of the company, many newer employees wonder, "What are you talking about?"

Our inquiry into Holacracy suggests that friction fixers battle such convoluted crap in three ways. First, as Buffer, Medium, and Zappos did, they abandon their efforts to live by this obtuse constitution. Second, as Convert does, they rely on specialists who understand how to translate the complicated rules and all that—but still mesh with the company's business model and culture. That way, every organization member is not burdened with becoming an expert on Holacracy's intricacies.

Third, they can embrace the editor-in-chief role and improve the language. Extensive editing of the constitution has been overseen by Brian Robertson. His consulting company, Holacracy-One, has spearheaded refinements in the governance model and efforts to make the constitution simpler, clearer, and easier to apply. For example, the legalese *herein* appears more than a dozen times in version 2.1, but never in version 5.0.

Alas, the updated version still all sounds like "blah, blah, blah" to our ears. Consider this gem: "A Role may link into another Circle if a Policy of that other Circle or any Super-Circle thereof invites it."

Meaningless Bullshit

Philosopher Harry Frankfurt's 2005 bestseller *On Bullshit* inspired "the growing field of 'bullshitology'," as André Spicer put it. In his book *Business Bullshit,* André defines such talk as "empty and misleading communication" usually crafted "to serve the bullshitter's purpose." In their 2019 analysis, "Bullshit and Organizational Studies," Lars Christensen and his colleagues add that such talk is meaningless to both the bullshitter and the bullshittee. Convoluted crap such as the Holacracy Constitution is hard to comprehend, but it is neither empty nor meaningless.

The vacuous and seemingly impressive language dissected by Gordon Pennycock's team in his studies of receptivity to bullshit fits André Spicer's definition well. Gordon found that tweets from new age guru Deepak Chopra provided a treasure trove of "pseudo-profound bullshit" for their experiments. Including, "Attention and intention are the mechanics of manifestation" and "Imagination is inside exponential space time events." This nonsense appears to serve Deepak Chopra's interests as it attracted over three million Twitter followers—although Gordon's research found that people who believed that such bullshit was profound (rather than meaningless) had lower cognitive ability and were more likely to believe in fake conspiracy theories.

Mondelez, a company that sells snacks including Oreo cookies and Ritz crackers, spewed out meaningless language after they paid Ogilvy, an advertising agency, big bucks to help them invent the word *humaning* and develop an advertising campaign around it. Here's how Mondelez explained *humaning*: "We are no longer marketing *to* consumers, but creating connections *with* humans." We have no idea what that means. We doubt they do either. The same goes for the equally hollow *brand heat, idea hamsters, hypertelling,* or hundreds of other meaningless yet familiar phrases you will hear from consulting firms or can produce with online tools such as the Corporate B.S. Generator or the Gobbledygook Generator. Our favorites include *organic synergies, thought shower,* and *chief pollinator.*

Bullshit scholars, including André Spicer and Lars Christensen, note that such nonsense is often expected and harmless, and can have some constructive consequences. Some people bullshit just to make money. Like "bullshit merchants" who sell "prepackaged concepts that they try to market to others." And people who use bullshit for collective amusement, "as stupid things for the sake of saying stupid things."

Bullshit also provides personal protection. André points to a study of middle managers in a large company where the art of bullshitting one another, senior management, and customers was viewed as essential for making unpleasant and unflattering information less damning and interesting. Expressing and responding to bullshit was a game that all middle managers played. As André explains, skilled players responded to it with just the right amount of seriousness: "If you took bullshit too seriously, you ran the risk of being seen as a chump. Likewise, if you challenged bullshit too frequently, you risked being seen as an asshole."

The trouble with bullshit, however, is that it generates so much confusion and wasted effort by the bullshitter and bullshittee. The nonsense cranked out by executives and spokespeople provides no useful guidance about how people ought to do their work and weave it together. When people detect that others are spewing out meaningless talk, it takes a lot of effort to confront the bullshitters and convince them their words are nonsense, get them to stop, and persuade their befuddled targets to ignore the monoxide. This is known as Brandolini's law, or the bullshit asymmetry principle: "The amount of energy needed to refute bullshit is an order of magnitude bigger than that needed to produce it." Italian programmer Alberto Brandolini proposed the law after watching Italy's former prime minister, the late Silvio Berlusconi, being interviewed on TV.

Brandolini's law is evident in a story we heard about a project manager in a small company. Her new boss had worked in big corporations for years, but never before for a small one. That boss spewed out a constant stream of biz buzz. His emails and presentations were packed with phrases like *pressure test,* *synergy,* and *mission critical.* The project manager was precise with language and thus confused about the implications of such terms for what she and her colleagues should *do.* Whenever she didn't understand what her boss meant, she asked him to pause and define the word or phrase—and the implications for action. About 50 percent of the time, her boss couldn't answer such questions—or answered them with more bullshit, which the manager then asked him to explain, too.

Meaningless bullshit can also prompt cynicism and disdain. Mondelez was mocked in *The New York Times* for *humaning.* So was Cisco CEO John Chambers when *Financial Times* columnist Lucy Kellaway deemed him the "Chief Obfuscation Champion" of 2012. John wrote to employees, "We'll wake the world up and move the planet a little closer to the future," which Lucy found a "concoction of sublime arrogance and cheesiness" that stood out in a "bumper year for guff, cliché, euphemism, and verbal stupidity."

In-Group Lingo

Specialized and well-defined jargon used by insiders can bolster communication, fast action, and feelings of belonging. Sociologists Ron Burt and Ray Reagans found that members of virtual teams developed in-group lingo as they engaged in more rounds of communication and did their work under time pressure—which created a "shared incentive to find shorthand terms (i.e., jargon) that enable faster exchange of accurate information." Similarly, the acronyms, abbreviations, and other

technical jargon that surgeons use are meaningless to the un-
initiated, but can trigger instant and coordinated action. When
a doctor says "Stat, MI," fellow healthcare workers understand
those six letters mean it's urgent to treat the patient immediately
because the patient is having a heart attack (or myocardial in-
farction).

Yet in-group language has many drawbacks. It creates communication and coordination troubles when unindoctrinated people
can't figure what those in the club are talking about. That's what
happened to a contractor that the Fire Department of New York
(FDNY) hired to fix a data glitch at their emergency dispatch
center in Brooklyn. The *New York Post* reported, "The repairman
mistook a glass-enclosed button, marked 'EPO' for 'emergency
power off,' for an electronic door release button, so he opened
the lid and accidentally shut down the system." As a result, communication by dispatchers via radio and the mobile terminals
in vehicles operated by firefighters, police, and emergency medical technicians was impossible for hours. Dispatchers had to
use "pens, paper, and telephones rather than digital systems—to
gather facts and get word to first responders as 911 calls came in."

No deaths were reported because of the chaos, but ambu-
lances and fire engines were dispatched far more slowly than
usual because the system was gummed up. Like the firefighters
in Queens who "spent an hour performing CPR on a patient
until an ambulance could arrive." Lightpath, the company that
sent the repairman who didn't know what EPO meant, has as-
sured the city that he would "no longer be handling its FDNY
work."

In-group lingo can also generate destructive conflict with
outsiders. Economists Roberto Weber and Colin Camerer
found, much as Ron Burt and Ray Reagans did, that student
duos worked more efficiently over time as they developed

shorthand terms that sped communication and guided fast decisions. But when a third member was added, the work slowed because of the newcomer's ignorance of the shorthand. Tension and hostility also flared in the expanded teams, and new and established members blamed one another for performance troubles.

Journalist Gillian Tett documented how in-group lingo created destructive dynamics in big investment banks, which helped fuel the global financial meltdown in 2007. In 2005 and 2006, Gillian devoted many hours talking to the "geeky and dull" people who developed the risky mortgage-backed securities that were widely blamed for the meltdown. These specialists worked in siloed departments, generated massive earnings for their banks, and were rewarded with fat bonuses. They fancied themselves revolutionaries and belittled colleagues in other departments as risk-averse wimps who couldn't comprehend or appreciate their brilliant work. As Gillian put it, their "world of complex credit was swathed in jargon and permeated with advanced mathematical techniques." Members of such departments loved their specialized language and work because it made them feel so smart, bonded them together, and rendered it almost impossible for other departments or superiors to understand what they did.

Gillian adds, because "they spoke a jargon that was impenetrable to others," they had an upper hand in political battles against other departments. She explains, "Banks were supposed to be run as coordinated units"; instead, different departments operated "like warring tribes" that competed for "resources against other departments," and such "oddly segregated" departments had no incentive for sharing information, resources, and power with others.

Gillian found that specialists in the young and technical field of "complex credit" weren't held accountable, in part, because their leaders, colleagues in other silos, and members of the press didn't understand such terms as *collateralized debt obligations* (CDOs) or *SIVs* (structured investment vehicles)—and didn't comprehend the wild risks. She adds an interesting twist: colleagues in other silos didn't bother to get to know these specialists or learn about their investments because they seemed like boring people who did boring things.

As a result, even senior executives who were "theoretically supposed to watch risk-taking" didn't understand what these hotshots did and let them do as they pleased. Financial instruments called super-senior CDOs resulted in massive losses for UBS. Yet UBS board member Peter Kurer said that, before 2007, "frankly most of us had not even heard the word *super-senior*. . . . We were just told by our risk people that these instruments were triple-A, like Treasury bonds. People did not ask too many questions."

We suggest three ways to dampen the damage inflicted by in-group lingo. The first stems from the power of generalists, who, as David Epstein shows in his book *Range,* play a crucial role in a world with so many specialists. You need to find and develop generalists who, apparently unlike UBS's Peter Kurer and his colleagues, know enough about the jargon and work of key specialists to discern the virtues and risks, and who understand how to weave their varied efforts together.

Mary Barra, CEO of General Motors, is an exemplary generalist. One reason Mary has been an effective leader of this huge and challenging firm is that she understands the lingo and methods used in so many different silos and specialties. Her past GM leadership roles include head of the Detroit/Hamtramck Assembly Plant, vice president of Global Manufacturing Engineering, executive vice president of Global Product Development, and just before taking charge, head of Global Human Resources. It isn't just Mary's experience that enables her to grasp varied in-group lingo—her penchant for listening and asking questions means she keeps learning more specialized jargon and methods. A former GM executive who worked with Mary for years told us she "always starts with listening to the room and trying to understand before declaring her position," often pulling in "people that hadn't spoken."

The second solution is for people to slow down and translate their in-group lingo for one another—and, when possible, to agree on a common language. That project manager from the small company who hounded her new boss to define his biz buzz found—while much was bullshit—many of his terms were useful. But they needed to be translated so that people in the company could grasp and act on them. So, she created a "Lexicon of Terms" after hashing out the meaning of dozens of words and phrases with her new boss and colleagues. The company's CEO told us this lexicon helped everyone work together more efficiently and to have fewer exasperating arguments. It ran more than three thousand words and was filled with definitions of key terms—including those of *health metrics, strategic goal,* and *sustainability*—so that two hundred employees in ten departments would be on the same page.

The third solution is to translate in-group jargon into plain English to avoid confusing or alienating outsiders who need to understand it. The switch flipped by the repairman that shut down the emergency dispatch center in Brooklyn was just labeled EPO—with no explanation that it meant "emergency power off." Spelling out EPO and adding a warning sign that explained what the switches did would have made it harder for him, or anyone else, to unwittingly shut the system down.

Translating in-group lingo into plain language also enhances communication between specialists and nonspecialists—as an experiment with sixty patients in New Zealand who suffered from chronic health conditions showed. After all patients received the usual jargon-filled letter from a doctor that described their condition and suggested treatment, thirty were randomly selected to get a "translated letter" two weeks later—with jargon from the first letter replaced by plain language. For example, "peripheral edema" was translated into "ankle swelling," "tachycardia" into "fast heart rate," and "idiopathic" into "unknown cause." Patients appreciated the translations: 78 percent preferred it to the jargon-filled letter, 69 percent said it had a positive impact on their relationship with their physician, and 80 percent reported it increased their "ability to manage their chronic health condition." Patients were asked to draw a circle around terms in their letters they didn't understand. Patients with untranslated letters circled an average of eight terms; those with translated letters circled an average of two terms.

Jargon Mishmash Syndrome

Destructive friction abounds when people use so many different labels and phrases, which mean so many different things to so many different people in an organization, that people can't distinguish between signal and noise. As Nobel Prize winner Daniel Kahneman and his coauthors show in their book *Noise*, when a system devolves into such a "random scatter of ideas" (their definition of noise), decision-making and coordination suffer, and dysfunctional conflict may abound, because people can't agree on what to do, how to do it, and what bad or good work looks like.

That's what happened to the word *agile*. We are big fans of the agile software movement. In 2001, seventeen software developers met in Snowbird, Utah, and published the "Manifesto for Agile Software." The four main values in the manifesto remind us how the best friction fixers think and act: (1) *"individuals and interactions* over processes and tools"; (2) *"working software* over comprehensive documentation"; (3) *"customer collaboration* over contract negotiation"; and (4) *"responding to change* over following a plan." Agile software teams deliver their work in small increments rather than in one "big bang" launch. Rather than following a rigid plan, they constantly evaluate results and constraints and update the software, and how they work, along the way.

We've studied and worked with companies including Adobe, Google, and Salesforce that use this iterative approach to help teams build good software and do it fast. Yet, while we were enamored with the agile software movement for years, we avoid using the word *agile* in *The Friction Project*. That's because so many idea merchants have spewed out such a bewildering array of jargon, sold so many tools, books, and speeches under the *agile* banner, and touted it all as cures for so many varied workplace maladies, it is impossible to comprehend and untangle the onslaught.

As Kahneman would put it, there is so much variation in the terms and methods that people deem *agile* that it has devolved into a noisy "random scatter of ideas."

Australian agile coach Craig Smith didn't intend to document such noise in his widely praised speech "40 Agile Methods in 40 Minutes." But that was our takeaway. The 105 slides in Craig's deck describe SCRUM, Scrum plop, TDD/ATD/BDD/ SBE, Holacracy, Rightshifting, Squadification, Beyond Budgeting, Programmer Anarchy, and thirty-two more methods. Craig unwittingly demonstrates that the term *agile* means so many different things to so many different people that it now means nothing. All that noise muddies communication, decision-making, and coordination. The variation in lingo, solutions, and skills makes it difficult for people who use different methods to work together or judge one another's performance. In some places, it triggers endless arguments about "what agile really means" and "how to really do agile."

There is no all-powerful jargon police force with the authority to enforce a narrow and precise definition of the word *agile* in our organizations. Alas, when a term like this has devolved into a random scatter of ideas, and it's too late to develop a uniform "Lexicon of Terms" to get everyone on the same page, it's often best to just stop saying or writing it. That's why we stopped using *agile*.

Powerful Words

Friction fixers replace hollow, stifling, impenetrable, and noisy babble with language that inspires others to make the right things easier and the wrong things harder and erases doubts about what ought to be done. Behavioral scientists have conducted hundreds of studies about the differences between powerful and powerless words and phrases. We are especially smitten with research led by Jonah Berger at the University of Pennsylvania and by our Stanford colleague Jennifer Aaker. We draw mostly on their work to generate five tips about the kind of talk that provokes people to act, persist, and develop imaginative solutions.

Powerful Words

Talk That Prompts Others to Act, Persist,
and Generate Imaginative Solutions

Say This	Not That	Why
"We've shortened all thirty-minute meetings to twenty-five and sixty-minute meetings to fifty."	"We've made our meetings shorter."	*Concrete language* is more persuasive than vague language because it demonstrates more knowledge about the details of a situation and gives more tangible guidance about what to do.
"The subtraction game is great."	"The subtraction game was great."	The *present tense* is more persuasive than the past tense because it suggests greater confidence and certainty about what is best to do now and about how to respond to current challenges.
"I don't want to waste your time."	"I am not allowed to waste your time."	Use terms that suggest you have *chosen to act this way,* that you are doing it because you have the power to do it, and you believe it is the right thing. Avoid terms that imply your actions are imposed against your will by rules, laws, or norms you can't change or by powerful people.
"Your employees are cold and callous and made my mom cry [😢]."	"Your employees are unpleasant and hurt my mom's feelings."	*Sensory metaphors*, words and phrases that express concepts by linking them to bodily experiences such as touch, smell, pain, hearing, smiles, and tears, are easier to remember, more persuasive, and more contagious.

Say This	Not That	Why
"We've completed our journey, but our friction fixing will continue."	"We've reached our destination, and we did some mighty fine friction fixing."	People *who frame accomplishments as a journey* are more likely to think about and learn from the path they took and persist after reaching a milestone; people who focus on the destination tend to treat it as "mission accomplished" and disengage.

As our table shows, these hallmarks include using *concrete language* rather than vague words and phrases, *talking in the present tense* rather than the past tense, using terms that suggest people have *chosen to engage in friction fixing* rather than are forced to do so, using *sensory metaphors* that are linked to bodily experiences, and talking about *friction fixing as a journey* rather than a destination.

Paul O'Neill was a master of powerful language when he led a turnaround of Alcoa, a large producer of aluminum. During the years that Paul led Alcoa, between 1987 and 2000, the value of the company increased by over 900 percent, from $3 billion to $27.5 billion. When Paul took over, he didn't talk much about efficiency, productivity, profits, or the stock price. He focused on improving a narrow and *concrete metric:* employee safety. Alcoa had better than average safety for the industry: about two workers out of every hundred were injured each year (the national average was about five workers out of every hundred). He announced that his goal was zero injuries, that "no one should get hurt here."

We noticed, as we read and listened to Paul's words, that whether he was talking about worker safety at Alcoa or patient safety in hospitals, he didn't talk in the past tense; instead, he framed safety as a "non-arguable goal" that *people ought to pursue right now* and in the future. Right after he took over as CEO of Alcoa, Paul met with bewildered Wall Street stock analysts and said, "The first thing I want talk to you about is safety." When those investors and business journalists asked questions about traditional financial matters including profit margins, Paul responded, "I'm not certain you heard me. If you want to understand how Alcoa is doing, you need to look at our workplace safety figures."

Paul said, again and again to different groups, that this focus on safety would inspire employees to *choose to devote more of their "discretionary energy"* to their jobs, that "you don't actually have to ask for, you need to turn them loose." He argued that creating a place where no one ever gets hurts is a "down payment" on treating people with dignity and respect—which creates pride "that swells up into everything you do."

Paul used *sensory metaphors* such as "swells up" routinely, especially when talking about the safety challenges workers faced in Alcoa's plants, which included "clanging overhead cranes" and "two-thousand-degree metal flowing around the plant," where it is "one hundred and thirty degrees and almost one hundred percent humidity" and "people get heat prostration." Finally, when Paul talked about how safety at Alcoa under his leadership improved from about two injuries per hundred workers to one injury per thousand workers a year, he didn't frame it as a mission that was accomplished or a destination the company reached. He described safety as an *ongoing journey,* a path everyone in the company travels each day.

Paul did a lot more at Alcoa than use powerful words. He and fellow company leaders dismissed managers who didn't turn knowledge about process improvements into action or, worse yet, covered up safety problems. As business author David Burkus argues, the genius of zeroing in on safety is "you can't improve safety without understanding every step in the process—understanding each risk—and then eliminating it." As a result, hundreds of process improvements "made the plants run more efficiently," and Paul "gradually changed the systems and the culture" so that "executives began sharing other data and other ideas more rapidly as well."

Paul was effective not only because of the powerful language he used to fire up employees and focus their attention on the details of Alcoa's production processes. What Paul *didn't say* provides an equally important lesson for friction fixers: we can't detect even a whiff of jargon monoxide in his words after reviewing numerous speeches, interviews, and written statements. For example, when a worker died from a preventable accident at an Alcoa plant in Arizona, he flew to the plant that day and told the executives who ran it, "We killed this man." And added, "It's my failure of leadership. I caused his death. And it's the failure of all of you in the chain of command." He didn't muddy that message with any convoluted crap, bullshit, in-group lingo, or "random scatter" of jargon.

Fast and Frenzied
When and How to Apply Good Friction

As we've seen throughout *The Friction Project,* an essential and vexing leadership challenge is figuring out when you and your colleagues are plodding along too slowly, making things too difficult, and are hobbled by "paralysis by analysis." Versus when you are too hurried and harried and pressing the people around you to go ever faster—even if it means doing crummy work, taking risky shortcuts, or breaking rules or laws. This chapter digs into how and when to apply constructive friction so that your team and organization can slow down at the right times. So people can do good work now, go faster and farther later, and maintain their health and sanity.

Too much speed at the wrong time kills people. In 2020, a study by the U.S. Highway Traffic Safety Administration found that excessive speed contributed to 29 percent of all fatalities from traffic accidents.

Putting the pedal to the metal is dangerous for organizations, too. London Business School's Dana Kanze and her colleagues compared managers who were urged by their leaders to rush ahead, to focus on "locomotion goals," to managers who were urged to slow down and evaluate their actions, to focus on "assessment goals." One of their studies tracked Equal Employment Opportunity Commission (EEOC) violations over a ten-year stretch by 559 U.S. franchises—corporations such as 7-Eleven, McDonald's, Marriott, and Ace Hardware that sell, license, and oversee businesses that operate under their brands. Dana and her colleagues classified corporations as focused on locomotion when their mission statements were packed with terms such as *do it, fast, urgent, hurry, can't wait,* and *launch.* They classified corporations as focused on assessment when mission statements were filled with terms including *careful, consider, right, evaluate, think,* and *thorough.*

Of those 559 franchises, the 148 fined for violations including age, gender, and racial discrimination and sexual harassment used far more locomotion language in their mission statements than the other 411 franchises that weren't fined. Dana's team also found that "just do it" lingo (compared "do the right thing" language) caused more unlawful discrimination in a controlled experiment. They "randomly assigned 717 U.S.-based online participants to act as a manager of a franchise with a mission statement either high in locomotion or assessment." When participants "read a mission statement that emphasized urgent action over thoughtful consideration," it quadrupled their odds of taking unethical actions, including age discrimination against a sixty-one-year-old job applicant.

The tale of Zenefits illustrates the symptoms and perils of such hustlemania. The moral of the story is that, when leaders start taking sleazy and unlawful shortcuts, it's a sign that it's time to hit the brakes. But they can become so infected with hurry sickness that it doesn't occur to them to slow down until it is too late. Zenefits was founded by Parker Conrad in 2013 to sell online software that automates human resources chores including health insurance and payroll. As *The New York Times* put it, "Mr. Conrad sought to turn a company's human resources busywork into the sort of one-step, paperless operation we've come to expect from most other parts of our app-driven, on-demand world."

In their frenzy to build and sell software to reduce friction for thousands of small businesses, Zenefits employees lived their misguided company motto "Ready. Fire. Aim." Ironically, they took shortcuts that created frustration and inefficiency for themselves and their customers. Their fixation with moving fast above all else got Zenefits in legal trouble that slowed the company down even further, damaged its reputation, and squelched growth and performance.

Venture capitalists, led by Lars Dalgaard from Andreessen Horowitz, poured more than $580 million into Zenefits. In 2015, the company was valued at $4.5 billion. Parker said, in 2014, his initial plan was to hire twenty sales reps in 2014 and hit $10 million in revenue. As Parker told it, Lars's reaction was "Why are you guys so fucking bush league?" Lars pressed Parker to hire one hundred reps and hit $20 million and said, "You guys gotta get your heads out of your asses, start focusing on going big here." As a result, Parker said he felt "constant pressure to keep moving faster, and faster and faster."

Zenefits hit Lars's aggressive sales target of $20 million in 2014. But the company did so by taking unethical actions that were reminiscent of the "just do it" corporations in Dana Kanze's locomotion research—including, apparently, shady shortcuts by Parker himself. For example, each U.S. state requires people to pass a licensing exam before they can sell insurance or advise clients. In California, brokers take a mandatory online training course that takes at least fifty-two hours to finish. *Bloomberg* reported, "Conrad created a Google Chrome browser extension that allowed people to bypass the fifty-two-hour rule by making it appear as if they were working on the course when they weren't." Zenefits was fined $7 million for such license violations by the California Department of Insurance.

The lust for speed also meant that, rather than slowing down to build automated systems that made it easy to transfer customer data quickly and accurately, staffers using the crummy Zenefits software often had to manually retype information from customers' records into Excel spreadsheets. As a result of rushing to ship a system that wasn't finished, and to sign up hundreds of customers that the company wasn't prepared to serve, constant errors were made by the inexperienced and overloaded back-office employees who typed in customer information. One customer complained, "Mistakes by Zenefits staff in entering payroll deduction information caused a string of erroneous paychecks to be issued." Another found, after submitting employee information, "names appear in records incorrectly. Dates are wrong. I don't know where the breakdown is, but the biggest problem is there's no quality check." Dissatisfied customers abandoned Zenefits in droves, and press reports about the company's flawed product and lousy service scared off new customers.

By 2016, the company failed to hit multiple revenue targets, 60 percent of its employees were laid off, and Parker was forced to resign. New CEO David Sacks changed Zenefits' motto from "Ready. Fire. Aim" to "Operate with Integrity." That and other changes came too late. Zenefits did operate as an independent company until 2021, when it was acquired by Francisco Partners, a private equity firm. Francisco didn't disclose the purchase price, but *Forbes* reported "venture-capital investors, including Andreessen Horowitz and Founders Fund, have already marked their investments in the firm to zero." In 2022, Francisco Partners sold Zenefits to TriNet, which announced it would operate the company as TriNet Zenefits.

Excessive Speed: Consequences for Individuals

Efficiency, frictionless experiences, and making the right things easier are hallmarks of good workplaces. But the Zenefits saga shows the dangers of fixating on locomotion that results in sloppy and sleazy work, which makes it harder to go faster later. Hundreds of studies show the ugly effects of feeling harried and overloaded, and focusing on working fast rather than well.

Here are five ways that excessive speed brings out the worst in people, which in turn damages organizations.

1. Burnout

Burned-out employees feel tired, down, frustrated, hopeless, cynical, and numb—and their performance and productivity suffer. A 2018 Gallup survey of seventy-five hundred employees found that 67 percent experienced regular episodes of burnout; and 23 percent felt burned out often or always. Employees with high levels of burnout were 63 percent more likely to take a sick day, 23 percent more likely to visit an emergency room, and 250 percent more likely to seek a new job. In this survey Gallup researchers Ben Wigert and Sangeeta Agrawal report, as have many prior researchers, that the onslaught of "mental quicksand" that drags down overloaded people fuels burnout. Their findings also suggest that slowing down to ease overload provides protection because, "when employees say they often or always have enough time to do all of their work, they are 70 percent less likely to experience high burnout."

2. Selfishness

When people are in a big hurry, they fixate so much on tasks that they don't slow down to offer a kind word or lend a hand to others and become oblivious to people who need their help.

That's what John Darley and Daniel Batson found in a classic 1973 experiment. They recruited Princeton Theological Seminary students to deliver a talk on the Good Samaritan—a New Testament parable on helping others in need. Each student was given the assignment and then instructed to walk outside on the cold December day through a narrow alley, where they encountered a person (planted by the researchers) who was "sitting slumped in a doorway, head down, eyes closed, not moving."

The researchers randomly assigned students to one of three groups. In one group, students were told there was no need to hurry; in a second group, they were asked to hurry a bit; and in a third group, they were urged to rush because they were late. Sixty-three percent of those theology students who were in no hurry stopped to help, compared to 45 percent of those in a bit of a hurry, and a measly 10 percent of those in a big hurry. Ironically, 90 percent of the harried theology students passed inches from a person (apparently) in dire need of help because they were late to give a speech on the virtues of being a Good Samaritan.

At work, when rushed people don't check on one another, they miss opportunities to help colleagues who are having personal struggles or need help doing their jobs. Surveys of hundreds of employees in seventeen industries by Christine Porath, author of *Mastering Civility,* found "more than 40 percent say they have no time to be nice." Many employees feel so rushed that they don't even take a second to smile and say hello, let alone to pause and ask if a colleague could use their help.

3. Bullying

Ohio State's Ben Tepper developed a measure of abusive supervision more than twenty years ago, which has since been used in many studies on the causes and consequences of such nasti-ness. Ben's measure lists fifteen behaviors that nightmare bosses heap on subordinates, including "is rude to me," "expresses an-ger at me when he/she is mad for another reason," "tells me I am incompetent," and "puts me down in front of others." Once again, time pressure is a major culprit. Dozens of studies that use this and related measures find that exhausted bosses stressed by constant struggles with deadlines are prone to abuse their subordinates—who respond by becoming anxious, depressed, physically ill, and less productive, and by quitting their jobs. Overloaded bosses who sleep poorly are more likely to bully employees, too—who respond to such nastiness by disengaging from work.

Since Bob Sutton published *The No Asshole Rule* in 2007, he's received hundreds of emails about harried leaders who treat others like dirt. A Ph.D. student we'll call "Ruth," for example, wrote Bob about her overbearing and uncaring supervisor, "Clay," an assistant professor at a prestigious university who worked "day and night" to compile a strong research record. Clay was determined to become renowned in his field and be promoted to a tenured professorship. Clay pressed Ruth to work "twelve hours a day, six or seven days a week." When Ruth asked for a day off to take care of herself, Clay responded by "ques-tioning my commitment." Ruth quit after a year of such abuse. She suffered from "insomnia, stress, and gaining twenty pounds from emotional eating."

4. Bad Decisions

When people try to accomplish things too fast, don't pause to think, and trigger a cycle of recrimination and anxiety, the frenzy imposes a "bandwidth tax" that results in lousy deci-sions. Worse, their narrow focus on current troubles hinders them from confronting new problems before they get out of control and prevents people from doing the kinds of long-term thinking and planning that separates good friction fixers and organizations from bad ones.

This syndrome pervades findings of "time poverty" studies. A team led by psychologist Eldar Shafir studied Princeton undergraduates who played a game based on the American game show *Family Feud*. The undergraduates were randomly assigned to be time rich (fifty seconds) or time poor (fifteen seconds) in answering questions. When time-poor students were given the option to borrow ahead to get extra time, they consistently borrowed too much, borrowed at the wrong times, and got deeper and deeper into debt. As psychologist Maria Konnikova explained, time-poor students "were so focused on operating under scarcity that they couldn't think their way through to a strategy—or, indeed, even realize that an opportunity to do so was available."

Daniel Kahneman's research, cited in chapter 2, shows that when you are in a "cognitive minefield," when you don't know what to do or things are going badly, it is best to slow down, ask for advice, and weigh pros and cons. The first decision that pops into your mind is probably flawed because it's based on biases and a shallow understanding of your choices. The hazards of time pressure also pervade research on locomotion, which, as we saw earlier in this chapter, shows that when people fixate on speed, they take shortcuts and even break laws.

These findings help explain the damage inflicted by Zenefits' "Ready. Fire. Aim" culture, which drove leaders to make unethical decisions, ship products that weren't ready, and, as *Buzzfeed* reported, create a high-pressure sales culture in which "almost nothing mattered as much as closing deals." As a result, work by Zenefits' staffers was inefficient and riddled with errors. Their customers suffered time-consuming ordeals, including stretches when their employees went without health insurance. Zenefits quickly plummeted from a unicorn that was once valued at $4.5 billion, to a flop that was then sold to new owners.

5. Kills Creativity

As we showed in chapter 2, creativity is slow, difficult, and frustrating. And that's if you are doing it right. As Jerry Seinfeld said, when it comes to creating comedy, "If you're efficient, you're doing it the wrong way. The right way is the hard way."

Teresa Amabile and her colleagues reached a similar conclusion after analyzing nine thousand daily diary entries from 177 employees on twenty-two project teams. Theresa's team developed a nuanced measure of daily creativity based on employee reports of discovery, generating ideas, thinking flexibly, learning, and enhanced self-awareness. Their findings revealed that "when creativity is under the gun, it usually ends up getting killed." Each day, participants rated how much time pressure they felt on a seven-point scale. "On the days rated a seven, people were 45 percent less likely to think creatively than they were on any of the lower-pressure days." Teresa's team found that time pressure may drive people to work longer hours, get more done, and "*feel* more creative." Yet, the pressure caused them to think less creatively, as indicated by that nuanced measure.

Time pressure was most destructive when people felt they were "on a treadmill" because their schedules were packed with fragmented and unimportant tasks, unnecessary meetings, and constantly shifting plans. The resulting frustration, anxiety, and inability to concentrate on their work undermined creativity. In contrast, time pressure didn't undermine creativity when people felt their team was on an important mission and members had long stretches to focus on essential solo work.

In the worst projects that Teresa's team tracked, even though it was clear to members that the original time frame was unrealistic, management kept pushing them to work at a frenzied pace. Members were too exhausted and anxious to slow down and dissect complex problems. Or to engage in the messy and unpredictable trial and error required to develop solutions that could save such projects. A member of one failing project was informed by his leader that, in the coming weeks, he should plan to work from 8:00 A.M. to 7:00 P.M., seven days a week. He wrote in his diary, "The project is now officially a death march in my mind. I can't fathom how much work we have left. . . . At every turn, we uncover more things that are unsettled, incomplete, or way more complex than we ever thought."

Excessive Speed: The Downward Spiral of Organizational Debt

As the damage caused by excessive speed ripples throughout an organization, it can turn into a vicious downward spiral that, once it gains momentum, is hard for leaders to reverse. As harried leaders make bad decisions and errors that create more pressing problems that are left unsolved, and one overwhelmed member after another burns out, turns selfish and nasty, makes more flawed decisions, and becomes less creative, everyone tangled up with the organization suffers.

Excessive speed also harms organizations when people postpone necessary work on the system, culture, or technology for too long—or never get around to it at all. In the world of software development, when coders defer necessary work, organizations incur "technical debt." It builds up, for example, when engineers rush to ship code that has bugs or isn't well-documented and tell themselves, "We will get to that later," "Next time," or "By the time it becomes a big problem, we will be working someplace else."

Similarly, veteran tech executive Steve Blank wrote that many fast-moving and growing companies have excessive "organizational debt"—which "can kill the company even quicker" than technical debt. Steve defines organizational debt as compromises made to "just get it done." Sometimes it's necessary, and smart, to prioritize the most important work and get to the rest later. Yet, like borrowing too much money, so much organizational debt can accumulate that your company struggles to pay it down. Then, Steve says, "just when things should be going great, organizational debt can turn a growing company into a chaotic nightmare."

Our case study of Uber documents how the wild growth of this ride-sharing company was fueled by hundreds of fast-moving teams—but spawned technical and organizational debt that ballooned until the chaos that Steve predicted reared its ugly head. Thuan Pham, Uber's chief technology officer from 2013 to 2020, said that, at first, dividing the company into fast-moving decentralized teams to build software, and to open Uber operations in new cities, helped the company scale fast. Former CEO Travis Kalanick had divided software teams into independent groups, each dedicated to a product area and gave them nearly complete autonomy. Travis also trumpeted company values that were brimming with locomotion language including *superpumped, let builders build, toe-stepping,* and *always be hustlin'.*

As Thuan and his coworkers told us in 2019, incurring massive "technical and organizational debt" spurred the fast growth that helped Uber gain the upper hand against Lyft and other competitors. As Thuan pointed out, "If we lived in a debt-free world, we probably would move very, very slowly." But Uber waited too long to "pay it down." By 2017, as Thuan explained, "each team was a speedboat, racing ahead at full throttle" with light oversight from executives and little concern about coordination across teams. This failure to slow down and fix things nearly killed the company.

As individual teams kept racing ahead, Uber's overall "organizational velocity" kept getting slower. There were three signs that the company was stalling. First, engineers were spending more time "wrestling with fixing things or dealing with mundane maintenance issues" and less time writing new code. Second, more teams had trouble implementing new features because they needed help from other teams, but weren't getting it. Or were blocked by other teams that were opposed to the new feature. Third, software outages were on the upswing. "Engineers and developers were responsible for their own code and on call for their services. That meant one proxy for technical debt was sleep debt." The sleep debt kept getting worse. Skilled engineers "mired" in such "grunt work" kept leaving for companies such as Google, because they didn't like being "woken up in the middle of the night fifteen times a week."

As Thuan explained, this "technical debt" resulted from a structure that was too decentralized and norms that encouraged people to charge ahead without collaborating and coordinating with other teams—so more and more employees engaged in firefighting to make temporary and local repairs that kept the system running but didn't fix root causes. Thuan added that further organizational debt was created because, as the company raced to scale fast, it hired and promoted too many inexperienced managers. These inexperienced managers were too focused on racing ahead and achieving short-term wins and were not focused (or skilled) enough to understand when to slow down and do things right and to coordinate their work with other teams.

This deadly brew of inexperience, pressure to move fast, and permission for people and teams to do as they pleased not only reduced Uber's overall velocity. It also fueled unchecked dumb and unethical behavior in many corners of the company. Uber faced legal problems throughout the world for bending and breaking laws, and its reputation suffered when engineer Susan Fowler spoke out about sexism and sexual harassment that she and other women faced—which stemmed, in part, from male-dominated teams filled with tech bros who felt free to break the rules and do as they pleased.

Travis was forced to resign in the wake of these troubles. CEO Dara Khosrowshahi, who replaced Travis, spent years struggling to pay down Uber's technical and organizational debt—and to develop a profitable business model. The company lost more than $4 billion in fiscal year 2017, and while it posted almost $1 billion in profits in 2018, it lost more than $8 billion in 2019. The COVID pandemic was rough on Uber, and losses continued through the first three quarters of 2022. Yet, by 2023, there were signs that Uber was turning things around, as the company posted record revenue and a modest profit in the last three months of 2022 and revenue from its ride-share and food-delivery services continued to rise through 2023. Dara implied that Uber had begun to reverse its downward spiral and was finally on the road to long-term profitability.

We don't know if Uber will become consistently profitable. But we do know that Dara's job would have been a lot easier if the company had hit the brakes a few years earlier and begun paying down all that technical and organizational debt.

Hitting the Brakes: On Creating Constructive Friction

"For fast-acting relief, try slowing down." That advice from actress and comedian Lily Tomlin captures the essence of this chapter. As a friction fixer, you can apply this advice when you are trying to help others and it is unclear what they ought to do. When they lack the will, skill, money, or tools to do it. When they are doing things too fast to do them well. Or when they are so far down the road that these and other sins haven't been rectified and the shit has hit the fan.

Unless immediate action is essential, your job is to get them to slow down or stop. Here are six ideas about how and when to inject constructive friction.

1. Pause to Start Right

When you launch a new project, team, or organization, pause to consider the talent, roles, norms, and resources that you will need to succeed. A great way to begin is to harness the human capacity for imaginary time travel: Pause to pretend that you have succeeded (a "previctorem") or failed (a "premortem") and write a story about the events that led to your wonderful or awful fate. Then build those lessons into how you design and do your work.

Psychologist Gary Klein uses premortems to help teams identify dangerous risks and delusions. Gary asks teams to imagine that it is, say, a year after they've made a decision, and it is a massive and unambiguous failure. People look back from that terrible future and develop lists and stories to explain what happened. Gary's research finds that premortems are "a low-cost, high-payoff" method for making better decisions and running better projects. Huggy Rao and his Stanford colleagues conducted a "back to the future" study that suggests doing a previctorem, in which you pause to look back from an (imaginary) successful future, may be even more effective than doing a premortem. Both forms of time travel can improve decisions and designs because treating an event as if it *did* rather than *might* happen—thinking about it in the *past tense*—makes it seem more concrete and likely to happen, which motivates people to unpack its nuances.

For their research, Huggy Rao and his colleagues did a field experiment with approximately a thousand aspiring entrepreneurs who were randomly assigned to 348 virtual teams. Each team was charged with developing an idea for a health-and-wellness product and creating an advertisement for it. Teams were randomly assigned to do a previctorem or a premortem before starting their project. There was also a placebo condition, in which teams were asked to review business operations rather than engage in time travel. In addition to paying team members for their efforts, the researchers cranked up the motivation with a $5,000 prize for the top team.

Huggy and his colleagues then measured two indicators of how well each team performed. First, how much members of each team made sacrifices for the greater good when negotiating about commitments, including the project start date and the amount of time members would work. Second, they measured the quality of the advertisement that each team created for their product, based on evaluations from panels of U.S-based adults, who assessed how interesting and effective an ad was, and how likely they were to click on it.

The highest-performing teams were those that wrote previctorems, where each member wrote about the team in the *past tense*—imagining it was a year later and their project had been a big success. Then these teammates spent fifteen minutes reflecting on the people dynamics that fueled their success. We believe such teams performed better because they agreed on how they would do their work and define performance and developed a shared language, which boosted coordination. And the focus on success boosted collective optimism and persistence.

The lesson from this research is, before the members of your new team or organization start their work, it's worth the trouble to pause, do some imaginary time travel, pretend that you've been a great success (or a great failure), tell a story about why it happened, and then live the lessons you conjure up.

2. Ask Questions That Make People Stop to Think— Before They Do Something Stupid

To help people break out of that "just do it" locomotion mode, to consider if their first instinct about an important decision or action is dumb or dangerous, teach and press them to pose questions that trigger assessment. Questions that activate what Daniel Kahneman calls System 2, that slow, deliberative, and rational way of thinking that, he says, we humans only use about 2 percent of the time.

Psychologist Jennifer Eberhardt led a study that shows how pausing to ask questions can dampen racist stereotypes and behavior. Jennifer's team worked with Nextdoor, an online application with over sixty million users, which enables people who live in the same neighborhood to share information, give and get help, and connect with nearby residents and businesses. Unfortunately, when a black person was spotted in a predominantly white neighborhood, Nextdoor users often assumed the person was up to no good, even in the absence of behavior suggesting otherwise. The cofounder of Nextdoor reached out to Jennifer and her colleagues, and, as Jennifer put it, "to reduce racial profiling, they realized that they were going to have to add friction." Nextdoor redesigned the app so, before users could report a person, they had to pause and think about such questions as "What was this person doing that made him suspicious?" Nextdoor provided users a definition of racial profiling and urged them, "If you see something suspicious, say something specific." After such friction was injected to slow Nextdoor users down, analysis by Jennifer Eberhardt's team found that racial profiling dropped by more than 75 percent.

3. Where's Your Times Square?

Since publishing *Scaling Up Excellence* in 2014, we've taught, coached, and studied hundreds of people who are bent on expanding organizations and spreading good things inside them. Unfortunately, as we saw with the Zenefits mess and the Google Glass fiasco earlier in the book, smart people sometimes forget a ridiculously obvious truth: to spread excellence, you must have excellence to spread.

We learned this lesson from Becky Margiotta, who led the 100,000 Homes Campaign that we talked about in chapter 1. Becky is now CEO of the Billions Institute, where she advises leaders of nonprofits and government organizations on how to imagine and implement large-scale change. Becky has many impatient clients who want to go big with half-baked and unproven ideas. She asks them, "Where's your Times Square?" That's because, before she led the nationwide 100,000 Homes Campaign, Becky was hired by Rosanne Haggerty, founder of the nonprofit Community Solutions, to reduce the homelessness problem in New York City's Times Square by two-thirds over a three-year period. That goal turned out to be unrealistic—it took five years.

Becky's team spent from 2003 to 2007 on the Street to Home initiative in Times Square. It took them until 2007 to develop the mindset, skills, and methods for tackling the problem, but that year, they surpassed their original goal and achieved an 87 percent reduction in street homelessness. It was a long, frustrating slog. Becky's team tried many methods that failed before they figured out what worked. For example, it took them years to identify who was homeless in Times Square. They finally learned the best way to "get the count" wasn't to visit Times Square during the day and to ask people if they were homeless. It was to go out at 5:00 A.M. and count the people sleeping there. They also learned to find homes first for people who had been homeless the longest and who suffered from the most severe health problems—because they faced the greatest risk of premature death.

Becky says that, without those five years of frustration, failure, and—eventually—development of a "playbook" that would work elsewhere, she and Rosanne couldn't have launched the 100,000 Homes Campaign in 2010. And the campaign wouldn't have reached its goal of finding homes for one hundred thousand chronically homeless Americans as it did on June 14, 2014.

Parker Conrad, the Zenefits CEO who was forced out in 2016, learned a similar lesson. The errors and lousy service that Zenefits gave clients happened, in part, because the company sold software and services to clients before it was automated. Many transactions that Zenefits employees used to link clients to insurance companies were done on paper or with emailed PDFs—which required time-consuming manual work to review and transfer information. Zenefits sold a system to hundreds of customers that was slow, hard to use, and easy to mess up—and the massive time pressure placed on Zenefits employees exacerbated such problems.

Just months after Parker left Zenefits, he started a similar company called Rippling, which uses an automated system to manage an array of employee data including payroll and benefits.

Rippling also offers a "device management platform" that allows "customers to retrieve, wipe clean, and store employee computers when staffers part ways with a company."

At Rippling, Parker's approach was the opposite of what he did at Zenefits. In 2021, Parker admitted, "it was almost too easy for us to close customers early on" at Zenefits, and leaders made the mistake of believing that their employees could do the manual work for clients "with an eye toward automating those processes afterward." They were wrong. The bigger Zenefits got, the harder it was to automate processes. Parker said that employees were doing so much manual work that costs soared and profits plummeted, and "that's when a lot of things started to come apart."

In contrast, during Rippling's first two years, Parker said, it was "basically me and like fifty engineers." They focused on building a robust product, on "pruning any operational function and trying to replace it with software." Parker prohibited employees from doing the manual chores that Zenefits employees did. Parker insisted, instead, that Rippling employees work with customers until they developed sound automated solutions. To assure that engineers understood customers' needs and challenges (and to save money), Rippling didn't hire any customer support staffers in those early years. Parker said, "I was personally doing—and the engineering team was personally doing—all of the customer support." Parker learned other lessons from Zenefits that he applies at Rippling, including selling bundles of software to customers rather than individual products—and developing each kind of software, from the start, so it is easy to integrate with other Rippling products.

Parker's focus on getting things right before going big, and other lessons he learned the hard way at Zenefits, seems to be working. By May of 2022, venture-capital firms had invested almost $700 million in Rippling, and it was valued at $11.25 billion—nearly twice as much as Zenefits' $6.5 billion in its (brief) heyday.

4. Do a Relaunch

When the COVID pandemic hit in early 2020, it triggered un-planned and massive changes in where and how employees worked and lived. As we wrote in the *McKinsey Quarterly* in August of 2020, "in a sense, are *all new hires,* into organizations that are *all* materially different than they were just a few months ago." Yet many teams kept racing ahead without pausing to re-flect on how these tectonic changes had altered the context in which their business operated.

The struggles that we've seen in so many teams provoked us to suggest, and sometimes coach and lead, an exercise that Har-vard Business School's Tsedal Neeley calls "a team relaunch." This intentional pause entails convening one or two meetings in which a team considers its goals, norms, rhythms, rituals, and use of resources. The team starts by discussing what is working and what isn't. Then members decide what ought to change and how to implement their decisions.

Tsedal convinces teams to do relaunches by sharing research that shows when mature teams face performance or interper-sonal problems, they benefit from hitting the pause button and engaging in reflection and self-criticism. Unfortunately, too many leaders are like the frazzled CEO of a nonprofit we met. Disgruntled star employees were quitting in droves, cynicism was rampant, and the organization was hemorrhaging cash. Yet the CEO told us her top team was "too busy" to follow our ad-vice and hit pause for an hour or two. When we told Tsedal about that troubled CEO, she said to us, "It's like not stopping the car to fuel up, even though you know you are out of gas."

We developed a relaunch for virtual teams with our colleague Dr. Kathryn Velcich. Kathryn has conducted this forty-five-to-ninety-minute Team Refresh exercise with some half a dozen clients of Teamraderie (a company we advise). After explaining the logic and evidence for resets, Kathryn leads six-to-twelve-person teams in the Subtraction Game. Members generate wild and practical ideas about norms and practices that once worked but now get in the way. The team then selects up to three of these "targets" and commits to getting rid of each. Next, Kathryn guides them in "the strengths game," following Gallup research that shows the best employees and teams play to their strengths. The team identifies and rallies around a few cherished norms, skills, or strategies that are (and will continue to be) crucial to their performance and sanity.

Several of these teams implemented substantial changes. A team from a software company that had default meeting lengths of thirty or sixty minutes shortened them to twenty or forty-five minutes. A team from a computer hardware firm designated a "chief of prioritization" charged with identifying projects and initiatives that shouldn't get any attention right away.

5. Use Friction to Create Cadence

Friction fixers can dampen confusion, reduce wasted effort, enhance coordination, and strengthen relationships by slowing down to implement routines and rituals that create a shared cadence. Rhythmic marching, dancing, and singing have an evolutionary basis: groups whose members are "in sync" have stronger emotional bonds and are more adept at the coordination and cooperation required to gather and grow food and defend themselves—and thus more likely to survive and breed.

After the COVID crisis hit the United States in March 2020, a software developer in our class explained how his team's cadence of stand-up meetings helped them shift to remote work. When they worked in person, every morning at nine all of the eight team members gathered for a stand-up meeting in which they described their goals for that day and asked for advice. The team continued this practice when they switched to remote work—except that members stood up in front of their laptops at home (instead of congregating in-person). After a few weeks of remote work, problems arose because teammates were no longer having the informal and accidental conversations they had when they worked side by side—which facilitated quick problem-solving, coordination, and banter packed with jokes, friendly teasing, and serious talk about personal matters. Members were also having trouble figuring out when to quit work for the day. When they all worked in the same place, everyone left at 5:30 P.M. After switching to remote work, people's hours became more variable—some quit at 3:00 P.M., while a few "workaholics" routinely worked past 8:00 P.M.

The team paused for a relaunch. They spent an hour discussing the need for more interaction, unclear expectations about when their workday ended, and tensions among "workaholics" and people who "had a life." They decided to add a second daily remote stand-up meeting at 4:30 P.M. Each engineer showed the team what he or she had accomplished that day, asked for and gave help, wove his or her work with that of others, and made plans for the next day—interspersed with the usual banter. This second ritual not only enhanced social bonds and coordination, it helped create a company cadence: after it ended, most members stopped working for the day unless some crisis couldn't wait until morning.

Cadence is a central theme in the "Start Up People Operations" class that Huggy teaches with John Lilly—who was CEO of Mozilla (producer of the open-source browser Firefox) as it grew from twelve to more than five hundred employees. John emphasizes that, as Mozilla grew from one team to multiple teams, rather than adding a lot of rules and specialized roles to bolster coordination and communication, his leadership team developed a "drumbeat that the organization marches to."

As Mozilla grew to roughly fifty people, confusion emerged—especially among newcomers—about how to fit in, whom to talk to and work with, and when to ship changes in code. Life got less chaotic after Mozilla's leaders added a "closed" meeting every Monday where they made decisions and plans. Later that day, the leadership team convened a company lunch and an all-hands meeting where they announced goals, answered questions, and talked about challenges Mozilla faced. When Mozilla grew to about eighty people, the leadership team added more "pacing mechanisms," including data reports every night at seven (to help people make short-term decisions) and quarterly company goals (to help people blend individual and collective efforts). Then, when Mozilla grew to about 120 people, and company-wide goals were too vague, the top team added quarterly group goals. Mozilla also started holding a worldwide summit every two years for employees, people from outside the company who wrote open-source code for Mozilla, and other key stakeholders, as a "time to see everyone, reconnect, and remember humanity."

6. Communicate a Lot, or Not at All

Shared rhythms also help people get work done and avoid exhaustion because they know when to work with others and when to work alone. That's what Christoph Riedl and Anita Woolley's "bursty communication" study found. Christoph and Anita randomly assigned 260 software workers from fifty countries to fifty-two five-person virtual teams. Each team developed algorithms to recommend the optimal contents of a medical kit for space flight. Cash prizes didn't improve performance. Rather, in the best teams, people exchanged many messages for short periods and then returned to solo work for long stretches—using "bursty communication." The worst teams communicated constantly, but at a slower pace, and switched back and forth among topics rather than tackling one at a time.

The implication for friction fixers is to make clear when bursts ought to start and stop, for example, by saying, "Everyone ought to work on this right now" or "We are done until next week, no need to do anything until then."

Take Time to End Things Right

Anthropologists and sociologists document how, when something ends, people benefit from pausing to reflect on the past, what they've lost, what comes next, and what matters most and least to them—and to support one another. Be it the end of a meeting, a day, a game, a career, a life, a team, a project, or an organization.

We humans are wired to care about and be swayed by how things end. Another insight from Daniel Kahneman's research is the "peak-end rule": When people judge if a past experience is good or bad, they put the strongest weight on how they felt during the best and worst times, and at the end. They don't simply judge the experience based on an average of how they felt throughout.

Friction fixers build good endings. In addition to writing a to-do list at the end of the day or week, you might encourage your colleagues to write a "ta-da list"—a ritual suggested by Gretchen Rubin, author of the book *The Happiness Project*. Gretchen says after listing your accomplishments—tasks you completed, people you helped, and ways you took care of yourself—you will feel proud and that it's time for a well-deserved break, and you will be ready to go the next day or week.

The routines used to end meetings can help assure that everyone is on the same page and understands what to do next. Such as Patty's Parting Questions, which we talked about in chapter 4. Patty McCord, who was Netflix's chief talent officer for the company's first fourteen years, told us, "The most important role I played at Netflix was, at the end of every executive meeting, to say, 'Have we made any decisions in the room today, and if we have, how are we going to communicate them?'"

Endings can reinforce the most precious values in a group, organization, or society. Such as the Sweeping the Shed ritual used by the All Blacks, New Zealand's national rugby team. The All Blacks have been a superpower in rugby for more than a hundred years. Through 2020, they had an all-time winning percentage of 77 percent, the highest of any professional sports team in the world. James Kerr, who studied the team's culture, says Sweeping the Shed is a mantra and ritual that reinforces "a tradition that says that no individual is bigger than the team and its ancestors." After every training session or match, no matter what role a person has on the team—janitor, player, manager—everyone pitches in and cleans the locker room. All Blacks' legendary superstar Dan Carter explained, "From the very start, you learn humility . . . like the fact that we always leave the changing room as clean as it was when we walked in."

At Roche, a giant pharmaceutical company, executives host a fancy celebration lunch at the end of every big project—including a champagne toast to the team. Leaders take particular care to celebrate failures. Roche depends on a creative process where "nine out of ten potential new drugs turn out to be flops." This ritual enables leaders to thank scientists for their hard work whether a project failed or succeeded, helps scientists accept that the project is over and it's time to start the next, and helps scientists think about lessons that might increase their (low!) odds of success next time. Roche CEO Severin Schwan says, "I would argue, from a cultural point of view, it's more important to praise the people for the nine times they fail than for the one time they succeed."

The differences between well-crafted and badly crafted endings are striking during employee layoffs. If you must lay people off, pause and remember there is a difference between what you do and how you do it. Bird, the San Francisco–based electric scooter company, laid off more than four hundred employees in March 2020 at the start of the pandemic. The employees to be let go were invited to a generic-sounding Zoom meeting titled "COVID 19 update." When employees logged on at 10:30 A.M., they encountered a slide that said, "COVID 19." Then, a two-minute audio-only meeting was led by a woman with a robotic voice—who didn't identify herself and who few employees recognized. She began, "This is a suboptimal way to deliver this message," then announced all employees on the call were losing their jobs—immediately. "Then their screens suddenly went dark and their company issued MacBooks restarted. By 10:40 A.M. everyone was locked out, just as employees were frantically trying to exchange personal numbers and emails on Slack and take screenshots of their contacts."

After the layoffs, Bird's CEO, Travis VanderZanden, was silent, and most fired employees heard little from the company. *Except* management was *very* concerned about getting back "company assets," especially Mac laptops, which were useless to former employees as they were locked out.

In contrast, consider the layoffs led by CEO Brian Chesky at Airbnb. On May 5, 2020, about a month after the Bird fiasco, Brian sent a memo to Airbnb employees announcing that about nineteen hundred people, 25 percent of the company, would lose jobs because of the abrupt drop in travel prompted by the COVID-19 crisis. Airbnb, he explained, would provide them generous severance benefits, including at least fourteen weeks of pay, twelve months of health insurance, and full vesting of company stock. Brian also wrote, "We have great people leaving Airbnb, and other companies will be lucky to have them. The result is that we will have to part with teammates that we love and value. . . . Please know this is not your fault. The world will never stop seeking the qualities and talents that you brought to Airbnb."

The memo explained, if employees worked in the United States or Canada and lost jobs, each would be informed in a personal, one-on-one meeting with a senior manager—and their invitation would be sent in the next few hours. The last official workday for laid-off employees was May 11, 2020, to "give people time to begin taking next steps and say goodbye." Brian announced a team of Airbnb recruiters would be dedicated to connecting laid-off alums with new employers, and each alum would get four months of support from RiseSmart, a career-services firm. All laid-off employees were allowed to keep their Airbnb laptop because it "is an important tool to find new work."

That layoff was still a brutal blow to many Airbnb employees, who were disappointed that management had done so little to protect their jobs. And employees who still had jobs feared Airbnb's caring and fun culture would never be the same again. Yet, after a few months, the wisdom of slowing down to do an orderly and compassionate layoff was clear—as was the need for a smaller and more nimble company. This "lesson in how to talk to your team in hard times," as *Inc.* put it, helped remaining Airbnb employees regain confidence in their company's leaders and culture. Most laid-off employees got good jobs within weeks. And Airbnb's earnings bounced back as people began traveling again.

During the downturn in 2022 and 2023, several leaders of tech firms whom we know read Brian's 2020 memo and talked with their top teams about the lessons for doing layoffs in their companies. They used it as a model for making cuts so that employees would still see their companies as good places to work and to protect the leaders' personal reputations.

Both Travis VanderZanden at Bird and Brian Chesky at Airbnb were determined to build companies that eliminated as much friction—and brought as much joy and satisfaction—as possible for their customers. A big difference between the two was that Brian realized that, to build a company that achieved those goals, the onset of the pandemic was not a juncture where the easy way was the best way, or where the fast eat the slow. Brian was much like other skilled friction fixers in this book, hitting the gas and the brakes at the right moments. He knew that, to steer his company through treacherous obstacles, Airbnb was at a crossroads where it was best to slow down. To pause and figure out how to give the people his company was laying off the time, resources, and compassion they needed to help them land on their feet. While Brian was widely praised, Travis VanderZanden was vilified in the press and made excuses including blaming employees for spreading false rumors. (He tweeted, "We did NOT let employees go via a pre-recording.")

The lesson for friction fixers, in the words of UCLA's legendary basketball coach John Wooden (who won ten national championships in his final twelve years as coach), is "If you don't have time to do it right, when will you have time to do it over?"

Part IV

THE WRAP-UP

Your Friction Project

We wrote *The Friction Project* because organizations that are filled with people who make the right things easier and the wrong things harder are more humane, productive, and innovative. We started our project because we were inundated with bad news about organizations that were plagued by friction troubles. As our seven-year research effort unfolded, however, we met and learned of so many friction fixers who implemented so many sound remedies in so many places that we became downright optimistic about the prospects for dampening such problems in most workplaces.

Each of these leaders created their own custom concoction tailored to the challenges faced by the organization that they labored to fix. Yet we found striking similarities in how these leaders thought and acted. We've boiled these themes down to three leadership principles that they followed and spread to others—which can help equip you to design and run your own friction project.

The first principle such leaders follow is *we serve as trustees of others' time.* As chapter 1 shows, thinking and acting like a trustee means focusing (and guiding your colleagues) on finding and repairing obstacles that squander others' time and money, frustrate them, and leave them pissed off and worn-out. Serving as a trustee also means knowing how to get people to stop and think about what the hell they are doing. And to inject friction when things ought to be hard or impossible.

Skilled trustees are adept at cranking up awareness of friction troubles among people who have the power to fix them—and doing it in ways that motivate such people to think like trustees and to start necessary repairs. These leaders also help others get beyond fretting over how hard it is to solve such problems or making excuses. For example, Michael Brennan, CEO and cofounder of Civilla knew that, for his little nonprofit to lead a successful effort to fix that grueling government benefits form completed by more than two million Michigan residents each year, they needed support from executives at Michigan's Department of Health and Human Services (MDHHS)—the organization responsible for that application form.

The Civilla team invited the top six MDHHS executives for a meeting and kicked it off by asking each executive to complete the forty-two-page form—something that none of them had attempted before. Terry Beurer, who was head of MDHSS and had worked there for thirty-five years, only got to page eight before he gave up. Terry told Michael it was one of the most humbling experiences of his career. Terry said, "Up until that point, I'd always believed the way we were doing things was the best way. I thought it was the best way because we'd developed it. Well . . . how much more wrong could I have been?"

To Terry's credit, rather than becoming defensive or making excuses about how hard it was to change a giant government bureaucracy, he signed MDHHS up for Civilla's Project Re:form on the spot and provided his time, departmental resources, and political support throughout this difficult, and ultimately successful, four-year redesign project.

Trustees practice their craft in endless ways. Winston Churchill sent out that "Brevity" memo to pressure British bureaucrats to be less long-winded. The leaders of the Cancer Center invited patient activists to tell their cancer tax horror stories to generate concern and motivation among doctors, nurses, and administrators. All trustees are similar, however, in that they keep finding ways to increase awareness of how they and their colleagues shape what is hard and easy for others, and to increase the will, resources, and skills required to keep making things better for people in their cone of friction.

The second leadership principle is that *our project is powered by ownership and accountability for friction fixing.* To paraphrase former Yum! Brands CEO David Novak, the idea is to build workplaces where accountability is a two-way street, where people feel "I own the place and the place owns me." When it comes to friction fixing, skilled leaders are keenly aware that, all too often, making the right things easier and the wrong things harder are treated as orphan problems, obstacles and ordeals that everyone on a team or organization believes are important but that no one takes responsibility for averting or repairing.

That's what happened at the Cancer Center until leaders were goaded by the patient advocates who told their cancer tax horror stories. Before that, many center leaders, administrators, and healthcare workers knew about the coordination burden the system imposed on patients and their families, but few felt accountable for reducing it, and it was widely seen as low-priority work. The tax only began to wane after executives acknowledged the importance of such work, took responsibility for developing remedies, and assigned CarePoint administrators to coordinate services for each patient.

Leaders who create cultures of accountability and owner-ship blend three strategies. First, they are relentless about com-municating and modeling expectations that friction fixing is important work. CEO Satya Nadella at Microsoft, for example, has been downright dogged and repetitive about reversing the company's decades-long history of siloism and dysfunctional internal competition. Before Satya took charge in 2014, few employees felt obligated to support collaboration and coordi-nation across Microsoft groups and businesses. Instead, people were rewarded for treating colleagues as enemies rather than friends. There was, as one veteran Microsoft employee told us, a "backstabbing bonus."

It's not like that any longer. Satya's been talking about what it means to embrace "One Microsoft" to people throughout the company for a decade. After hearing the message over and over, employees know they are expected to "come together as a team" and "build on the ideas of others and collaborate across bound-aries to bring the best of Microsoft to our customers as one."

Second, leaders use rewards and punishments to encour-age accountability and ownership. Microsoft has put serious teeth behind Satya's "One Microsoft" talk. Employees get raises and promotions now by doing great work and helping others succeed—not by dragging others down as in the bad old days when Steve Ballmer led the company. As we saw in chapter 1, nonfinancial rewards were used to bolster account-ability in the 100,000 Homes Campaign. Becky Margiotta's team gave out dozens of "chicken-f'er awards"—the metal rooster they presented to community members who stepped up and found homes for unhoused people. And Becky's team learned to (gently) ignore those "hollow Easter bunnies" who blabbed about great ideas and plans but never took ownership for turning them into action.

Third, leaders are keenly aware that friction fixing can become an orphan problem when it is treated as something that is "nice" for everyone to help out with but isn't owned by any person or team. To battle this problem, leaders design their projects and organizations so that everyone understands which friction fixing work they are accountable for doing and managing. That's why *The Friction Project* is packed with such "directly responsible individuals," or DRIs, Apple lingo for the person (or team) "responsible for getting the tasks done, making crucial decisions, and keeping the project on track." The buck stops with them, and when questions or concerns arise, the DRI is the go-to person or team. Examples include the administrators in the Cancer Center's CarePoint program, who are responsible for coordinating patient care; Pushkala Subramanian's Center for Simplification Excellence at AstraZeneca during the campaign that saved the company two million hours; and that brave U.S. Department of Defense administrator, Lt. Col. David Shoemaker, who blocked Theranos from installing its unproven blood-testing gizmo on army helicopters (despite pushback from U.S. Army general Jim "Mad Dog" Mattis).

The third leadership principle is *organizational design is the highest form of friction fixing.* Most of the time, leaders don't have the luxury of designing a workplace from scratch. So most must find ways to manage in existing and imperfect systems. The bottom three levels of the Help Pyramid in chapter 3 show how leaders can reduce the damage inflicted by badly designed teams and organizations—problems they can't fix (at least for now). This work entails *reframing* friction troubles as less soul crushing for victims of lousy systems, helping people *navigate* bewildering and broken systems, and *shielding* others from inefficiencies and indignities. This is essential work for leading any friction project because all systems have flaws.

Yet the leaders we celebrate and learn the most from in *The Friction Project* find ways to build better systems—not make the best of crappy ones. That's why we put *neighborhood design and repair* and *system design and repair* at the top two levels of our Help Pyramid. Tweaking and transforming teams and organizations so they don't drive people crazy, don't stifle productivity, and do bolster better decisions, coordination, and innovation is the kind of leadership work that matters most when it comes to friction fixing.

It's also why each of the five chapters at the heart of this book dissects the causes and remedies for a friction trap. Chapters 4 through 8 each focus on solutions for designing and redesigning leadership behavior, employee roles, teams, and organizations. Each is an on-ramp that leaders can use to target their design efforts, including subtraction tools for ridding systems of bad friction, solutions for improving how the roles, teams, and departments in an organization mesh together to avoid coordination snafus, and methods for designing organizations that routinely create constructive friction at the right times and in the right ways.

For many leaders, most such design work is done by their teams. That's not only true for leaders in charge of one team or just a few teams. It's also true for leaders of large and complex organizations because most rely on their executive teams to make and implement systemwide design decisions. Research by the late J. Richard Hackman, who devoted much of his fifty-year career to understanding what drives team performance, shows why team design decisions are so important. Richard's years of research led him to develop the "60–30–10 rule." He found that the day-to-day "tweaking" by team leaders and members only determines about 10 percent of performance. That 30 percent stems from the design at the launch—at least in teams that have a short life, such as the cockpit crews in commercial airlines.

And a whopping 60 percent of performance is determined by what Richard called "prework": ongoing design choices including strategy, size, rewards, norms, routines, rituals, how work is divided up and coordinated, and who makes which decisions. For teams that endure for months and years, ongoing design choices pack an even bigger wallop.

That's why, following Tsedal Neeley's advice about the power of periodic team "relaunches" in chapter 8, well-run teams routinely pause to assess, argue over, and make decisions about what still works and what needs to change in their organization as a whole—not just on their teams. That's what happened when Alcoa CEO Paul O'Neill insisted that employees slow down and focus on improving safety. The ongoing discussions and healthy arguments on the factory floor, in safety meetings, and in committees at Alcoa, and resulting changes in procedures and equipment, not only led to a dramatic decrease in injuries. The associated upswing in communication and psychological safety also generated numerous solutions that boosted Alcoa's innovation, efficiency, and financial performance.

This closing chapter digs deeper into how to lead and implement your friction project—and how, whether your influence is modest or massive, you can build and bolster workplaces where making the right things easier and the wrong things harder are ways of life. We unpack five leadership lessons to live by and to spread to others.

Lessons for Leaders to Live By

1. Focus on the Journey, Not the Destination

"The journey is the reward" is ancient Chinese wisdom that, thanks perhaps to Steve Jobs's affection for it, you've probably heard before.

Most friction fighting adventures have milestones, such as when AstraZeneca set and then exceeded their goal of saving a million hours of employees' time. Yet it's leadership work that never ends. Hard-won lessons from past journeys help you succeed in new ones. Sheri Singer, a veteran Hollywood executive producer of more than forty films, emphasized this point on our *Friction* podcast. After suffering through delays in her early films, Sheri learned how to avoid "the first thing that can go wrong" on shoot days. She explained, "Your talent goes into hair and makeup every morning. And if they don't come out in time, your day starts out and you're late already, right? You're forty-five or fifty minutes late and you haven't started."

Research by Szu-chi Huang and Jennifer Aaker supports our focus on means rather than ends. They conducted six experiments with more than sixteen hundred participants "in activities ranging from dieting and fitness to executive training courses" and found that "thinking of an achieved goal as a journey" made people more likely to continue "behaviors that enabled them to attain their goal." For example, executives who completed an education program in Ghana "went through a thirty-minute exit interview in which they were guided by the interviewer to contemplate and discuss the learning experience using either the journey metaphor, the destination metaphor, or no metaphor at all." A six-month follow-up found that executives prompted with the journey metaphor were more likely to turn their knowledge into action, for example, by "improving supply chains to help their companies scale."

The journey metaphor helps you persist after achieving a milestone because it turns attention to "the ups and downs along the way," what you've learned, and how to handle similar challenges in the future—rather than celebrating your achievement and slacking off. As Steve Jobs said, "I think if you do something and it turns out pretty good, then you should go do something else wonderful, not dwell on it for too long." He understood the hazards of fixating on how fantastic it will be to achieve a goal and resting on your laurels when you do.

2. Link Little Things to Big Things

Zen in the Art of Archery provides a lovely analogy to help leaders focus on the journey rather than the destination during friction projects. And to concentrate on doing the right little things along the way that, when woven together, fuel ongoing success. Author and philosopher Eugen Herrigel lived in Japan in the 1920s and studied archery under Zen master Awa Kenzo. It took Herrigel years to grasp the joys and nuances of breathing properly, attaching the string, putting the arrow in the bow, waiting a few moments to clear his mind, drawing the arrow back, releasing it, and watching its flight—and not to "grieve over bad shots" or "rejoice over the good ones." By doing so, he took pleasure from each little task, and because he mastered the details, he hit the target more often, too.

The lesson from Eugen Herrigel, and leaders including Sheri Singer and Steve Jobs, is that they not only focus on the journey, they obsess along the way over the *right* little things that, when fused together, lead to success. For Sheri, it was learning the key warning signs that her tight film schedule was about to slip and when to take preventive action.

Steve Jobs was renowned for linking little things to big things. A former senior Apple executive told us that Steve spent hours and hours arguing and dreaming up prototypes with Ron Johnson (who led retail operations) about every tiny detail of the customer experience at Apple Stores—including how to eliminate needless friction, make visits inspiring and fun, and display products to look beautiful and irresistible. One result was that

Apple Stores eliminated cash registers. Instead, employees with handheld devices move around the store and help customers select, set up, and buy products on the spot—eliminating steps including waiting in line to pay for their purchases.

To propel friction fixing, your job is to fret over and keep tweaking the little steps that you, your team, and your customers take. And, along the way, to draw on lessons from those moments of discomfort, conflict, and pleasure. It helps you enjoy the journey, figure out which little things to link to big things, and pump up your chances of long-term success.

3. Put "Grease People" and "Gunk People" in the Right Places

Even if your organization is well designed in other ways, friction problems will fester and flare up if the right people aren't in the right roles. To avert such troubles, skilled leaders work to put "grease people" in places where friction ought to be low and "gunk people" in places where friction ought to be high. Research on personality and culture reveal differences in responses to *rules, risk,* and *monitoring* that can help you figure out where people (including you) fall on our grease-gunk continuum:

Grease People	Gunk People
Rules: "Unbureaucratic personalities" or "Chaos Muppets" who ignore, bend, defy, and remove rules, norms, and traditions.	**Rules:** "Bureaucratic personalities" or "Order Muppets" who follow, create, and enforce rules, norms, and traditions.
Risk: Comfortable with taking chances, focus on the upside of trying new things. Encourage others to take risky actions.	**Risk:** Uncomfortable with taking chances, focus on what can go wrong, hesitate to try new things. Discourage others from taking risky actions.
Monitoring: Scrutinize others lightly. Quick to trust others and assume good intent. Downplay and encourage errors, setbacks, and rule breaking.	**Monitoring:** Scrutinize others closely. Wary about trusting others and assume bad intent. Call out and punish errors, setbacks, and rule breaking.

In *Rule Makers, Rule Breakers,* psychologist Michele Gelfand documents how those we call "grease people" bolster creativity by embracing failure and setbacks and taking pride bending and breaking rules. Michele's research reminds us of the creative teams that pitch stories for Pixar's animated films. They take pride in bouncing back from one failed pitch after another. And in trying ridiculous things, such as a story about a rat who cooks great French food, and for their research, interviewing a woman who lives with thirty-six rats. Or the veteran Disney "imagineers" who were undaunted by all their failed prototypes, and who enjoyed making senior executives squirm by developing Space Mountain, an indoor roller coaster that was more disorienting and frightening than any past Disney attraction.

Yet, to maintain and operate Space Mountain, you want gunk people, who are bent on enforcing proven safety procedures, abhor putting guests at risk, and monitor one another closely to stomp out errors or forbidden improvisations. Similarly, we love the antics of Tom Cruise's "Maverick" character in the *Top Gun* movies, such as flying upside down, under bridges, and within inches of other planes. But we don't want our United Airlines pilot doing that stuff.

Dahlia Lithwick made a similar distinction in *Slate* with her tongue-in-cheek Muppet Theory: "Every living human can be classified according to one simple metric: every one of us is either a Chaos Muppet or an Order Muppet." Chaos Muppets including Cookie Monster and Ernie are "out-of-control, emotional, volatile." Order Muppets such as Bert and Kermit the Frog are "neurotic, highly regimented, averse to surprises." Dahlia argues that neither is superior to the other. Chaos and Order Muppets balance one another out because "a well-functioning family and a productive place of work" need both the flexibility and spontaneity that comes from breaking rules and taking risks and the stability and safety provided by rules and plans.

Leisha DeHart-Davis's study of government employees in four U.S. cities found that civil servants with "unbureaucratic personalities," who routinely bent and broke rules, were a useful counterforce to their rigid counterparts with "bureaucratic personalities." Such as the "unbureaucratic" foreman who confessed, "Only streets that are dedicated to the city are supposed to be maintained by the city. But if there's a hole in town, whether it's dedicated or not, I deal with it. I'll just sneak out and fill the hole. I try to make the town look better." If every civil servant flaunted every rule, inefficiency and confusion would be rampant. But having a few employees like that foreman who defied rigid rules for the greater good made that town a safer and more attractive place.

Friction fixers also coach, critique, and, when necessary, banish destructive grease and gunk people. In well-run organizations, even the most powerful executives are held accountable for their sins, including those committed by gunk people who clog up organizations. Like the workplace vigilantes studied by Katy DeCelles and Karl Aquino who appoint themselves "judge, jury, and deliverer of justice" and punish and tattle on colleagues and customers for petty and imagined offenses.

Leaders who are friction fixers don't let these sadistic Order Muppets get away with their antics. That's what happened to one rule freak who plagued us for years. When we tried to spend Stanford funds on legitimate expenses such as teaching assistants, a manager we'll call Larry routinely laid down a gauntlet of unnecessary bureaucratic hoops and treated us as if we were criminals. Then Larry got a new boss, who advised him that, sure, everyone must follow Stanford rules. But his job was to reduce, not inflict, friction on people who do the organization's work. That boss kept a close eye on Larry and coached him to desist when he created unnecessary ordeals. Magically, within months, the worst of Larry's obstruction stopped.

Larry's boss also realized that this Order Muppet didn't feel appreciated and took care to praise his work. Research led by Nate Fast suggests that such respect may have helped Larry abandon his vigilante ways—because some gunk people frustrate and demean others as payback for their lack of prestige. In Nate's experiment, some undergraduates were randomly assigned as "Workers" and told that their job entailed menial tasks and that fellow students "tend to look down on the Worker role and don't have admiration or respect for it." Other undergraduates were assigned as "Idea Producers" and told that they performed crucial tasks and that fellow students looked up to them. Then, students in each group dictated one or more hoops that a partner had to jump through to qualify for a $50 drawing—selected from a list of ten choices presented to them by the researchers. These hoops ranged from activities that weren't demeaning at all ("Tell the experimenter a funny joke") to creepy and humiliating ("Say, 'I am filthy,' five times" and "Bark like a dog three times"). The lowly Workers took out their resentment by imposing more demeaning hoops.

So, if your organization is plagued by vigilantes who make you jump through hoops akin to "Say, 'I am filthy,' five times" consider how they are treated. Are they ignored or underappreciated? If so, firing them isn't the answer; their replacements will probably act the same way. Try what Larry's boss did and show them some respect.

4. The Best Friction Fixers Are Friction Shifters

The best leaders and teams, despite their predilections for grease or gunk, learn what to make easy, hard, or impossible and how to switch between modes. They avoid being held hostage by their inner Chaos or Order Muppet and master the craft of friction shifting, which includes using "friction forensics"—those eight diagnostic questions in chapter 2 for assessing what ought to be hard and what ought to be easy.

Jeff Bezos, Amazon's founder and former CEO, champions a variation of our question "Is failure cheap, safe, reversible, and instructive?" Jeff asks whether decisions are "one-way" or "two-way" doors. As he wrote Amazon shareholders in 2015, one-way doors are "consequential and irreversible or nearly irreversible." Such as selling or buying a company, where "if you walk through and don't like what you see on the other side, you can't get back to where you were before." So, "these decisions must be made methodically, carefully, slowly, with great deliberation and consultation." In contrast, two-way doors require less friction because "they are changeable, reversible." That means "you can reopen the door and go back through."

The organizational redesign at IDEO that we talked about in

chapter 1 is a good example of a two-way door. CEO David Kelley calmed employees (and made them laugh) by shaving off his trademark Groucho Marx mustache. And telling them that, just as he could grow back his mustache, IDEO's new studio model was reversible.

Jeff argued that big companies that apply a heavyweight, high-friction decision process to two-way doors are doomed to invent less because they move too slowly. He added that small companies that use a lightweight decision process for one-way doors are screwing up, too, and will "go extinct before they get large." In short, when decision-makers get stuck in either gunk or grease mode, the road ahead is rough.

Leading friction shifting in your team or organization also requires sending clear signals that it's time for more or less friction, making sure your intentions are understood and shape behavior. You may believe that others hear your message, but as chapter 4 shows, people, especially those with a lot of power, often have a dim understanding of how others interpret and respond to their decisions, orders, and suggestions. Organizations muddy the waters further by pummeling people with confusing, conflicting, and excessive information—making it tough to distinguish "signal" from "noise." That means, to trigger friction shifting, a leader's job is to craft simple and crisp signals that it's time to work in grease or gunk mode.

That's what Paul Anderson did in 1998 when he became CEO of BHP, a giant Australian mining and energy company that was losing billions of dollars a year. Paul implemented big changes, including closing unprofitable operations, improving safety, and working with fellow executives to write a charter that spelled out the company's strategy and "values, goals, and paths to success." By 2001, BHP posted a record $2.2 billion in profits, and the employee injury rate had fallen by nearly 30 percent.

Paul told us, when you take charge of a troubled company, "you have to assess the situation rather than act quickly. Everyone wants you to do something, so the first thing you say, very calmly, is, 'We're not going to do anything today.'" During his first months on the job, Paul hit the brakes and asked "each of the top eighty people in the company to write a two-page document that answered, first, 'Who are you? What are you responsible for?' And then: 'What issues do you believe are most pressing? What would you do if you were me?'" After speaking to all eighty and figuring out what was broken, who the best (and worst) people were, and what was required to fix BHP, Paul let his charges know that it was time to shift gears and start those changes, which, in just a few years, turned the company around.

5. Friction Fixing Is Fueled by Civility, Caring, and Love

We've documented how you, as a friction fixer, can make strategic use of emotions, including warmth, laughter, disdain, and fury. We've shown how to detect and shape the emotions felt by people in your "cone of friction," to dampen their aggravation and despair, and to crank up their psychological safety. A related leadership lesson we've implied is that friction fixing is accelerated by shared civility, caring, and love. When such emotions pervade an organization, people form stronger bonds, develop trust, focus on the best qualities of colleagues and customers, and devote more energy to helping others and less to satisfying their selfish needs.

Civility, caring, and love reflect a rough hierarchy of collective compassion. As Christine Porath documents in *Mastering Civility*, when organizations are plagued with rudeness, it causes employee commitment, cooperation, and coordination to plummet. While tensions, disagreements, and power struggles rear their ugly heads in every group and organization, that doesn't mean that people are destined to treat one another like dirt. As Peter Drucker said, "It is a law of nature that two moving bodies in contact with each other create friction." But civility can help bring out the best in people because, as Drucker put it, "manners are the lubricating oil of an organization." When employees—and the customers and citizens they serve—treat one another with outward respect, it helps everyone avoid open warfare and backstabbing, resolve (or at least tolerate) tensions, and be more amenable to collaboration.

Christine's research confirms that when civility is pervasive, employees get more done; they go the extra mile to help others and enjoy better physical and mental health. Christine dissects how leaders build civil cultures by modeling desired behaviors, hiring, rewarding, and promoting people for civility, and developing programs that spread respectful actions. She shows how seemingly small interventions pack a wallop. Like the upswing in civility at Ochsner Health in Louisiana. It was sparked partly by the "Ochsner 10/5 way," which means if an employee is within ten feet of a colleague or patient, the employee is expected to make eye contact and smile. And to say hello if the employee is within five feet.

Every organization (and family) would be more civil if we all followed Christine's advice when we encounter a difficult person: "Before shutting down, saying no, or displaying frustration, try to appreciate where the other person is. You might even go one step further and ask yourself, *How can I help them?*"

Caring is a more powerful form of collective compassion than civility. It entails deeper empathy and concern than surface civil behavior. In caring cultures, people feel obligated to help others avoid and overcome obstacles—they expect one another to take that extra step Christine suggested. That's why Garry

Ridge, who served as CEO of WD-40 for twenty-five years, talks about two kinds of lubricants: the spray oil his company sells in those blue cans with the red top *and* the power of WD-40's culture of caring.

Garry says, when he took charge in 1997, too many managers tried to squeeze the most out of people with fear, which damaged their productivity, undermined their trust, and left them unhappy at the end of each workday. Garry revamped WD-40 and filled it with leaders who put people first. Garry says such collective caring oils the company's wheels in two ways. The first is "I care about you enough to reward you and applaud you doing great work," which fuels pride, effort, and cooperation. The second is "I'm also brave enough to redirect you when the work you're doing isn't helping you succeed." When leaders help others flourish, they avoid what Kim Scott calls "ruinous empathy": fuzzy, sugarcoated critiques and fake praise that prevents individual learning and organizational improvement. At WD-40, caring entails *radical candor,* which is the title of Kim's book. That means telling people the hard truths so they can learn from mistakes and amplify strengths—and doing so in ways that leave them feeling supported and respected.

Garry believes this culture of caring and candor is the key reason that, during his tenure, WD-40's revenues tripled and shareholder return grew at an average annual rate. Garry is especially proud of employee surveys that showed 97 percent of WD-40 employees respect their "coach" (their term for a boss).

Research led by the late Sigal Barsade explored cultures of "companionate love," workplaces with strong "feelings of affection, compassion, caring, and tenderness for others." Sigal's surveys of thirty-two hundred employees in seventeen organizations from seven industries found when "employees felt and expressed companionate love toward one another, people reported greater job satisfaction, commitment, and personal accountability for work performance." Her sixteen-month study of a long-term care facility found, in units with cultures of companionate love, employee teamwork was superior and burnout was lower. Patients also reported being more satisfied with the quality of care in their lives, they were in better moods, and they took fewer unnecessary trips to the emergency room.

Todd Park, who—as we saw in chapter 6—is renowned for leading the charge to fix the Obamacare website, believes that love is the secret ingredient for banishing bad friction. In 2017, Todd and his brother Ed launched Devoted Health to help older Americans get "all-in-one healthcare" with a "coordinated system" that weaves together benefits including care from doctors and dentists, prescription medicines, over-the-counter health products such as toothpaste and vitamins, and eyewear. Devoted Health helps seniors navigate the convoluted and "discombobulated" U.S. healthcare system. Todd says, "While it may seem impossible to understand and get around the system, that's what Devoted is designed to do."

Todd is vehement that a marriage of love and logistics is crucial to designing and operating Devoted's system—so that customers are treated with care, affection, and tenderness by employees, are spared absurd waiting times and other ordeals, and get every penny they deserve. Devoted's mission is to "work like crazy to care for everyone like we would for own mom." Todd adds, "The standing order for the whole company is, when doing any action or making any decision, 'Close your eyes, imagine the face of someone in your family you love desperately, and ask yourself if you were making the decision to impact him or her directly, what would you do?'"

Parting Thought: Expect and Embrace the Mess

Back in about 2012, we had a friend who worked at Facebook (now Meta). She read several articles about how employees loved their "move-fast-and-break-things" culture and how it fueled ultrafast and effective product development. She laughed and said, "That sounds like a great company, I wish I worked there." Every organization, no matter how celebrated or profitable, stumbles and makes key actions too hard or too easy—and pisses off employees and customers. After we gave a speech at a big law firm, a partner told us about "the grass is browner club" that he'd formed at the firm with several of his current partners. The members of that club had all, in recent years, left for seemingly greener pastures at other law firms. These quitters left because they were disgusted with how hard it was to get things done in the firm, and because of other problems including power struggles and unfair compensation. Each partner returned because, as they learned the hard way, the grass was browner in their new firms.

Our last lesson, then, is that smart friction fixers expect organizational life to be messy, try to clean up what they can, and embrace (or at least endure) the rest. That means accepting that, as those lawyers did, no matter where you are, there will always be unavoidable and aggravating friction. As that partner who told us about the "grass is browner club" suggested, it helps to remember the old military acronym SNAFU (Situation Normal: All Fucked Up): although some places are better or worse than others, it describes every organization. That's the advice we've heard from David Kelley again and again over the past twenty-five years about the organizations he's founded and led. He tells frustrated and confused people (including us) at IDEO and the Stanford d.school, "Life is messy sometimes. Sometimes the best you can do is to accept that it is a mess, try to love it as much as you can, and move forward."

Clara Shih is the founding CEO and executive chair of Hearsay Systems and the CEO of Salesforce AI. She agrees "with the notion of embracing the mess while working to clean it up." Clara adds that, especially when you are doing something new, even though you don't know which messes will arise, it's best to expect that things will go wrong. Rather than being shocked or freaking out, be ready to make repairs if you can, but as David Kelley suggests, keep moving forward through the muck.

Clara suggests three methods to fortify people for impending messes, which she used when Hearsay Systems launched its first product and continues to refine at Hearsay and Salesforce. The first is "We had every team member brainstorm ahead of time what might go right and what might go wrong." That prepared people to be on the lookout for unexpected opportunities and troubles, to see their jobs as making the best out of every surprise, and to develop ways to tackle messes they didn't believe were likely—but might just rear their ugly heads.

The second method echoes Becky Margiotta's Times Square approach in the 100,000 Homes Campaign—getting the prototype right (or at least less wrong) before you go big. Clara's Hearsay team "decided to launch to a smaller group first before opening it to the public, which allowed us to practice cleaning up a smaller mess before creating a bigger mess."

Third, and finally, Clara designated certain team members to clean up messes, such as "fixing bugs in real time." She assigned other engineers to focus on developing new features and other promising solutions. Clara explained, "In computer science, we call this 'separation of concerns' because the cleanup crew could focus on the mess and other engineers could devote their energy to imagining what just might go well and as expected."

Like so many other leaders we've learned from in *The Friction Project,* Clara takes responsibility for making the right things easier and the wrong things harder. She behaves as if it's on her to help curate solutions that are tailored to her companies' troubles, opportunities, and idiosyncrasies. By doing so, and enticing others to join her on the journey, Clara believes that she will build better companies and that their employees and customers will live better lives.

That's what it takes to be a friction fixer.

Acknowledgments

Many people helped us during the long journey that created *The Friction Project*. This seven-year adventure was sparked, shaped, and nourished by advice, questions, and critiques from hundreds of people, including students, colleagues, friends, relatives, and friction fixers from organizations of every stripe. We thank each of you and apologize to those we have omitted. We couldn't have written this book without you.

For starters, we thank our wonderful academic colleagues. Rebecca Hinds played key roles at every stage in this adventure. First as a research assistant when she was a Stanford graduate student, then as a coauthor of multiple articles, and lately, since completing her Ph.D., in her role as head of Asana's Work Innovation Lab, leading friction-fixing interventions including the "meeting reset" and "collaboration cleanse." We are grateful to Rebecca for her warmth, encouragement, imagination, and relentless hard work during this long and sometimes trying journey.

We thank John Lilly, a venture capitalist at Greylock and board chair at Code for America, and Sujay Jaswa, founder of WndrCo. We are grateful for their wisdom about friction, especially when teaching with Huggy in their Stanford Graduate School of Business (GSB) course "People Operations: From Startup to Scaleup." Huggy also thanks Michael Ross, former chief human resources officer at Visa, and Prasad Setty, former vice president of People Analytics at Google, for their insights about friction when they teach "Disruptions to the World of Work: A Lab for Startup Hypotheses" together at Stanford GSB.

Other supportive Stanford colleagues over the years include Steve Barley, Tom Byers, Peter Glynn, Lindy Greer, David Kelley, Perry Klebahn, Laura McBain, Maggie Neale, Charles O'Reilly III, Jeffrey Pfeffer, Bernie Roth, Lisa Solomon, Sarah Stein Greenberg, Tina Seelig, Sarah Soule, Baba Shiv, Jeremy Utley, Kathryn Velcich, and Melissa Valentine. Bob thanks Pamela Hinds (chair of Stanford's Department of Management Science and Engineering) and Jennifer Widom (dean of the Stanford Engineering School) for their support, humor, and tolerance of his quirks and flaws. Huggy thanks Dean Jonathan Levin and Senior Associate Dean Amit Seru at Stanford GSB for their encouragement and support.

Davina Drabkin, David Hoyt, and Julie Makinen at Stanford GSB did the writing and research for many cases that we've drawn on for this book—they are masters of this craft and a delight to work with. And we thank their GSB colleagues, including Mehrdad Azim and Justin Willow, for helping to produce these multimedia cases. We are indebted to the spirited team at the Stanford Technology Ventures Program who produced two seasons of the Friction Podcast in 2016 and 2017, especially Matt Harvey, Asher Julkowski, Ali Rico, Eli Shell, and Ryan Shiba. We thank Owen Modeste, Ronie Shilo, and Robyn Woodman from the Stanford Center for Professional Development who have supported our various harebrained ideas for learning and teaching about leadership, scaling, and friction—

notably the "The Fixers" webinars (once called "The Shitfixers") in 2022 and 2023. Bob appreciates the support from dedicated staffers at Stanford's Department of Management Science & Engineering, including Lori Cottle, Jim Fabry, Sarah Michaelis, and information technology guru extraordinaire Tim Keely. Huggy especially appreciates Tina Bernard and Jeannine Williams, both role models of excellence.

A host of former and current Stanford students supported and taught us in varied ways, including Sarah Alexander, Deirdre Clute, Bob Eberhart, Liz Gerber, Olivia Hallisey, Paul Leonardi, Steven Li, Katharina Lix, Joachim Lyon, Govind Manian, Danielle Pensack, Olivia Rosenthal, Jeff Spight, Ryan Stice-Lusvardi, Bobbi Thomason, Monica Tsien, Elizabeth Woodson, Ron Tidhar, and Joe Tobin.

A number of colleagues outside of Stanford shaped our ideas in crucial ways. Adam Grant (Wharton Business School) was supportive at every turn, and we hope he will forgive us for not naming this book "The Shitfixers." When we needed help with ideas, introductions, or emotional support, we could always count on Rob Cross (Babson College), Jerry Davis (University of Michigan), Katy DeCelles (Rotman School of Management), Amy Edmondson (Harvard Business School), Leidy Klotz (University of Virginia), Rita McGrath (Columbia Business School), Christine Porath (Georgetown University), and Tsedal Neeley (Harvard Business School). Bob offers special thanks to his late mentor and dissertation advisor Robert L. Kahn, who lived to be one hundred years old and was a model of graceful and productive aging, for his warmth, wisdom, and unwavering support.

The research and writing for this book entailed constant conversation with executives, technologists, advisors, authors, and consultants who wrestled with and fixed all kinds of friction troubles. There were hundreds, perhaps thousands, and we apologize to those we haven't listed. We thank Jennifer Anastasoff (executive director, Tech Talent Project), Michael Arena (former chief talent officer, General Motors), Safi Bahcall (author of *Loonshots*), Michael Brennan (CEO, Civilla), Shona Brown (former Google executive vice president), Ed Catmull (former Pixar president), Amy Coleman (corporate vice president, Microsoft), Michael Dearing (founder, Harrison Metal), Karen Dillon (coauthor of *The Microstress Effect*), Irina Egorova (cofounder Teamraderie), V. R. Fersoe (senior vice president, SAP), Kaye Foster (advisor, board member, and former head of HR at Johnson & Johnson and Onyx), Carl Liebert (veteran senior executive at companies including 24-Hour Fitness, Home Depot, and USAA), Ben Horowitz (cofounder of Andreessen-Horowitz), Drew Houston (CEO, Dropbox), Becky Margiotta (cofounder and president, Billions Institute), Joe McCannon (cofounder, Billions Institute), Michael McCarroll (CEO, Teamraderie), Lenny Mendonca (former chief economic and business advisor at State of California and owner of the Half Moon Bay Brewing Company), Shantanu Narayen (CEO, Adobe), Josh Nicholls (Microsoft), Thuan Pham (former CTO, Uber), Joel Podolny (CEO, Honor Education), Dominic Price (Atlassian), Diego Rodriguez (former IDEO partner and Intuit executive), David Sanford (CEO, Hypothesis Fund), Adam Selzer (cofounder, Civilla), Lena Selzer (cofounder, Civilla), Bonny Simi (head of air operations and people, Joby Aviation), Peter Sims (founder and CEO, Black Sheep), Kim Scott (author of *Radical Candor*), Clara Shih (CEO, Salesforce AI), Beth Steinberg (chief people officer, Chime), Deb Stern (publicist extraordinaire), Pushkala Subramaniam (former vice president at AstraZeneca), Ben Wigert (director of research and strategy, Gallup), and Chris Yeh (coauthor of *Blitzscaling* and all-around creative person).

We are also grateful to Tom Neilssen and Les Tuerk from Bright-Sight for working with us to arrange workshops and speeches, which helped to develop our ideas about friction and many other matters. Bob is also grateful to Charlotte Perman, Sondra Ulin, and Daria Wagganer for helping to arrange his speaking engagements.

This book would not have survived the journey from half-baked idea, to proposal, to finished manuscript without our relentless and practical literary agent—Christy Fletcher—who has served as guide, friend, and shield. We appreciate the remarkable support provided by her colleagues at Fletcher & Company, which is now part of the United Talent Agency. Sarah Fuentes edited multiple versions of our book proposal—she repaired the language and logic and asked the hard questions. We are also grateful to the help provided by Christy's talented colleagues, including Melissa Chinchillo, Victoria Hobbs, and Yona Levin.

Tim Bartlett, our editor at St. Martin's Press, has remarkable skill and patience. He is the best editor we've ever worked with at spotting and fixing big problems, while at the same time working on the little changes in words and sentences that help carry the reader along. We thank him for putting up with our quirks, worries, nagging, and occasional crankiness. We are also grateful to Kevin Reilly, who helped us produce and improve this manuscript and shepherded it through production at St. Martin's. And for Laura Clark's wisdom about how to get people to notice and buy this book and apply the ideas to their workplaces.

Bob gives his love to his three adult children, Tyler, Claire, and Eve, for putting up with their father's obsession with another book—and offering so much encouragement, even though he is a strange man who, in their view, serves long stretches of solitary confinement in the garage. Huggy is grateful to his brothers, Sandila and Bhargava, for how they so generously helped with elder care and reduced friction for all.

Finally, *The Friction Project* would never have been written without our loving and (usually) patient wives, Marina and Sadhna. They were our not-very-silent partners through every twist and turn of this long adventure. These remarkable women gave us affection and encouragement, shielded us from demands, taught us what ought to be hard and easy in life, and, as we finished the book, Marina gave us precious advice that improved the language on nearly every page. We dedicate our book to these two skilled and caring friction fixers.

Teach Us More, Learn More

Dear Reader,

The publication of *The Friction Project* is a major milestone on our learning journey about how people can make the right things easier and the wrong things harder in organizations. But it's not the end. We invite you to join us as this adventure continues. Tell us about the lessons you've learned about fixing friction troubles in your workplace. Share your stories, studies, and ideas about how friction fixers can practice their craft. We'd love to hear your questions and feedback. You can reach us at bob@bobsutton.net. Note that, by sending us your story, comment, or observation, you are giving us permission to use it in the things we write and say. But we promise not to use your name unless you give us explicit permission.

Please visit our websites at bobsutton.net and huggyrao.com to read about what we've been learning and fretting over lately. You can follow Sutton (@work_matters) and Rao (@huggyrao) on Twitter. Or, better yet, follow and connect with Sutton (linkedin.com/in/bobsutton1/) and Rao (linkedin.com/in/hayagreevarao/) on LinkedIn.

Thanks so much. We look forward to hearing from you and to continuing the friction project together.

ROBERT I. SUTTON
HUGGY RAO
Stanford University

Notes

Introduction

3. **all 1,266 words:** This email was sent by Stanford vice-provost and dean of research Kathyrn Ann Moler to "all university tenure line faculty" (including the two authors) on January 25, 2021, and was titled "More Details on Faculty Input on the New School."

5. **convoluted forty-two-page:** "Project Re:form: Removing Barriers to Benefits by Transforming the Longest Assistance Application in America," Civilla, https://civilla.org/work/project-reform-case-study.

5. **three hundred thousand hours:** Marcus Buckingham and Ashley Goodall, "Reinventing Performance Management," *Harvard Business Review* 93, no. 4 (2015): 40–50.

7. **"meeting reset":** Rebecca Hinds and Robert I. Sutton, "Meeting Overload Is a Fixable Problem," *Harvard Business Review*, October 28, 2022, https://hbr.org/2022/10/meeting-overload-is-a-fixable-problem.

7. **"Alexa, can you play dollhouse":** Jennifer Earl, "6-Year-Old Orders $160 Dollhouse, 4 Pounds of Cookies with Amazon's Echo Dot," CBS News, January 5, 2017, www.cbsnews.com/news/6-year-old-brooke-neitzel-orders-dollhouse-cookies-with-amazon-echo-dot-alexa/.

8. **Google Glass prototype:** Nick Bilton, "Why Google Glass Broke," *New York Times*, February 4, 2015, www.nytimes.com/2015/02/05/style/why-google-glass-broke.html.

9. **Ed believes:** Personal communication between Ed Catmull and the authors, July 6, 2022.

10. **"robotic bureaucracy":** Barry Bozeman and Jan Youtie, "Robotic Bureaucracy: Administrative Burden and Red Tape in University Research," *Public Administration Review* 80, no. 1 (2020): 157–62.

10. **leaders at Jumbo:** Adita Bora, "Dutch Supermarket Introduces Unique Slow Checkout Lane for Lonely Seniors Who Want to Have a Chat," *Upworthy*, December 9, 2022, https://scoop.upworthy.com/dutch-supermarket-introduces-a-unique-slow-checkout-lane-to-help-fight-loneliness.

10. **"labor leads to love"**: Michael I. Norton, Daniel Mochon, and Dan Ariely, "The IKEA Effect: When Labor Leads to Love," *Journal of Consumer Psychology* 22, no. 3 (2012): 453–60.

11. **Drucker was right:** David J. Hickson and Derek S. Pugh, *Great Writers on Organizations: The Third Omnibus Edition* (Aldershot, UK: Gower, 2012), 163.

Our Friction Project

13. **tracked close to two thousand agile teams:** Rebecca Hinds and Hayagreeva Rao, "Core Teams in Multiteam Systems: An Observational Study of Performance," working paper, Graduate School of Business, Stanford University, 2019.

13. **"prenups for start-ups":** Andrea Freund et al., "Enabling Success or Cementing Failure: When and Why Team Charters Help or Hurt Team Performance," working paper, Graduate School of Business, Stanford University, 2021.

14. **AstraZeneca saved two million hours:** Hayagreeva Rao and Julie Makinen, "AstraZeneca: Scaling Simplification," case HR45 (Stanford, Calif.: Stanford Graduate School of Business, 2017), www.gsb.stanford.edu/faculty-research/case -studies/astrazeneca-scaling-simplification.

14. **CEO at BHP:** Robert I. Sutton, "The CEO Who Led a Turnaround Wearing a Helmet," *Harvard Business Review*, November 22, 2013, https://hbr.org/2013/11 /the-ceo-who-led-a-turnaround-without-wearing-a-helmet.

14. **Uber got in big trouble:** Hayagreeva Rao, Robert I. Sutton, and Julie Makinen, *Uber: Repaying Technical and Organizational Debt* (Stanford, Calif.: Stanford Graduate School of Business, 2018).

14. **"How Bosses Waste Their Employees' Time":** Robert I. Sutton, "How Bosses Waste Their Employees' Time," *Wall Street Journal*, August 12, 2018, www.wsj .com/articles/how-bosses-waste-their-employees-time-1534126140.

14. **"Too Many Teams":** Robert I. Sutton and Ben Wigert, "Too Many Teams, Too Many Bosses: Overcoming Matrix Madness," Gallup.com, October 19, 2021, www .gallup.com/workplace/354935/teams-bosses-overcoming-matrix-madness.aspx.

14. **"Our To-Do Lists":** Leidy Klotz and Robert I. Sutton, "Our To-Do Lists Can't Grow Forever. It's Time to Try Subtraction," *Times Higher Education*, March 24, 2022, www.timeshighereducation.com/blog/our-do-lists-cant-grow-forever-its-time-try -subtraction.

14. **"Why Your Job":** Bob Sutton, "Why Your Job Is Becoming Impossible to Do: The Tragedy of Well-Intentioned Organizational Overload," LinkedIn, December 17, 2015, www.linkedin.com/pulse/why-your-job-becoming-impossible-do-tragedy -overload-bob-sutton/.

14. **"How Do You End a Meeting?":** Bob Sutton, "How Do You End a Meeting? Netflix's HR Rebel Asks Two Simple Questions," LinkedIn, February 10, 2015, www.linkedin.com/pulse/how-do-you-end-meeting-netflixs-hr-rebel-asks-two -simple-bob-sutton/.

14. **"Meeting Overload Is a Fixable Problem":** Rebecca Hinds and Robert I. Sutton, "Meeting Overload Is a Fixable Problem," *Harvard Business Review*, October 28, 2022, https://hbr.org/2022/10/meeting-overload-is-a-fixable-problem.

14. *Parkinson's Law:* C. Northcote Parkinson, *Parkinson's Law* (London: Murray, 1957).

15. *The Mythical Man-Month:* Frederick P. Brooks, Jr., *The Mythical Man-Month,* anniversary ed. (White Plains, N.Y.: Addison-Wesley Professional, 1995).

15. **Sludge:** Cass R. Sunstein, *Sludge: What Stops Us from Getting Things Done and What to Do About It* (Cambridge, Mass.: MIT Press, 2021).

15. *Administrative Burden:* Pamela Herd and Donald P. Moynihan, *Administrative Burden: Policymaking by Other Means* (New York: Russell Sage Foundation, 2019).

16. **Leidy Klotz's *Subtract*:** Leidy Klotz, *Subtract: The Untapped Science of Less* (New York: Flatiron Books, 2021).

16. **"rule of halves":** Klotz and Sutton. "Our To-Do Lists."

16. *Necessity of Friction:* Nordal Åkerman, *The Necessity of Friction* (New York: Routledge, 2018).

17. **"Friction: A Manifesto":** Huggy Rao and Kate Larson, "Friction: A Manifesto," Filene, June 15, 2020, https://filene.org/learn-something/reports/friction-a-manifesto.

17. **Saul Gurdus and Elizabeth Woodson:** Robert I. Sutton and David Hoyt, "Better Service, Faster: A Design Thinking Case Study," *Harvard Business Review,* January 6, 2016, https://hbr.org/2016/01/better-service-faster-a-design-thinking-case-study.

18. **Adam put it:** Based on our online video interview with Adam and Lena Selzer, March 16, 2022.

18. **Project Re:form:** "Project Re:form."

18. *Friction* **podcast:** Bob Sutton, *Friction Podcast on Organizational Culture,* https://ecorner.stanford.edu/series/friction/.

18. *Lean Startup:* Eric Reis, *The Lean Startup* (New York: Crown Business, 2011).

19. **43 percent of their time:** Krisda H. Chaiyachati et al., "Assessment of In-patient Time Allocation Among First-Year Internal Medicine Residents Using Time-Motion Observations," *JAMA Internal Medicine* 179, no. 6 (2019): 760–67.

20. **Getting Rid of Stupid Stuff:** Melinda Ashton, "Getting Rid of Stupid Stuff," *New England Journal of Medicine* 379, no. 19 (2018): 1789–91.

21. *Thinking, Fast and Slow:* Daniel Kahneman, *Thinking, Fast and Slow* (New York: Macmillan, 2011).

21. **Waze CEO:** Noam Bardin, "What's a Start-Up CEO's Real Job?" LinkedIn, January 3, 2015, www.linkedin.com/pulse/what-early-stage-startup-ceos-real-job-noam-bardin/.

22. *Bad Blood:* John Carreyrou, *Bad Blood* (Paris: Larousse, 2019).

22. **Cloosterman–van Eerd:** "Dutch Market Introduces a Chat Checkout Lane for Seniors to Combat Loneliness," *La Voce di New York,* January 24, 2023, https://lavocedinewyork.com/en/lifestyles/2023/01/24/dutch-market-introduces-a-chat-checkout-lane-for-seniors-to-combat-loneliness/.

23. **human penchant to add:** Gabrielle S. Adams et al., "People Systematically Overlook Subtractive Changes," *Nature* 592, no. 7853 (2021): 258–61.

24. **"I own the place and the place owns me":** Robert I. Sutton and Hayagreeva Rao, *Scaling Up Excellence: Getting to More Without Settling for Less* (New York: Random House, 2016), 144.

Chapter 1: A Trustee of Others' Time

29. **"Brevity" memo:** Laura Cowdrey, "Churchill's Call for Brevity," National Archives, October 17, 2013.

30. **"Armeetingeddon":** Rebecca Hinds and Bob Sutton, "Dropbox's Secret for Saving Time in Meetings," *Inc.,* March 11, 2015, www.inc.com/rebecca-hinds-and-bob-sutton/dropbox-secret-for-saving-time-in-meetings.html.

31. **Rohm and Haas:** Elena Lytinkia Botelho and Sanja Kos, "Unexpected Companies Produce Some of the Best CEOs," *Harvard Business Review,* January 10, 2022, https://hbr.org/2020/01/unexpected-companies-produce-some-of-the-best-ceos.

32. **Dr. Macarena C. García:** Macarena C. García et al., "Declines in Opioid Prescribing after a Private Insurer Policy Change—Massachusetts, 2011–2015," *Morbidity and Mortality Weekly Report* 65, no. 41 (2016): 1125–31.

32. **systemic changes:** For example, see State of California, Department of Motor Vehicles, "Improving the Department of Motor Vehicles," Work Action Plans, April 23, 2019, https://htv-prod-media.s3.amazonaws.com/files/improving-the-department-of-motor-vehicles-final-042319-1-1557879964.pdf.

35. **David Kelley:** These observations of IDEO are based on an eighteen-month ethnography of the company conducted by Robert Sutton and Andrew Hargadon during 1995 and 1996. Sutton and Hargadon spent an average of two days a week at the company during this stretch, attending many meetings and brainstorming sessions (including at least thirty Monday-morning meetings) and having informal conversations and semi-structured interviews with most members of the company. Sutton attended the meeting described here and spoke with Kelley right before it started and just after it ended. Sutton continued to learn about the company's people, culture, and design in his role as an IDEO Fellow from 1997 to 2017.

36. **"majority of my adult life":** Becky Margiotta, "I've Spent My Life Unf—king Problems," *Got Your Six,* November 11, 2014, www.youtube.com/watch?v=1H-4x-gj_8s.

36. **100,000 Homes Campaign:** Sarah Soule et al., "The 100,000 Homes Campaign," case L30 (Stanford Calif.: Stanford Graduate School of Business, 2016), www.gsb.stanford.edu/faculty-research/case-studies/100000-homes-campaign.

37. **"smart-talk":** Jeffrey Pfeffer and Robert I. Sutton, "The Smart-Talk Trap," *Harvard Business Review* 77, no. 3 (1999): 135–36.

39. **"brilliant but cruel":** Teresa M. Amabile, "Brilliant but Cruel: Perceptions of Negative Evaluators," *Journal of Experimental Social Psychology* 1, no. 2 (1983): 146–56.

39. **As Adam tells it:** Based on our online video interview with Adam and Lena Selzer, March 16, 2022.

40. **Project Re:form:** "Project Re:form."

41. **riddled with inefficiency and quality problems:** Nelson P. Repenning and John D. Sterman, "Nobody Ever Gets Credit for Fixing Problems That Never Happened: Creating and Sustaining Process Improvement," *California Management Review* 43, no. 4 (2001): 64–88.

42. **Boeing 737 MAX jets crashed:** Chris Hamby, "How Boeing's Responsibility in a Deadly Crash 'Got Buried,'" *New York Times,* January 20, 2020, www.nytimes.com/2020/01/20/business/boeing-737-accidents.html; Natalie Kitroeff, "Boeing Employees Mocked F.A.A. and 'Clowns' Who Designed 737 Max," *New York Times,* January 29, 2020, www.nytimes.com/2020/01/09/business/boeing-737-messages.html?action=click&module=RelatedCoverage&pgtype=Article&region=Footer; David Gelles, "Boeing Expects 737 Max Costs Will Surpass $18 Billion," *New York Times,* July 15, 2020, www.nytimes.com/2020/01/29/business/boeing-737-max-costs.html.

43. **Ed Pierson:** Adam Grant, "Is It Safe to Speak Up?" *WorkLife with Adam Grant* (podcast), July 20, 2021, www.ted.com/podcasts/worklife/is-it-safe-to-speak-up-at-work-transcript.

44. **"textbook case of how the absence of psychological safety":** Amy Edmondson, "Boeing and the Importance of Encouraging Employees to Speak Up," *Harvard Business Review*, May 4, 2019, https://hbr.org/2019/05/boeing-and-the-importance-of-encouraging-employees-to-speak-up.

44. **John Sterman explained:** Repenning and Sterman, "Nobody Ever Gets Credit," 82.

44. **Anita Tucker and Amy Edmondson:** Anita L. Tucker and Amy C. Edmondson, "Why Hospitals Don't Learn from Failures: Organizational and Psychological Dynamics That Inhibit System Change," *California Management Review* 45, no. 2 (2003): 55–72.

46. **"I've delivered programs under duress":** Repenning and Sterman, "Nobody Ever Gets Credit," 81.

46. **rallying cry:** Andrew Russell and Lee Vinsel, "Let's Get Excited About Maintenance!" *New York Times*, July 22, 2017, www.nytimes.com/2017/07/22/opinion/sunday/lets-get-excited-about-maintenance.html.

47. **Mierle Laderman Ukeles:** Jillian Steinhauer, "How Mierle Laderman Ukeles Turned Maintenance Work into Art," *Hyperallergic*, February 10, 2017, https://hyperallergic.com/355255/how-mierle-laderman-ukeles-turned-maintenance-work-into-art/.

48. **"authentic pride":** See Jessica L. Tracy and Richard W. Robins. "Emerging Insights into the Nature and Function of Pride," *Current Directions in Psychological Science* 16, no. 3 (2007): 147–50; Eric Mercadante, Zachary Witkower, and Jessica L. Tracy, "The Psychological Structure, Social Consequences, Function, and Expression of Pride Experiences," *Current Opinion in Behavioral Sciences* 39 (2021): 130–35.

49. **Charles Darwin:** Tracy and Robins, "Emerging Insights," 147.

Chapter 2: Friction Forensics

50. **"IKEA effect":** Michael I. Norton, Daniel Mochon, and Dan Ariely, "The IKEA Effect: When Labor Leads to Love," *Journal of Consumer Psychology* 22, no. 3 (2012): 453–60.

51. **"looked friction in the face and laughed":** Dina Chaiffetz, "3 Ways Friction Can Improve Your UX," invision, www.invisionapp.com/inside-design/3-ways-friction-can-improve-your-ux/.

53. **PreCheck program:** Sunstein, *Sludge*, 14–15.

53. **"Learn from the mistakes of others":** "You Must Learn from the Mistakes of Others. You Will Never Live Long Enough to Make Them All Yourself," Quote Investigator, September 18, 2018, https://quoteinvestigator.com/2018/09/18/live-long/.

54. **first-mover advantage:** See, for example, Fernando Suarez and Gianvito Lanzolla, "The Half-Truth of First-Mover Advantage," *Harvard Business Review*, 2005; Marvin B. Lieberman and David B. Montgomery, "Conundra and Progress: Research on Entry Order and Performance," *Long Range Planning* 46, no. 4–5 (2013): 312–24; Elena Vidal and Will Mitchell, "When Do First Entrants Become First Survivors?" *Long Range Planning* 46, no. 4–5 (2013): 335–47.

54. **Swedish cooking show:** Ali Ahmed, "Don't Be First! An Empirical Test of the

First-Mover Disadvantage Hypothesis in a Culinary Game Show," *Social Sciences & Humanities Open* 1, no. 1 (2019): 100004. Note that the total number of winners adds up to less than 100 percent because these are "sole winners" only; winning contestants who tied with one or more others are excluded.

55. **kill creativity:** Teresa M. Amabile, *How to Kill Creativity* (Boston: Harvard Business School, 1998).

55. **Jerry Seinfeld:** Daniel McGinn, "Life's Work: An Interview with Jerry Seinfeld," *Harvard Business Review* 95, no. 1 (2017): 172.

56. **Laszlo Bock:** This story about Google is based on an email exchange between Robert Sutton and Laszlo Bock on August 27, 2022. It is also summarized in Robert I. Sutton, "Why Bosses Should Ask Employees to Do Less—Not More," *Wall Street Journal*, September 25, 2022, www.wsj.com/articles/bosses-staff-employees-less-work-11663790432.

58. **forty-two emergency-department physicians:** Jillian A. Berry Jaeker and Anita L. Tucker, "The Value of Process Friction: The Role of Justification in Reducing Medical Costs," *Journal of Operations Management* 66, no. 1–2 (2020): 12–34.

60. **Mark Zuckerberg's boast:** Robert Hof, "LIVE with Mark Zuckerberg at F8: Facebook Is Your Life," *Forbes*, September 22, 2011, www.forbes.com/sites/roberthof/2011/09/22/live-with-mark-zuckerberg-at-facebook-f8/?sh=3d3e9ed4432e.

60. **"citizen-saboteurs":** U.S. Office of Strategic Services, *Simple Sabotage Field Manual* (1944; repr., New York: HarperOne, 2015).

62. **darkpatterns.org:** Harry Brignull, "Types of Deceptive Design," www.deceptive.design/types. Note that the name of this site was changed from darkpatterns to deceptive.design in late 2022.

62. **"Stopping the Manipulation Machines":** Greg Bensinger, "Stopping the Manipulation Machines," *New York Times*, April 21, 2021, www.nytimes.com/2021/04/30/opinion/dark-pattern-internet-ecommerce-regulation.html.

62. **documented the ordeal:** Nir Eyal, "The New York Times Uses the Very Dark Patterns It Derides," Nir and Far, www.nirandfar.com/cancel-new-york-times/.

63. **new California law:** Amanda Beane et al., "California Passes Updated Automatic Renewal Law," *Consumer Protection Review*, November 21, 2021, www.consumerprotectionreview.com/2021/11/california-passes-updated-automatic-renewal-law/.

63. **Eric told us:** Personal communication from Eric Colson, March 21, 2022.

64. **Patty believes:** Personal communication from Patty McCord, March 19, 2022.

65. **Fast List:** Patrick Collison, "Some Examples of People Quickly Accomplishing Ambitious Things Together," https://patrickcollison.com/fast.

66. **Dee Hock explains:** Dee Hock, *One from Many: Visa and the Rise of Chaordic Organization*, 2nd ed. (Oakland, Calif.: Berrett-Koehler, 2005).

66. **now 3.9 billion:** "Visa Fact Sheet," Visa.com, https://usa.visa.com/dam/VCOM/global/about-visa/documents/aboutvisafactsheet.pdf.

67. **elite team of warriors:** Hayagreeva Rao, Carter Bowen, and Gib Lopez, "Navy SEALs: Selecting and Training for an Elite Fighting Force," case HR40 (Stanford, Calif: Stanford Graduate School of Business, 2014).

Chapter 3: How Friction Fixers Do Their Work

71. **cognitive behavioral therapy:** Aaron Beck authored or coauthored twenty-five books and more than six hundred articles in his lifetime, most on elements of

cognitive behavioral therapy. A nice summary of this method is found in his daughter's book, Judith S. Beck, *Cognitive Behavior Therapy: Basics and Beyond* (New York: Guilford, 2020).

72. **Rumana Jabeen:** Personal communications from Rumana Jabeen to Robert Sutton, discussions that took place between April and August 2021.

72. **six intertwined studies:** Emma Bruehlman-Senecal and Özlem Ayduk, "This Too Shall Pass: Temporal Distance and the Regulation of Emotional Distress," *Journal of Personality and Social Psychology* 108, no. 2 (2015): 356.

73. *Humor, Seriously:* Jennifer Aaker and Naomi Bagdonas, *Humor, Seriously: Why Humor Is a Secret Weapon in Business and Life (and How Anyone Can Harness It. Even You)* (New York: Crown Currency, 2021).

74. **"workplace vigilantes":** Katy DeCelles and Karl Aquino, "Vigilantes at Work: Examining the Frequency of Dark Knight Employees," SSRN, April 30, 2017, https://papers.ssrn.com/sol3/papers.cfm?abstract_id=2960941.

74. **"taking a tissue":** Alexander Alonso, "The High Price of Pettiness at Work," *HR Magazine,* September 4, 2019, www.shrm.org/hr-today/news/hr-magazine/fall2019/pages/the-high-price-of-pettiness-at-work.aspx.

75. **"Getting a Permit":** Heather Knight, "S.F.'s Building Department Is a Mess. It's No Wonder Pay-to-Play Rules the Day," *San Francisco Chronicle,* December 12, 2020, www.sfchronicle.com/bayarea/heatherknight/article/The-S-F-building-department-is-a-mess-Its-ties-15796068.php.

76. **Out of money and hope:** Heather Knight, "He Spent $200,000 Trying to Open an S.F. Ice Cream Shop, but Was No Match for City Bureaucracy," *San Francisco Chronicle,* April 21, 2021, www.sfchronicle.com/local/heatherknight/article/S-F-ice-cream-shop-hopeful-sees-dreams-melted-by-16116082.php.

76. **Research on newcomers:** W. Brad Johnson and Gene R. Andersen, "Mentoring in the US Navy: Experiences and Attitudes of Senior Navy Personnel," *Naval War College Review* 68, no. 3 (2015): 76–90.

78. *Organizations in Action:* James D. Thompson, *Organizations in Action: Social Science Bases of Administrative Theory* (1967; repr., New York: Routledge, 2017).

78. **half in jest:** Henry Mintzberg, "The Manager's Job: Folklore and Fact," *Harvard Business Review* 53, no. 4 (1975).

78. **"shit umbrellas":** Matt J. Davidson, "Shit Umbrella," *Matt J. Davidson Blog,* June 9, 2018, https://mattjdavidson.github.io/shit-umbrella/.

79. **Ed and Alvy "saved our jobs":** Bob Sutton, "Real Heroes at Pixar: When Leaders Serve as Human Shields," LinkedIn, December 18, 2013, www.linkedin.com/pulse/20131218225944-15893932-real-heroes-at-pixar-when-leaders-serve-as-human-shields/.

80. **"dragons behind the desk":** Sara Arber and Lucianne Sawyer, "The Role of the Receptionist in General Practice: A 'Dragon Behind the Desk'?" *Social Science & Medicine* 20, no. 9 (1985): 911–21.

80. **flak catchers:** Paul G. Friedman, "Hassle Handling: Front-Line Diplomacy in the Work-Place," *ABCA Bulletin* 47, no. 1 (1984): 30–34.

80. **"fights before flights":** Katherine A. DeCelles et al., "Helping to Reduce Fights Before Flights: How Environmental Stressors in Organizations Shape Customer Emotions and Customer–Employee Interactions," *Personnel Psychology* 72, no. 1 (2019): 49–80.

82. **Josh Nicholls:** Personal communication between Josh Nicholls and Robert Sutton, July 18, 2022.

82. **LaunchPad class:** This description is based on our intermittent conversations over the years with Perry Klebahn, who cofounded the LaunchPad class in 2010, and on occasional class visits over the years. In addition, when Perry Klebahn and Jeremy Utley taught the class in the spring of 2022, Robert Sutton visited nearly every class session and, where he could, helped out with the teaching and coaching. The history, design, and principles of this class are described on the detailed LaunchPad website: www.LaunchPad.stanford.edu/#what-is-LaunchPad.

84. **LaunchPad grad Greta Meyer:** Based on our online video interview with Greta Meyer, April 14, 2022.

85. **fired every general manager:** Joel M. Podolny and Morten T. Hansen, "How Apple Is Organized for Innovation," *Harvard Business Review* 98, no. 6 (2020): 86–95.

86. **Million Hours Campaign:** Hayagreeva Rao and Julie Makinen, "AstraZeneca: Scaling Simplification," case HR45 (Stanford, Calif.: Stanford Graduate School of Business, 2017), www.gsb.stanford.edu/faculty-research/case-studies /astrazeneca-scaling-simplification.

86. **crash of a B-17 bomber:** Walter J. Boyne, "The Checklist," *Air & Space Forces Magazine,* August 1, 2015, www.airandspaceforces.com/article/0813checklist/.

87. **100,000 Lives Campaign:** David Hoyt and Hayagreeva Rao, "Institute for Healthcare Improvement: The Campaign to Save 100,000 Lives," case L13 (Stanford, Calif.: Stanford Graduate School of Business, 2008), www.gsb.stanford.edu/faculty-research /case-studies/institute-healthcare-improvement-campaign-save-100000-lives.

87. **"play jazz":** Joe McCannon, Becky Margiotta, and Abigail Zier Alyesh, "Unleashing Large-Scale Change," *Stanford Social Innovation Review,* June 16, 2017, https:// ssir.org/articles/entry/unleashing_large_scale_change#.

87. **prepackaged daily prep meeting:** Jillian Chown, "The Unfolding of Control Mechanisms Inside Organizations: Pathways of Customization and Transmutation," *Administrative Science Quarterly* 66, no. 3 (2021): 711–52.

Chapter 4: Oblivious Leaders

96. **strategist Rob Kleinbaum:** Frank Langfitt, "Thousands of GM Workers Get Company Cars, Gas," *Morning Edition,* National Public Radio, March 25, 2009, www.npr.org/2009/03/25/102316176/thousands-of-gm-workers-get-company -cars-gas.

97. **"absence of inconvenience":** John Amaechi, "What Is White Privilege?," BBC Bitesize, July 2020, www.bbc.co.uk/bitesize/articles/zrvkbqt.

98. **"The Office of Tom Karinshak":** This email was sent from "Rich P." from "The Office of Tom Karinshak" on May 3, 2021. It was followed by multiple emails and phone calls with several *very* nice and helpful "personal account representatives," who not only provided prompt and excellent service but waived at least one $125 fee for a home installation visit that other customers are charged.

98. **the very bottom:** Adrianne Jeffries, "The Worst Company in America," *Verge,* August 19, 2014, www.theverge.com/2014/8/19/6004131/comcast-the-worst-company -in-america.

98. **2022 "horror stories":** Jon Brodkin, "Comcast Debacles Dominate *Ars Technica*'s Biggest ISP Horror Stories of 2022," *Ars Technica,* December 28, 2022,

https://arstechnica.com/tech-policy/2022/12/comcast-debacles-dominate-ars
-technicas-biggest-isp-horror-stories-of-2022/.

99. **Jimmy Cayne:** Deborah Solomon, "The Bear Market: Questions for Alan C. Greenberg," *New York Times,* May 13, 2010, www.nytimes.com/2010/05/16 /magazine/16fob-q4-t.html.

99. **Richard Fuld:** Larry McDonald and Patrick Robinson, *A Colossal Failure of Common Sense: The Incredible Inside Story of the Collapse of Lehman Brothers* (New York: Random House, 2009).

100. **fallacy of centrality:** Ron Westrum, "Social Intelligence About Hidden Events: Its Significance for Scientific Research and Social Policy," *Knowledge* 3, no. 3 (1982): 381–400.

100. **conclude, wrongly:** Karl E. Weick, "Faith, Evidence, and Action: Better Guesses in an Unknowable World," *Organization Studies* 27, no. 11 (2006): 1723–36.

100. **happening:** Ibid., 1723.

100. **leaders did penalize consultants:** Erin Reid, "Why Some Men Pretend to Work 80-Hour Weeks," *Harvard Business Review,* April 28, 2015, https://hbr.org/2015 /04/why-some-men-pretend-to-work-80-hour-weeks

101. **selfishness:** Dacher Keltner, *The Power Paradox: How We Gain and Lose Influence* (New York: Penguin, 2016).

103. **leaders rarely notice:** James G. March, "Footnotes to Organizational Change," *Administrative Science Quarterly* (1981): 563–77.

103. **"more forcefully":** Ibid., 563.

103. **every twenty or thirty seconds:** Lionel Tiger, "Dominance in Human Societies," *Annual Review of Ecology and Systematics* 1, no. 1 (1970): 287–306.

103. **most of the interpretative labor:** David Graeber, *The Utopia of Rules: On Technology, Stupidity, and the Secret Joys of Bureaucracy* (New York: Melville House, 2015), 81.

103. **studied 7-Eleven stores:** See Robert I. Sutton and Anat Rafaeli, "Untangling the Relationship Between Displayed Emotions and Organizational Sales: The Case of Convenience Stores," *Academy of Management Journal* 31. no. 3 (1988): 461–87; Robert I. Sutton and Anat Rafaeli, "How We Untangled the Relationship Between Displayed Emotion and Organizational Sales: A Tale of Bickering and Optimism," *Doing Exemplary Research,* 1992, 115–28.

104. **"email urgency bias":** Laura M. Giurge and Vanessa K. Bohns, "You Don't Need to Answer Right Away! Receivers Overestimate How Quickly Senders Expect Responses to Non-urgent Work Emails," *Organizational Behavior and Human Decision Processes* 167 (2021): 114–28.

106. **Cofounder Callum Anderson:** Megan Carnegie, "The Rise of the 15-Minute Meeting," *Wired,* March 5, 2022, www.wired.co.uk/article/15-minute-meeting -burnout.

108. **Patty McCord:** Sutton, "How Do You End a Meeting?"

109. **"the act of calling 'dibs'":** Urban Dictionary, August 30, 2013, s.v. "cookie licking," www.urbandictionary.com/define.php?term=cookie%20licking.

109. **"Microspeak":** Steven Sinofsky, "Innovation Versus Shipping: The Cairo Project," *Hardcore Software,* April 18, 2021, https://hardcoresoftware.learningbyshipping .com/p/020-innovation-versus-shipping-the.

111. **Steve Barley joined a committee:** A version of this story was first published in

The Wall Street Journal; though it didn't name Steve Barley, we do so here with his permission. Robert I. Sutton, "The Biggest Mistakes Bosses Make When Making Decisions—and How to Avoid Them," *Wall Street Journal,* October 29, 2018, www .wsj.com/articles/the-biggest-mistakes-make-when-making-decisionsand -how-to-avoid-them-1540865340.

112. **George Washington's death:** Howard Markel, "Dec. 14, 1799: The Excruciating Final Hours of President George Washington," *PBS News Hour,* December 14, 2014, www.pbs.org/newshour/health/dec-14–1799-excruciating-final-hours-president -george-washington.

112. **invented the phrase MBWA:** Personal communication, via email, from John Doyle, October 29, 2019.

113. **eighteen-month experiment:** Anita L. Tucker and Sara J. Singer. "The Effectiveness of Management-by-Walking-Around: A Randomized Field Study," *Production and Operations Management* 24, no. 2 (2015): 253–71.

113. **"problems are like dinosaurs":** Wally Bock, "Leadership: Dinosaurs and Behavior," Connection Culture Group, June 30, 2018, www.connectionculture.com /post/leadership-dinosaurs-and-behavior-problems.

113. **"found that adverse events":** Tucker and Singer, "Effectiveness of Management-by-Walking-Around," 256.

113. **"easy-to-solve":** Ibid., 255.

114. **hog airtime and interrupt others:** Victoria L. Brescoll, "Who Takes the Floor and Why: Gender, Power, and Volubility in Organizations," *Administrative Science Quarterly* 56, no. 4 (2011): 622–41.

116. **Dan Cockerell:** This section is based on an email exchange between Dan Cockerell and Robert Sutton on May 21, 2022, and on Dan Cockerell, *How's the Culture in Your Kingdom? Lessons from a Disney Leadership Journey* (Garden City, NY: Morgan James, 2020).

116. **tracked 115 senior leaders:** Tsedal Neeley and B. Sebastian Reiche, "How Global Leaders Gain Power Through Downward Deference and Reduction of Social Distance," *Academy of Management Journal* 65, no. 1 (2022): 11–34.

117. **"invert the jobs":** Ibid., 17.

117. **"Please, trust us":** Ibid., 23.

117. **"I'm the expert":** Ibid.

118. **U.S. Navy SEALs:** Lindy Greer, interviewed by Frieda Klotz, "Why Teams Still Need Leaders," *MIT Sloan Management Review,* July 24, 2019, https://sloanreview .mit.edu/article/why-teams-still-need-leaders/.

118. **ten start-ups:** Lindred L. Greer, Nicole Abi-Esber, and Charles Chu, "Hierarchical Flexing: How Start-Up Teams Dynamically Adapt Their Hierarchy to Meet Situational Demands," University of Michigan working paper, 2023; also see Lindy Greer, Francesca Gino, and Robert Sutton, "You Need Two Leadership Gears: Know When to Take Charge and When to Get Out of the Way," *Harvard Business Review.*

119. **"bureaucracy must die":** Gary Hamel, "Bureaucracy Must Die," *Harvard Business Review,* November 4, 2014, https://hbr.org/2014/11/bureaucracy -must-die.

119. **hierarchy is inevitable:** This section is a descendant of Bob Sutton, "Hierarchy Is Good. Hierarchy Is Essential. And Less Isn't Always Better," LinkedIn, January 12,

2014, www.linkedin.com/pulse/20140112221140-15893932-hierarchy-is-good
-hierarchy-is-essential-and-less-isn-t-always-better/.

120. **hierarchies are evident:** Deborah H. Gruenfeld and Larissa Z. Tiedens, "Organizational Preferences and Their Consequences," *Handbook of Social Psychology,* 2010.

120. **we wrote:** Sutton and Rao, *Scaling Up Excellence,* 108.

121. **Mark Templeton:** Adam Bryant, "Paint by Numbers or Connect the Dots," *New
York Times,* September 22, 2012, www.nytimes.com/2012/09/23/business/mark
-templeton-of-citrix-on-the-big-career-choice.html?_r=0.

Chapter 5: Addition Sickness

122. **"My shit is stuff":** "George Carlin Talks About Stuff," CappyNJ, May 1, 2007,
www.youtube.com/watch?v=MvgN5gCuLac.

122. **"self-serving biases":** See, for example, Bruce Blaine and Jennifer Crocker, "Self-
Esteem and Self-Serving Biases in Reactions to Positive and Negative Events: An
Integrative Review," in *Self-Esteem: The Puzzle of Low Self-Regard,* ed. Roy F. Bau-
meister (New York: Springer, 1993), 55–85.

122. **"addition bias":** Adams et al., "People Systematically Overlook Subtractive," 258–61.

123. **"sandwich-like structure":** Leidy Klotz, "Subtract: Why Getting to Less Can Mean
Thinking More," *Behavioral Scientist,* April 12, 2021, https://behavioralscientist
.org/subtract-why-getting-to-less-can-mean-thinking-more/.

123. *Subtract:* Klotz, *Subtract.*

123. **economist Robert E. Martin:** Jenny Rogers, "3 to 1: That's the Best Ratio of Tenure-
Track Faculty to Administrators, a Study Concludes," *Chronicle of Higher Education,* November 1, 2012, www.chronicle.com/article/3-to-1-thats-the-best-ratio-of
-tenure-track-faculty-to-administrators-a-study-concludes/?cid=gen_sign_in.

123. **study of 117 universities:** Alison Wolf and Andrew Jenkins, "Managers and Academics in a Centralising Sector: The New Staffing Patterns of UK Higher Education," 2021, www.advance-he.ac.uk/knowledge-hub/managers-and-academics
-centralising-sector-new-staffing-patterns-uk-higher-education.

123. **Alison Wolf concludes:** Andrew Jack, "Are Universities Suffering from Management Bloat?" *Financial Times,* May 17, 2022, www.ft.com/content/338d7321
-bc87-4573-885e-565f34a80b30.

124. **Timothy Devinney:** Ibid.

124. **"Tragedy of the Commons":** Garrett Hardin, "The Tragedy of the Commons:
The Population Problem Has No Technical Solution; It Requires a Fundamental
Extension in Morality," *Science* 162, no. 3859 (1968): 1243–48.

125. **Michael was a guest:** Bob Sutton, "The Basic Hygiene of Management, with Michael Dearing," *Friction* podcast on organizational culture, July 5, 2017, https://
ecorner.stanford.edu/podcasts/the-basic-hygiene-of-management/.

125. **sludge audits:** Cass R. Sunstein, "Sludge Audits," *Behavioural Public Policy* 6, no.
4 (2022): 654–73.

125. **Identify "stupid stuff":** Lisa Bodell, "Get Rid of Stupid Workplace Rules in 30
Minutes," *Forbes,* February 28, 2018, www.forbes.com/sites/lisabodell/2018/02
/28/get-rid-of-stupid-workplace-rules-in-30-minutes/?sh=5a1c62f12bb0.

125. **Getting Rid of Stupid Stuff:** Ashton, "Getting Rid of Stupid Stuff," 1789–91.

126. **Meeting Reset:** Hinds and Sutton, "Meeting Overload Is a Fixable Problem."

126. **three hundred thousand hours:** Michael Mankins, "This Weekly Meeting Took Up 300,000 Hours a Year," *Harvard Business Review,* April 24, 2014, https://hbr .org/2014/04/how-a-weekly-meeting-took-up-300000-hours-a-year.

126. **"tallied the number of hours":** Buckingham and Goodall. "Reinventing Performance Management," 40–50.

126. **28 percent of their time:** Michael Chui et al., "The Social Economy: Unlocking Value and Productivity Through Social Technologies," McKinsey Global Institute, July 1, 2012, www.mckinsey.com/industries/technology-media-and-telecommunications /our-insights/the-social-economy.

126. **"refrain from sending emails":** "zzzMail," Vynamic Inizio Advisory, https:// vynamic.com/zzzmail/#:~:text=Vynamic's%20motto%20is%20%E2%80% 9CLife%20is,Sunday%2C%20and%20all%20Vynamic%20holidays.

126. **benefits form:** "Project Re:form."

127. **families of disabled children:** Sutton and Hoyt, "Better Service, Faster."

127. **the Perfectionist's Paradox:** John Gall, *The Systems Bible: The Beginner's Guide to Systems Large and Small* (Walker, Minn.: General Systemantics Press, 2002), 155.

127. **Rebecca Hinds's journey:** Hinds and Sutton, "Meeting Overload Is a Fixable Problem."

127. **Armeetingeddon:** Hinds and Sutton, "Dropbox's Secret for Saving Time."

128. **Cass tells us:** Sunstein, *Sludge,* 20.

129. **introduced guidelines:** Shalanda D. Young and Dominic J. Mancini, "Improving Access to Public Benefits Programs Through the Paperwork Reduction Act," Office of Management and Budget, M-22-10, April 13, 2022, www.whitehouse.gov /wp-content/uploads/2022/04/M-22-10.pdf.

129. **Twitter:** Twitter was rebranded as X just as we finished writing this book. We've decided to preserve all references to Twitter and tweets because those were the labels employed by the company and users at the time all examples in the book occurred.

129. **As did Don Moynihan and Pamela Herd:** Don Moynihan and Pamela Herd, "Transforming the Paperwork Reduction Act to Tackle Administrative Burden," Substack, April 26, 2022, https://donmoynihan.substack.com/p/transforming -the-paperwork-reduction?s=w.

130. **Simple subtraction rules:** Donald Sull and Kathleen M. Eisenhardt, *Simple Rules: How to Thrive in a Complex World* (New York: Houghton Mifflin Harcourt, 2015).

131. *Simple Rules:* Ibid.

132. **treated for heart attacks:** Andrew M. Carton, Chad Murphy, and Jonathan R. Clark, "A (Blurry) Vision of the Future: How Leader Rhetoric About Ultimate Goals Influences Performance," *Academy of Management Journal* 57, no. 6 (2014): 1544–70.

132. **"The rule of halves":** Klotz and Sutton. "Our To-Do Lists."

133. **"smashing the old ways":** Kursat Ozenc and Margaret Hagan, *Rituals for Work: 50 Ways to Create Engagement, Shared Purpose, and a Culture That Can Adapt to Change* (Hoboken, N.J.: John Wiley & Sons, 2019), 203–4.

133. **"mourning for the recently left":** Ibid., 208–9.

134. **Annette's "revolution":** Jeffrey Pfeffer and Robert I. Sutton, *The Knowing-Doing Gap: How Smart Companies Turn Knowledge into Action* (Boston: Harvard Business Press, 2000), 98–102.

135. **"czar of bad systems":** Ryan Holmes, "Why This CEO Appointed an Employee to Change Dumb Company Rules," *Fast Company,* March 14, 2017, www.fastcompany

.com/3068931/why-this-ceo-appointed-an-employee-to-change-dumb-company
-rules.

136. **Scaling Up Excellence:** Sutton and Rao, *Scaling Up Excellence.*

138. **collaborative work:** Robert L. Cross, *Beyond Collaboration Overload: How to Work Smarter, Get Ahead, and Restore Your Well-Being* (Boston: Harvard Business Review Press, 2021).

138. **Harvard Business School:** Evan DeFilippis et al., "Collaborating During Coronavirus: The Impact of COVID-19 on the Nature of Work," Harvard Business School, Organizational Behavior Unit Working Paper No. 21-006, July 16, 2020, https://ssrn.com/abstract=3654470.

138. **Meeting Doomsday:** Hinds and Sutton, "Meeting Overload Is a Fixable Problem."

140. **"quiet time":** Leslie A. Perlow, "The Time Famine: Toward a Sociology of Work Time," *Administrative Science Quarterly* 44, no. 1 (1999): 57–81.

140. **"async week":** Lisa Lee, "Can You Work Without Meetings? Salesforce Tried for Another Week," *360 Blog,* August 31, 2022, www.salesforce.com/blog/meeting-fatigue/.

140. **Lou's first moves:** Louis V. Gerstner, *Who Says Elephants Can't Dance? Inside IBM's Historic Turnaround* (New York: HarperCollins, 2002), 90.

141. **Steve Jobs returned to Apple:** Steve Jobs, speech given at DeAnza College's Flint Center, Cupertino, Calif., May 6, 1998.

142. **Stanford case study:** Rao and Makinen, "AstraZeneca: Scaling Simplification."

144. **ten-week LaunchPad:** "What Is LaunchPad?" https://www.LaunchPad.stanford.edu/.

144. **seven hundred start-ups:** David Kirsch, Brent Goldfarb, and Azi Gera, "Form or Substance: The Role of Business Plans in Venture Capital Decision Making," *Strategic Management Journal* 30, no. 5 (2009): 487–515.

145. **Burn the Business Plan:** Carl J. Schramm, *Burn the Business Plan: What Great Entrepreneurs Really Do* (New York: Simon & Schuster, 2018).

145. **"emotional trust":** Daniel J. McAllister, "Affect- and Cognition-Based Trust as Foundations for Interpersonal Cooperation in Organizations," *Academy of Management Journal* 38, no. 1 (1995): 24–59.

145. **better when they've worked together:** See, for example, Claudia Bird Schoonhoven, Kathleen M. Eisenhardt, and Katherine Lyman, "Speeding Products to Market: Waiting Time to First Product Introduction in New Firms," *Administrative Science Quarterly* 35, no. 1 (1990): 177–207; Robert S. Huckman, Bradley R. Staats, and David M. Upton, "Team Familiarity, Role Experience, and Performance: Evidence from Indian Software Services," *Management Science* 55, no. 1 (2009): 85–100; Robert S. Huckman and Gary P. Pisano, "The Firm Specificity of Individual Performance: Evidence from Cardiac Surgery," *Management Science* 52, no. 4 (2006): 473–88; and Brian Uzzi and Jarrett Spiro, "Collaboration and Creativity: The Small World Problem," *American Journal of Sociology* 111, no. 2 (2005): 447–504.

146. **Dean Keith Simonton documents:** D. K. Simonton, "Creativity as Heroic: Risk, Success, Failure, and Acclaim," in *Creative Action in Organizations,* ed. Cameron M. Ford and Dennis A. Gioia (Newbury Park, Calif.: SAGE Publications, 1995), 88–93.

146. **"green tape":** Leisha DeHart-Davis, "Green Tape: A Theory of Effective Organizational Rules," *Journal of Public Administration Research and Theory* 19, no. 2 (2009): 361–84.

147. **"I can refer":** Ibid., 365.

147. **"if people understand":** Ibid., 374.

Chapter 6: Broken Connections

149. **"Cancer Center":** The information about this research is based on a series of conversations with Melissa Valentine during the years that she conducted this research and analyzed the data. And in findings reported in the resulting academic paper: Melissa A. Valentine, Steven M. Asch, and Esther Ahn, "Who Pays the Cancer Tax? Patients' Narratives in a Movement to Reduce Their Invisible Work," *Organization Science*, October 2022.

152. *coordination neglect:* Chip Heath and Nancy Staudenmayer, "Coordination Neglect: How Lay Theories of Organizing Complicate Coordination in Organizations," *Research in Organizational Behavior* 22 (2000): 153–91.

153. **"technical people":** Deborah Dougherty, "Interpretive Barriers to Successful Product Innovation in Large Firms," *Organization Science* 3, no. 2 (1992): 179–202.

154. **stem U-boat attacks:** Eliot A. Cohen and John Gooch, *Military Misfortunes: The Anatomy of Failure in War* (New York: Simon & Schuster, 2012).

155. **Akshay Kothari and Ankit Gupta:** Sutton and Rao, *Scaling Up Excellence,* 102–3.

155. **Experiments show:** Robert B. Cialdini, *Influence, New and Expanded: The Psychology of Persuasion* (New York: HarperCollins, 2021).

156. **Microsoft engineer:** Herminia Ibarra and Aneeta Rattan, "Satya Nadella at Microsoft: Instilling a Growth Mindset," CS-18-008, London Business School, 2016.

156. **Satya Nadella took over:** Ibid.

157. **Satya's first moves:** Ibid.

158. **the Reputation Institute:** Julie Bort, "Microsoft's Reputation Is Soaring as Trust in the Tech Industry Flounders, According to New Research," *Business Insider,* November 19, 2019, www.businessinsider.com/microsoft-reputation-institute -soaring-research-2019-11.

158. **In Lindy's research:** Greer, Abi-Esber, and Chu, "Hierarchical Flexing."

159. **shared anger and pride:** These arguments draw on Sutton and Rao, *Scaling Up Excellence,* 68–97.

160. **new software developers:** See, for example, Gaurav G. Sharma and Klaas-Jan Stol, "Exploring Onboarding Success, Organizational Fit, and Turnover Intention of Software Professionals," *Journal of Systems and Software* 159 (2020): 110442.

160. **onboarding at Harvard Business School:** This information about the START program for new faculty members comes from a series of email and video exchanges in August of 2022 with a veteran HBS faculty member who asked not to be named and who has been involved in the program as a newcomer, teacher, and mentor. This faculty member reviewed this section and made multiple corrections and suggestions.

163. **"L6 strategy":** Michael Lewis, "Six Levels Down," *Against the Rules* (podcast), April 4, 2022, www.pushkin.fm/podcasts/against-the-rules/six-levels-down.

164. **worked on HealthCare.gov:** Steven Levy, "America's Tech Guru Steps Down— but He's Not Done Rebooting the Government," *Wired,* August 28, 2014, www .wired.com/2014/08/healthcare-gov/.

165. **Carl Liebert:** Personal communication between Carl Liebert and Robert Sutton, October 2022.

166. **storytelling:** Ian Tattersall, *Becoming Human: Evolution and Human Uniqueness* (New York: Houghton Mifflin Harcourt, 1999).

166. **members of Agta:** Daniel Smith et al., "Cooperation and the Evolution of Hunter-Gatherer Storytelling," *Nature Communications* 8, no. 1 (2017): 1853.

167. **turnaround at Best Buy:** Hubert Joly, *The Heart of Business: Leadership Principles for the Next Era of Capitalism* (Boston: Harvard Business Press, 2021).

168. **"dino baby":** Shannon McLellan, "Best Buy Employees Perform 'Surgery' on 3-Year-Old's Beloved Toy Dinosaur," *GMA*, March 5, 2019, www.goodmorningamerica .com/family/story/best-buy-employees-perform-surgery-year-olds-beloved -61389519.

168. **engages listeners:** Paul J. Zak, "Why Your Brain Loves Good Storytelling," *Harvard Business Review* 28 (2014): 1–5.

169. **described the program:** Valentine, Asch, and Ahn, "Who Pays the Cancer Tax?"

170. **Rudy Crespo:** Robert I. Sutton, *Good Boss, Bad Boss: How to Be the Best . . . and Learn from the Worst* (New York: Business Plus, 2010), 133–34.

171. **Crew chiefs:** Karl E. Weick, "Puzzles in Organizational Learning: An Exercise in Disciplined Imagination," *British Journal of Management* 13, no. S2 (2002): S7–S15.

172. **I-PASS method:** Amy J. Starmer et al., "Changes in Medical Errors After Implementation of a Handoff Program," *New England Journal of Medicine* 371, no. 19 (2014): 1803–12.

172. **complex work unfolds:** Beth A. Bechky and Gerardo A. Okhuysen, "Expecting the Unexpected? How SWAT Officers and Film Crews Handle Surprises," *Academy of Management Journal* 54, no. 2 (2011): 239–61.

175. *reciprocal interdependence:* Thompson, *Organizations in Action.*

175. **pooled interdependence:** Roger Schwarz, "Is Your Team Coordinating Too Much, or Not Enough?" *Harvard Business Review*, March 3, 2017, https://hbr.org /2017/03/is-your-team-coordinating-too-much-or-not-enough.

175. **emergency department:** Melissa A. Valentine and Amy C. Edmondson, "Team Scaffolds: How Mesolevel Structures Enable Role-Based Coordination in Temporary Groups," *Organization Science* 26, no. 2 (2015): 405–22.

176. **spared such intrusions:** Adam Lashinsky, *Inside Apple: How America's Most Admired—and Secretive—Company Really Works* (New York: Business Plus, 2012).

177. **collaboration overload:** Rob Cross, Scott Taylor, and Deb Zehner, "Collaboration Without Burnout," *Harvard Business Review* 96, no. 4 (2018): 134–37.

177. **Rob describes Scott:** Cross, *Beyond Collaboration Overload.*

Chapter 7: Jargon Monoxide

180. **consultants:** See, for example, Aaron De Smet, Sarah Klienman, and Kirsten Weerda, "The Helix Organization," *McKinsey Quarterly*, October 3, 2019; and Aaron De Smet, Michael Lurie, and Andrew St. George, "Leading Agile Transformation: The New Capabilities Leaders Need to Build 21st-Century Organizations," McKinsey & Company, 2018, 1–27.

181. **"upright striding vertical bipedality":** Zachariah C. Brown, Eric M. Anicich, and Adam D. Galinsky, "Compensatory Conspicuous Communication: Low Status Increases Jargon Use," *Organizational Behavior and Human Decision Processes* 161 (2020): 274–90.

183. **descriptions of new products:** Laura J. Kornish and Sharaya M. Jones, "Raw Ideas in the Fuzzy Front End: Verbosity Increases Perceived Creativity," *Marketing Science* 40, no. 6 (2021): 1106–22.

184. **"golden rule of Holacracy":** Marshall Hargrave, "Holacracy Meaning, Origins,

How It Works," *Investopedia*, December 27, 2022, www.investopedia.com/terms/h/holacracy.asp.

184. **"practicing Holacracy":** "Who's Practicing Holacracy?," Holacracy.org, www.holacracy.org/whos-practicing-holacracy.

184. **"either love it or hate it":** Diederick Janse, "Holacracy: A Framework, Not a Blueprint," *Corporate Rebels*, April 6, 2022, www.corporate-rebels.com/blog/holacracy-a-framework-not-a-blueprint.

185. **Both versions:** HolacracyOne, "Holacracy Constitution: Version 5.0," www.holacracy.org/constitution/5. Note we downloaded this version in October 2022. We also downloaded version 2.1 in 2015, and the text here draws on that version, but it appears to no longer be available for download.

185. **"anesthetizes a portion of one's brain":** George Orwell, "Politics and the English Language," in *The Collected Essays, Journalism, and Letters of George Orwell*, vol. 4: *In Front of Your Nose, 1945–1950*, ed. Sonia Orwell and Ian Angus (New York: Harcourt, Brace & World, 1968). Also available at www.orwell.ru/library/essays/politics/english/e_polit.

185. **"Holacracy Bootstrapper":** Jen Palmer, "Boss-Free Remote Work," *Medium*, August 15, 2022, https://blog.holacracy.org/boss-free-remote-work-568b4b53d93d.

186. **"getting in the way":** Andy Doyle, "Management and Organization at Medium," *Medium*, May 4, 2016, https://blog.medium.com/management-and-organization-at-medium-2228cc9d93e9.

186. **Zappos also struggled:** Molly Lipson, "It's Time to Get Rid of Managers. All of Them," *Business Insider*, May 12, 2022, www.businessinsider.com/great-resignation-get-rid-of-middle-managers-holacracy-2022-5.

186. **Holacracy coinventor:** Brian Robertson, "An Impersonal Process," *Medium*, January 2, 2014, https://blog.holacracy.org/an-impersonal-process-b618fc93b988.

187. **spearheaded refinements:** See, for example, Brian Robertson, "Part 2: Holacracy Constitution 5.0," September 13, 2018, https://m.facebook.com/HolacracyOne/videos/part-2-holacracy-constitution-50-brian-robertson-open-source-constitution-on-git/1858663140897782/?_se_imp=10n57xnEmpaChnB4D.

187. **2005 bestseller:** Harry G. Frankfurt, *On Bullshit* (Princeton, N.J.: Princeton University Press, 2005).

187. **"growing field of 'bullshitology'":** André Spicer, "Playing the Bullshit Game: How Empty and Misleading Communication Takes over Organizations," *Organization Theory* 1, no. 2 (2020): 2631787720929704.

187. **André defines:** André Spicer, "Shooting the Shit: The Role of Bullshit in Organizations," *Management* 5 (2013): 653–66; also see André Spicer, *Business Bullshit* (New York: Routledge, 2017).

188. **bullshitter and the bullshittee:** Lars Thøger Christensen, Dan Kärreman, and Andreas Rasche, "Bullshit and Organization Studies," *Organization Studies* 40, no. 10 (2019): 1587–1600.

188. **receptivity to bullshit:** Gordon Pennycook et al., "On the Reception and Detection of Pseudo-Profound Bullshit," *Judgment and Decision Making* 10, no. 6 (2015): 549–63.

188. **Mondelez:** Tiffany Hsu and Sapna Maheshwari, "'Thumb-Stopping,' 'Humaning,' 'B4H': The Strange Language of Modern Marketing," *New York Times*, November 25, 2020, www.nytimes.com/2020/11/25/business/media/thumb-stopping-humaning-b4h-the-strange-language-of-modern-marketing.html.

189. **Andre points:** Spicer, "Playing the Bullshit Game," 2631787720929704, 7.

189. **Brandolini's law:** Andrew Gelman, "The Bullshit Asymmetry Principle," *Statistical Modeling, Causal Inference, and Social Science,* January 28, 2019, https://statmodeling.stat.columbia.edu/2019/01/28/bullshit-asymmetry-principle/.

190. **"Chief Obfuscation Champion":** Lucy Kellaway, "The First Word in Mangled Meaning," *Financial Times,* January 6, 2013, www.ft.com/content/86f0383a-54f6-11e2-89e0-00144feab49a.

190. **in-group lingo:** Ronald S. Burt and Ray E. Reagans, "Team Talk: Learning, Jargon, and Structure Versus the Pulse of the Network," *Social Networks* 70 (2022): 375–92.

191. **New York (FDNY):** Rich Calder, Susan Edelman, and Larry Celona, "Oops! FDNY Contractor Presses Wrong Button, Shuts Down NYC's Emergency Dispatch System," *New York Post,* October 15, 2022, https://nypost.com/2022/10/15/fdny-contractor-presses-wrong-button-shuts-down-emergency-dispatch-system/.

192. **shorthand terms:** Roberto A. Weber and Colin F. Camerer, "Cultural Conflict and Merger Failure: An Experimental Approach," *Management Science* 49, no. 4 (2003): 400–415.

192. **big investment banks:** Gillian Tett, "Silos and Silences," *FSR Financial,* July 2010, 121.

193. **power of generalists:** David Epstein, *Range: Why Generalists Triumph in a Specialized World* (New York: Penguin, 2021).

193. **CEO of General Motors:** "How GM's Mary Barra Drives Value," Knowledge at Wharton, May 3, 2018, https://knowledge.wharton.upenn.edu/article/how-gms-mary-barra-drives-value/.

195. **patients in New Zealand:** M. Wernick et al., "A Randomised Crossover Trial of Minimising Medical Terminology in Secondary Care Correspondence in Patients with Chronic Health Conditions: Impact on Understanding and Patient Reported Outcomes," *Internal Medicine Journal* 46, no. 5 (2016): 596–601.

195. **"random scatter of ideas":** Daniel Kahneman, Olivier Sibony, and Cass R. Sunstein, *Noise: A Flaw in Human Judgment* (New York: Little Brown, 2021).

196. **"Manifesto for Agile Software":** Kent Beck et al., "Manifesto for Agile Software Development," February 2001, https://agilemanifesto.org/.

196. **105 slides:** Craig Smith, "Scrum Australia 2014: 40 Agile Methods in 40 Minutes," Craig Smith: Australian Agile Coach & IT Professional, October 21, 2014, https://craigsmith.id.au/2014/10/21/scrum-australia-2014-40-agile-methods-in-40-minutes/; also see Craig Smith, "40 Agile Methods Goes Viral," Craig Smith: Australian Agile Coach & IT Professional, December 1, 2021, https://craigsmith.id.au/2021/01/12/40-agile-methods-goes-viral/.

199. *concrete language:* Jonah Berger and Grant Packard, "Wisdom from Words: The Psychology of Consumer Language," *Consumer Psychology Review,* 2023 (forthcoming).

199. *present tense:* Grant Packard, Jonah Berger, and Reihane Boghrati. "How Verb Tense Shapes Persuasion," *Journal of Consumer Research,* January 23, 2023, https://doi.org/10.1093/jcr/ucad006.

199. *chosen to engage:* Cialdini, *Influence, New and Expanded.*

199. *sensory metaphors:* Ezgi Akpinar and Jonah Berger, "Drivers of Cultural Success: The Case of Sensory Metaphors," *Journal of Personality and Social Psychology* 109, no. 1 (2015): 20.

199. *journey:* Szu-Chi Huang and Jennifer Aaker, "It's the Journey, Not the Destination: How Metaphor Drives Growth After Goal Attainment," *Journal of Personality and Social Psychology* 117, no. 4 (2019): 697.

199. **read and listened:** For example, "Paul O'Neill, CEO of Alcoa—It's All About Safety," Charter Partners, June 12, 2015, www.youtube.com/watch?v=tC2ucDs_XJY; Fareed Zakaria, "Paul O'Neill Interview, Worker Safety at ALCOA," *Tough Decisions,* CNN, May 29, 2014, www.youtube.com/watch?v=56a3-Sc65M8.

200. **genius of zeroing in:** David Burkus, "How Paul O'Neill Fought for Safety at Alcoa," David Burkus, April 28, 2020, https://davidburkus.com/2020/04/how-paul-oneill-fought-for-safety-at-alcoa/.

Chapter 8: Fast and Frenzied

202. **29 percent of all fatalities:** NHSTA, U.S. Department of Transportation, "Speeding," www.nhtsa.gov/risky-driving/speeding.

202. **"locomotion goals":** Dana Kanze, Mark A. Conley, and E. Tory Higgins, "The Motivation of Mission Statements: How Regulatory Mode Influences Workplace Discrimination," *Organizational Behavior and Human Decision Processes* 166 (2021): 84–103.

204. **human resources busywork:** Farhad Manjoo, "Zenefits' Leader Is Rattling an Industry, So Why Is He Stressed Out?" *New York Times,* September 20, 2014, www.nytimes.com/2014/09/21/business/zenefits-leader-is-rattling-an-industry-so-why-is-he-stressed-out.html.

204. **Lars's reaction:** Claire Suddath and Eric Newcomer, "Zenefits Was the Perfect Startup. Then It Self-Disrupted," Bloomberg, May 9, 2016, www.bloomberg.com/features/2016-zenefits/.

205. **customer complained:** William Alden, "How Zenefits Crashed Back Down to Earth," *Buzzfeed,* February 18, 2016, www.buzzfeednews.com/article/williamalden/how-high-flying-zenefits-fell-to-earth.

205. **Francisco Partners:** Amy Feldman, "Zenefits, Once Worth $4.5 billion, Does Deal with Private-Equity Firm That Gives It Control," March 18, 2021, *Forbes,* www.forbes.com/sites/amyfeldman/2021/03/18/zenefits-once-worth-45-billion-does-deal-with-private-equity-firm-that-gives-it-control/?sh=48746d8c3873. Also: TriNet, "TriNet Completes Acquisition of Zenefits," February 15, 2022. https://www.trinet.com/about-us/news-press/press-releases/trinet-completes-acquisition-of-zenefits.

206. **Gallup survey:** Ben Wigert and Sangeeta Agrawal, "Employee Burnout, Part 1: The 5 Main Causes," July 12, 2018, Gallup, www.gallup.com/workplace/237059/employee-burnout-part-main-causes.aspx.

207. **Theological Seminary students:** John M. Darley and C. Daniel Batson, "'From Jerusalem to Jericho': A Study of Situational and Dispositional Variables in Helping Behavior," *Journal of Personality and Social Psychology* 27, no. 1 (1973): 100.

207. **"no time to be nice":** Christine Porath, *Mastering Civility: A Manifesto for the Workplace* (Sanger, Calif.: Balance, 2016).

208. **Ben's measure:** Bennett J. Tepper, "Consequences of Abusive Supervision," *Academy of Management Journal* 43, no. 2 (2000): 178–90.

208. **abuse their subordinates:** Bennett J. Tepper, Lauren Simon, and Hee Man Park,

"Abusive Supervision." *Annual Review of Organizational Psychology and Organizational Behavior* 4 (2017): 123–52.

208. **sleep poorly:** Christopher M. Barnes et al., "'You Wouldn't Like Me When I'm Sleepy': Leaders' Sleep, Daily Abusive Supervision, and Work Unit Engagement," *Academy of Management Journal* 58, no. 5 (2015): 1419–37.

209. **time-poor:** Maria Konnikova, "No Money, No Time," *New York Times,* June 13, 2014, https://archive.nytimes.com/opinionator.blogs.nytimes.com/2014/06/13/no-clocking-out/.

209. *Buzzfeed:* Alden, "How Zenefits Crashed Back Down."

210. **nine thousand daily diary entries:** Teresa M. Amabile, Constance N. Hadley, and Steven J. Kramer, "Creativity Under the Gun," *Harvard Business Review* 80 (2002): 52–63.

212. **"organizational debt":** Steve Blank, "Organizational Debt Is like Technical Debt—but Worse," *Steve Blank,* May 19, 2015, https://steveblank.com/2015/05/19/organizational-debt-is-like-technical-debt-but-worse/.

212. **case study of Uber:** Rao, Sutton, and Makinen, *Uber.*

214. **losses continued:** For a summary of Uber's financial performance through September 2022, see "Uber Technologies Net Income, 2017–2022," Macrotrends, www.macrotrends.net/stocks/charts/UBER/uber-technologies/net-income.

214. **record revenue:** Kellen Browning, "Uber Reports Record Revenue as It Defies the Economic Downturn," *New York Times,* February 8, 2023, www.nytimes.com/2023/02/08/business/uber-revenue.html.

214. **Dara implied:** https://www.reuters.com/markets/us/uber-confident-profit-ride-sharing-makes-strong-start-2023-2023-05-02/.

215. **uses premortems:** Gary Klein, "Performing a Project Premortem," *Harvard Business Review* 85, no. 9 (2007): 18–19; Tim Koller, Dan Lovallo, and Gary Klein, "Bias Busters: Premortems: Being Smart at the Start," *McKinsey Quarterly,* 2019.

216. **"back to the future":** Madison Singell et al., "Back to the Future: A 'Lab-in-the-Field' Experiment on Mental Time Travel and Collective Action in Startup Teams," working paper, Graduate School of Business, Stanford University, 2021.

217. **pausing to ask:** See Jennifer L. Eberhardt, *Biased: Uncovering the Hidden Prejudice That Shapes What We See, Think, and Do* (New York: Penguin, 2020); and Jennifer L. Eberhardt, "How Racial Bias Works—and How to Disrupt It," *TED: Ideas Worth Spreading,* June 22, 2020, www.ted.com/talks/jennifer_l_eberhardt_how_racial_bias_works_and_how_to_disrupt_it?language=en.

218. **100,000 Homes Campaign:** Sarah Soule et al., "The 100,000 Homes Campaign," case L30 (Stanford, Calif.: Stanford Graduate School of Business, 2016).

220. **Parker's approach:** Connie Lozios, "Parker Conrad's Rippling Is Now Valued at $6.5 billion—More Than Zenefits at Its Peak," TechCrunch, October 21, 2021, https://techcrunch.com/2021/10/21/parker-conrads-rippling-is-now-valued-at-6-5-billion-more-than-zenefits-at-its-peak/#:~:text=Startups-,Parker%20Conrad's%20Rippling%20is%20now%20valued%20at%20$246.5%20billion,than%20Zenefits%20at%20its%20peak&text=Founded%20by%20entrepreneur%20Parker%20Conrad,%244.5%20billion%20within%20three%20years.

221. **valued at $11.25 billion:** Sophia Kunthara, "Parker Conrad's Rippling Reaches $11.25B Valuation with Series D," *Crunchbase News,* May 11, 2022, https://news.crunchbase.com/startups/rippling-hr-funding-parker-conrad-zenefits/.

221. **all new hires:** Hayagreeva Rao and Robert Sutton, "From a Room Called Fear to a Room Called Hope: A Leadership Agenda for Troubled Times," *McKinsey Quarterly,* 2020, www.mckinsey.com/featured-insights/leadership/from-a-room -called-fear-to-a-room-called-hope-a-leadership-agenda-for-troubled-times.

221. **"team relaunch":** Tsedal Neeley, *Remote Work Revolution: Succeeding from Anywhere* (New York: Harper Business, 2021).

222. **Kathryn Velcich:** "Team Refresh | Energy, Focus and Progress for Your Team," Teamraderie, www.teamraderie.com/experiences/virtual-team-refresh/.

222. **"in sync":** See, for example, Scott S. Wiltermuth and Chip Heath, "Synchrony and Cooperation," *Psychological Science* 20, no. 1 (2009): 1–5; and Piercarlo Valdesolo, Jennifer Ouyang, and David DeSteno, "The Rhythm of Joint Action: Synchrony Promotes Cooperative Ability," *Journal of Experimental Social Psychology* 46, no. 4 (2010): 693–95.

223. **CEO of Mozilla:** John Lilly, "Cadence in Organizations," *Medium,* February 28, 2017, https://news.greylock.com/cadence-in-organizations-78a4b1637f12.

224. **"bursty communication":** Christoph Riedl and Anita Williams Woolley, "Teams vs. Crowds: A Field Test of the Relative Contribution of Incentives, Member Ability, and Emergent Collaboration to Crowd-Based Problem Solving Performance," *Academy of Management Discoveries* 3, no. 4 (2017): 382–403.

225. **"peak-end rule":** Daniel Kahneman et al., "When More Pain Is Preferred to Less: Adding a Better End," *Psychological Science* 4, no. 6 (1993): 401–5.

225. **"ta-da list":** Gretchen Rubin, "To-Do List Alternatives," *Gretchen Rubin,* November 21, 2021, https://gretchenrubin.com/articles/alternatives-to-to-do-list/.

226. **Sweeping the Shed:** James Kerr, *Legacy: What the All Blacks Can Teach Us About the Business of Life* (New York: Hachette, 2013).

226. **fancy celebration lunch:** Caroline Copley and Ben Hirschler, "For Roche CEO, Celebrating Failure Is the Key to Success," Reuters, September 17, 2014, www .reuters.com/article/us-roche-ceo-failure/for-roche-ceo-celebrating-failure-is -key-to-success-idUKKBN0HC16N20140917.

227. **laid off more than four hundred employees:** Ben Bergman, "'It Felt like a *Black Mirror* Episode': The Inside Account of How Bird Laid Off 406 People in Two Minutes via a Zoom Webinar," *dot.LA,* April 1, 2020, https://dot.la/bird-layoffs -meeting-story-2645612465.html.

227. **memo to Airbnb employees:** Brian Chesky, "A Message from Co-founder and CEO Brian Chesky," *Airbnb,* May 5, 2020, https://news.airbnb.com/a-message -from-co-founder-and-ceo-brian-chesky/.

228. ***Inc.* put it:** Jason Aten, "Lessons Behind Airbnb's CEO Email About Laying Off 1,900 Workers," *Inc.,* May 6, 2020, www.inc.com/jason-aten/lessons-behind -airbnb-ceos-email-about-laying-off-1900-workers.html.

229. **vilified in the press:** Bani Sapra, "Bird Employees Say They Were Locked out of Their Email and Slack Accounts as They Were Told Their Jobs Were Gone," *Business Insider,* April 2, 2020, www.businessinsider.com/bird-employees-locked-out -of-emails-layoffs-2020-4.

Chapter 9: Your Friction Project

234. **Michael Brennan:** See Melinda French Gates, "A 1,000-Question Form Stood Between People and Their Safety Net Benefits. These Advocates Designed a Better Ap-

proach," *Bill & Melinda Gates Foundation,* October 5, 2022, www.gatesfoundation
.org/ideas/articles/improving-lives-economic-mobility-opportunity; and Terry
Beurer, "You Can't Learn by Just Sitting in Your Chair" (interview), Civilla, https://
civilla.org/stories/interview-terry-beurer.

235. **David Novak:** Sutton and Rao, *Scaling Up Excellence,* 144.

236. **downright dogged and repetitive:** See Ibarra and Rattan, "Satya Nadella at Microsoft"; Todd Bishop, "Exclusive: Satya Nadella Reveals Microsoft's New Mission Statement, Sees 'Tough Choices' Ahead," *GeekWire,* June 25, 2015, www.geekwire
.com/2015/exclusive-satya-nadella-reveals-microsofts-new-mission-statement
-sees-more-tough-choices-ahead/.

237. **"directly responsible individuals":** See Lashinsky, *Inside Apple;* "What Are Directly Responsible Individuals? How to Set Up DRI Models?" Cloud Tutorial, 2023, www.thecloudtutorial.com/directly-responsible-individuals/#:~:text
=Conclusion-,What%20is%20a%20Directly%20Responsible%20Individual%20
(DRI)%3F,keeping%20the%20project%20on%20track.

238. **"60–30–10 rule":** J. Richard Hackman, *Collaborative Intelligence: Using Teams to Solve Hard Problems* (Oakland, Calif.: Berrett-Koehler, 2011).

239. **Alcoa CEO Paul O'Neill:** Paul H. O'Neill, Sr., *A Playbook for Habitual Excellence: A Leader's Roadmap from the Life and Work of Paul H. O'Neill, Sr.* (Value Capture, 2020).

240. **Sheri Singer:** Bob Sutton, "Productive Paranoia: Lights, Camera . . . Anxiety," *Friction,* season 2, episode 4, June 20, 2018, https://ecorner.stanford.edu/podcasts
/productive-paranoia-lights-camera-anxiety/.

240. **means rather than ends:** Huang and Aaker, "It's the Journey," 697; Patrick Kiger, "Redefining Success: Adopt the Journey Mindset to Move Forward, *Stanford Business,* August 30, 2019, www.gsb.stanford.edu/insights/redefining-success
-adopt-journey-mindset-move-forward.

240. **Steve Jobs said:** Mark Gurman, "Steve Jobs Legacy Lives on at Apple Campus with Posters and Quotes," *9to5Mac,* January 9, 2012, https://9to5mac.com/2012
/01/29/steve-jobs-legacy-lives-on-at-apple-campus-with-posters-and-quotes/.

241. **journey rather than the destination:** Eugen Herrigel, *Zen in the Art of Archery* (Digital Fire, 2021).

243. **Michele's research:** Michele Gelfand, *Rule Makers, Rule Breakers: Tight and Loose Cultures and the Secret Signals That Direct Our Lives* (New York: Scribner, 2019).

243. **lives with thirty-six rats:** "How Do Disney and Pixar Come Up with Those Ingenuous Stories? Through Research and Development," *No Film School,* November 9, 2016, https://nofilmschool.com/2016/11/how-research-and-development
-drive-story-creation-disney-pixar.

243. **Space Mountain:** Dan Heaton, "Former Disney Imagineer Bill Watkins on Designing Space Mountain," *Tomorrow Society,* August 22, 2018, https://
tomorrowsociety.com/disney-imagineer-bill-watkins/.

244. **Muppet Theory:** Dahlia Lithwick, "Chaos Theory: A Unified Theory of Muppet Types," *Slate,* June 8, 2012, https://slate.com/human-interest/2012/06/chaos
-theory.html.

244. **"unbureaucratic personalities":** Leisha DeHart-Davis, "The Unbureaucratic Personality," *Public Administration Review* 67, no. 5 (2007): 892–903.

245. **workplace vigilantes:** Katherine A. DeCelles and Karl Aquino, "Dark Knights:

When and Why an Employee Becomes a Workplace Vigilante," *Academy of Management Review* 45, no. 3 (2020): 528–48.

245. **payback for their lack of prestige:** Nathanael J. Fast, Nir Halevy, and Adam D. Galinsky, "The Destructive Nature of Power Without Status," *Journal of Experimental Social Psychology* 48, no. 1 (2012): 391–94.

246. **"Is failure cheap":** Jeff Bezos, "To Our Shareholders," Amazon, April 2015, www.sec.gov/Archives/edgar/data/1018724/000119312515144741/d895323dex991.htm; Jeff Hayden, "Amazon Founder Jeff Bezos: This Is How Successful People Make Such Smart Decisions," *Inc.*, December 3, 2018, www.inc.com/jeff-haden/amazon-founder-jeff-bezos-this-is-how-successful-people-make-such-smart-decisions.html.

247. **Paul implemented big changes:** Sutton, "CEO Who Led a Turnaround."

248. **plagued with rudeness:** Porath, *Mastering Civility.*

249. **"manners are the lubricating oil":** Peter Ferdinand Drucker, *Managing Oneself* (Boston: Harvard Business Review Press, 2008), 8–9.

249. **Christine's advice:** Christine Porath, "Frontline Work When Everyone Is Angry," *Harvard Business Review*, November 9, 2022, https://hbr.org/2022/11/frontline-work-when-everyone-is-angry.

249. **CEO of WD-40:** Chris Benguhe and RaeAnne Marsh, "For Former WD-40 CEO, Caring Oils the Wheels of Management," *International Business Times*, December 9, 2022, www.ibtimes.com/former-wd-40-ceo-caring-oils-wheels-management-3644876.

250. **"ruinous empathy":** Kim Scott, *Radical Candor: Fully Revised & Updated Edition: Be a Kick-Ass Boss Without Losing Your Humanity* (New York: St. Martin's Press, 2019).

250. **"companionate love":** Sigal G. Barsade and Olivia A. O'Neill, "What's Love Got to Do with It? A Longitudinal Study of the Culture of Companionate Love and Employee and Client Outcomes in a Long-Term Care Setting," *Administrative Science Quarterly* 59, no. 4 (2014): 551–98.

251. **Devoted Health:** Kevin Truong, "Why Devoted Health Has Put Family at the Center of Its Mission," *MedCity News*, January 7, 2019, https://medcitynews.com/2019/01/why-devoted-health-has-put-family-at-the-center-of-its-mission/; Robert I. Sutton, "The Fixers Presents: Todd Park," Stanford Online interview, February 1, 2022, https://event.on24.com/wcc/r/4093006/C652E63E63BB403B4BEA98D598166C9E.

253. **Clara Shih:** Personal communication to Robert Sutton, December 22, 2022, and January 24, 2023.

Index